America and the Politics of Insecurity

D0139590

THEMES IN GLOBAL SOCIAL CHANGE
Christopher Chase-Dunn, Series Editor

America
and the Politics of Insecurity

ANDREW ROJECKI

University of Illinois at Chicago

Johns Hopkins University Press

Baltimore

© 2016 Johns Hopkins University Press
All rights reserved. Published 2016
Printed in the United States of America on acid-free paper
2 4 6 8 9 7 5 3 1

Johns Hopkins University Press
2715 North Charles Street
Baltimore, Maryland 21218-4363
www.press.jhu.edu

Library of Congress Cataloging-in-Publication Data

Names: Rojecki, Andrew, 1946– author.
Title: America and the politics of insecurity / Andrew Rojecki.
Description: Baltimore : Johns Hopkins University Press, [2016] | Series:
    Themes in global social change | Includes bibliographical references
    and index.
Identifiers: LCCN 2015030261 | ISBN 9781421419602 (pbk. : acid-free paper)
    | ISBN 9781421419619 (electronic) | ISBN 1421419602 (pbk. : acid-free
    paper) | ISBN 1421419610 (electronic)
Subjects: LCSH: Globalization—United States. | United States—Social
    conditions. | United States—Foreign relations. | National security—
    United States.
Classification: LCC HN90.G56 R65 2016 | DDC 303.48/273—dc23
    LC record available at http://lccn.loc.gov/2015030261

A catalog record for this book is available from the British Library.

Special discounts are available for bulk purchases of this book.
For more information, please contact Special Sales at 410-516-6936 or
specialsales@press.jhu.edu.

Johns Hopkins University Press uses environmentally friendly book materials,
including recycled text paper that is composed of at least 30 percent
post-consumer waste, whenever possible.

For my parents, Władysław and Kazimiera

CONTENTS

FIGURES

TABLES

The idea for this book took root in the summer of 2001, when I attended a seminar on globalization led by historian Perry Anderson at the School for Theory and Criticism at Cornell University. For my fellowship to STC, I thank Stanley Fish, then dean of the College of Liberal Arts and Sciences at the University of Illinois at Chicago. While at Cornell, I was immersed in the flow of ideas from a group of eminent independent thinkers who inspired me to pursue an idea wherever it led me, even if it meant crossing ideological lines. My model there was Deirdre McCloskey, who I met after she spoke to a skeptical audience at STC on the virtue ethics of Adam Smith. Deirdre read an early draft of the proposal that became this book and generously helped me fashion and prune my argument.

Bob Entman, who I am fortunate to call a mentor and friend, helped me see the shape of the forest by asking the right questions and by his insistence that I see the fullness of the glass rather than its negative space. I am grateful to Bob's home institution, the School of Media and Public Affairs at George Washington University, for granting me a semester-long fellowship, and to Steve Livingston and Frank Sesno for their support.

Molte grazie to Gianpietro Mazzoleni for arranging a sabbatical in the Department of Social and Political Studies at the University of Milan and to Gianpietro's colleagues, professors Luisa Leonini and Marco Maraffi. The hospitality of my Milan colleagues, both intellectually and personally, added flavor and texture to the sabbatical experience.

At the University of Illinois, a number of graduate students were instrumental at various stages of the project. Michael Schandorf helped draft an early version of chapter 6 and applied his analytical skills in coding the voluminous text, as did Ryan Henke. Indira Neill provided expert help on bibliographic research. I would like to thank Mexhit Rexhepi, an energetic undergraduate who had heard about my project and wanted to learn as much as he could in preparation for his graduate studies at the University of Chicago. He showed up one day in my office and volunteered to help—and help he did. He spent numerous hours compiling poll data and chasing down research.

For their ongoing support and alliance for the duration of this project, my sincere appreciation goes to my department heads, Steve Jones and Zizi Papacharissi. They helped clear hurdles so the work could proceed. Victor Margolin, then in the School of Architecture and Art at UIC, contributed his boundless enthusiasm and intellectual curiosity. At Johns Hopkins University Press, Suzanne Flinchbaugh and Catherine Goldstead provided an unobtrusive web of support. I thank them and the anonymous reviewers for their incisive comments and for encouraging me to improve the quality of the book.

Key friends and family members endured conversations on the various topics addressed in this book and helped boost morale at crucial moments. Thank you Ralph, Bill, and Nils for your perspective-widening wit and humor. Special thanks to Edward Gubar at Indiana University for his wise counsel and suggestions for clarifying and simplifying. I am most grateful for the selfless and loving support of my wife, Susan. She read and reread multiple drafts without complaint and offered clarifying suggestions that helped me connect the dots. Her best advice was to get on with it, and so I did.

An earlier version of chapter 3 was published as "Media Discourse on Globalization and Terror," in *Political Communication*, 22 (2005): 63–82. An earlier version of chapter 4 was published as "Rhetorical Alchemy: American Exceptionalism and the War on Terror," in *Political Communication*, 25 (2008): 67–88. An earlier version of chapter 5 was published as "Political Culture and Disaster Response: The Great Floods of 1927 and 2005" in *Media, Culture, and Society*, 31 (2009): 957–76.

America and the Politics of Insecurity

CHAPTER ONE

Globalization and Insecurity

After the Great Recession of 2008, *New York Times* columnists Paul Krugman and David Brooks each took up contrasting themes in their analysis of the new economic realities facing Americans. A miniature of their differences appeared on the May 29, 2015, op-ed page. Paul Krugman's column was titled "The Insecure American," an analysis of the diminished resources of Americans enumerated in a report issued by the Federal Reserve. The finding that caught Krugman's attention was that nearly half of the population could not cover an emergency expense costing $400.

Brooks's column was titled "The Small Happy Life." In it, he reported samples of responses from readers to his request for what they found meaningful, the theme of a book he had recently written on the same topic. Brooks claimed to be surprised by the thrust of the essays: "I expected most contributors would follow the commencement-speech clichés of our high-achieving culture: dream big; set ambitious goals; try to change the world. In fact, a surprising number of people found their purpose by going the other way, by pursuing the small, happy life."

The contrasting analyses of post–Great Recession America could not be starker. For simplicity's sake, Krugman's position might be called the new insecurity and Brooks's the new normal. They defined alternative universes of diagnosis and remedy for a new reality, symptoms of the politics that had been dividing the nation since the end of the Cold War, a period during which feelings of forward-looking optimism slowly turned inward and pessimistic.

The Short End of History

In the glow of optimism that rose after the fall of the Berlin Wall, the concept of globalization gradually entered the US public sphere. By the mid-1990s, globalization had become part of the media lexicon, though not yet the public mind. Polls taken in the mid-1990s show that nearly half of Americans were unfamiliar with the term. Among those who were, they associated globalization with expanding prosperity in the United States as once-closed economies in Eastern Europe and elsewhere opened their markets to the West. Free trade became a magical term of reference and the most commonly understood dimension of globalization.

Among some scholars, the collapse of the Soviet Union and the export of free-market capitalism to such unlikely places as the People's Republic of China and the adoption of liberal democracy in former authoritarian regimes signaled a sea-change in history. Francis Fukuyama argued in his iconic book *The End of History and the Last Man* that the end of ideological evolution had yielded market capitalism as the solution to material security and liberal democracy as the solution to the need for recognition. By the mid-1990s, some nations had already adopted these solutions (others would follow), and an era of increased prosperity and peace would take hold.* As the world's largest economy and sole military hegemon, the United States became especially advantaged by globalization. Classical economists and other scholars echoed these themes in claims that free markets would promote economic development across the globe and deter civil wars (Fearon & Laitin, 2003; Barbieri & Reuveny, 2005; cf. Olzak, 2011). The optimism would be short-lived.

Speculative bubbles in Asia and later in the United States itself (the "dot.com" bubble) struck a discordant note and increased Americans' awareness of globalization, as it became associated with a new and unfamiliar class of problems. Scholars began to note the risks and discontinuities of globalization, qualitatively different from preceding eras. Anthony Giddens (1990) highlighted the greater number of *perceived* hazards and dangers owing to increased reliance on global systems and modes of exchange that warped traditional conceptions of time and space and whose complexity would lead to unforeseen and unintended consequences. One example is the mortgage-backed collateralized debt obligations (CDOs) traded in international markets that played a large role in the financial panic of 2007 and the Great Recession that followed. Similarly concerned with risk but with a contrasting view, Ulrich Beck (1992) noted the increased number of *objective* hazards from the proliferation of what economists term "bads"— for example, pollution and global warming—due to the production of sought-after "goods." The catastrophic consequences of the bads were unavoidable because of a now-accelerated drive for economic growth. Societies once conceived as protecting their citizens from risk, as in the rise of the welfare state (termed

---

* Fukuyama was not entirely optimistic. He could not dismiss the role of *thymos*, a chest-thumping need for recognition in human nature. Like Tocqueville, Fukuyama noted the alienation accompanying the disappearance of individuality under conditions of equality.

by economists as "embedded liberalism"), now face uncontrollable risk that arises from hazards that are indifferent to national boundaries.

The protests at the 1999 World Trade Organization meetings in Seattle marked the first popular resistance to a deregulated ("neoliberal") economy that threatened the wages of American workers. The terrorists who flew airliners into the World Trade Center and the Pentagon, symbols of US dominance in the new global order, demonstrated that globalization also provided a vector for importing bads of an unforeseen sort. Two oceans and Fortress America no longer afforded Americans peace of mind from foreign attack. Increased global flows of capital and the acceleration of the offshoring of labor raised doubts about US economic primacy that for two generations had led to expectations of a rising standard of living. By the 2000s, the disruptions of globalization had outrun the capacity of American political culture—pragmatic, optimistic, future oriented—to provide ways to think about and act effectively in a world that seemed increasingly fraught with risk. A transformed American economy, foreign-bred terrorism, and a rising sense of threat from global warming and related issues dominated media and public attention.

Poll data, indicators of salient themes in public discourse, show significant increases in attention to globalization-related issues. The Roper Poll database, for example, reveals that compared to the 1990s, the 2000s show a fourteenfold increase in polls regarding terrorism, a 40 percent increase on unemployment (before the Great Recession of 2008), and fivefold increases each on global warming, illegal immigration, and globalization itself.

Growing awareness of a new class of seemingly insoluble issues increased incentives for a politics of insecurity that trades on fear, resentment, and moral judgment, a staple of the partisan discourses on cable TV and talk radio. Politics becomes a zero-sum game in which heated disagreement on rival ends displace cooler discussions of rival means for attaining a common goal. In the politics of insecurity, those discourses that attain high levels of salience and cultural resonance overpower rivals that fail to inspire the same levels of passion. They also make it more difficult to understand the origins of the problems. This risks promoting policies that aggravate the conditions that led to the problems in the first place. Groups, movements, and policies that do not have the political resources or the advantage of cultural resonance to evoke the same passions as their rivals suffer a political disadvantage, no matter their merit.

One example is the hypernationalism following 9/11 that made it all but impossible for critics such as Susan Sontag to get a hearing for their efforts to understand the foreign policy context of the suicide attacks. Pressure to extend the walls on the Mexican border to restrict the flow of illegal immigrants drew from the same fear-based discourses that took root in the wake of 9/11. These discourses overpowered appeals for immigration reform, which were muted and diffuse by comparison.

While some problems such as global terrorism may be widely understood (albeit incompletely), others, especially in the economic domain, are not. The deeper and subtler effects of the economic dimension of globalization intensify the politics of insecurity. Aside from postincome redistributive policy, the state has fewer policy options for increasing employment or wages. US employment and income growth are now much more influenced by global conditions than in the past. Under these new circumstances, a distinction between domestic and foreign policy is analytically unproductive. For example, it risks categorizing movements like the Tea Party and Occupy Wall Street (OWS) as originating from domestic conditions rather than their interaction with global processes. The illegal immigration debate also represents a second-order reaction to economic globalization that is commonly framed as a domestic issue. Understood as reactions to undiagnosed global conditions, these issues embody the politics of insecurity.

Additionally, some classes of problems such as global climate change are more incremental and call to mind the story of the frog lolling in a pot of water atop a lit burner on a range. As citizens are exposed to ubiquitous messages of alarm, their thresholds of attention rise and become concerned only after spectacular destructive events, such as floods, hurricanes, and extreme heat waves. The disasters hold public attention for a time but have thus far failed to evoke the passion and commitment needed to support a corrective policy.

Thus, despite a scientific consensus on the link between greenhouse gases and rising global temperatures and the political will demonstrated by the 191 signatories to the Kyoto Accords, the United States—the world's biggest polluter—failed to ratify the treaty. Critics on the right pointed to the failure of China—the world's second largest polluter—to sign on and leveraged the dissent of a tiny number of climate scientists to block laws that would reduce carbon emissions. Critics on the left accused opponents of denial, ignorance, and knuckling under to oil interests but failed to energize the political passion of Americans, a majority who agree with scientists that climate change is real, poses a threat, and is the result of human action. Trading on increased perceptions of risk and uncertainty, the politics of insecurity explains this perplexing outcome. In this book, I propose a model of political communication—the uncertainty model—that explains the dynamics of this new political and information environment.

Using the model in the chapters that follow, I analyze the response of citizens and elites to a series of crises that confronted the United States in the first decade of the 2000s, a period that brought Americans face-to-face with extraordinarily difficult problems, compounded by their origin in seemingly uncontrollable global forces but especially by polarizing political discourses that traded on competing ends rather than common solutions. The discord has favored the right, which enjoyed several advantages in the conflict. Before addressing the reasons for the political paralysis and for the ascendance of the right, I first define the core concept of this book.

Risk, Uncertainty, and Insecurity

Insecurity is a feeling of vulnerability that arises when one is faced with an unfamiliar threat to well-being or from one that has no obvious means to defeat it. Insecurity occurs when there is a disruption in a socially constructed fabric of expectations and the ways by which they are ordinarily met. To say that perceptions of these threats are socially constructed is trivial only insofar as they do not have political significance. Mediated discourse links perceptions of individual insecurity to their political consequences, which may enter a feedback loop that aggravates the conditions that led to those perceptions.

To bridge the psychology of insecurity with the politics of insecurity, it is helpful to define security. Obvious at an intuitive level, it is surprisingly difficult to define analytically. This is because security defined at an individual level is subjective, varies from person to person, and is subject to the imperfections of human judgment, especially when contrasted with the consensual judgments of experts such as actuaries, whose job is to calculate statistically reliable estimates of risk. Risk is to be contrasted with *uncertainty* when even experts cannot offer calculable risk exposure because a situation has no comparative precedent. For nonexperts, the threshold between risk and uncertainty may be much lower.

When it comes to calculable risk, a wide range of research shows that we are unreliable judges of our own security when compared with those of experts. In his analysis of perceptions of risk, for example, Slovic (1987) contrasted actuaries' assessments of risk on such criteria as annual fatalities and probabilities with those of ordinary citizens who use ready mental shortcuts to invoke risk profiles. While experts calculate probabilities from annual casualties that result from annual events and accidents, citizens assess risk on the basis of perceived control and knowledge.

On the first dimension, the less control we have over an activity, the greater our perceived risk. Thus we feel safer driving than flying despite statistics that show that people are 72 times more likely to die in an auto accident than in a plane crash (Slovic, 1987). Slovic reports that the public is 1,000 times more likely to accept the risks of commonplace voluntary activities such as skiing rather than involuntary hazards from extremely rare events such as nuclear accidents.

The second dimension of risk assessment by ordinary citizens is information, and more specifically its absence. Known dangers such as fireworks are considered less risky than lesser-known threats such as new strains of influenza, such as bird flu. A function of information and control, the most dreaded threats—those that create extreme uncertainty—are both unfamiliar and over which citizens feel they have little control. Notable examples include the Al-Qaeda attacks of 9/11, the anthrax scare that followed, and the threat of an Ebola pandemic.

Absent the expert judgment needed to quantify the low risks posed by these threats, citizens may rely on mediated information, which is often driven less by actuarial risk than the catnip of sensationalism. As a signature example, the most widely reported media stories in the month prior to 9/11 were about shark attacks. Because dread is a major determinant of public perceptions of risk (Fischhoff et al., 1978; Slovic, 1987), it is a principal source of policy distortion. Under conditions of risk-driven insecurity, feelings dominate rational calculation because they are more available and efficient, especially for assessment of highly unlikely events that carry with them even the scantest possibility of strongly negative consequences (Slovic et al., 2004). They are politically significant insofar as they produce malleable anger, the latter a function of multiple factors including perceived fairness (Sandman, 1989).

Perceptions of perilous exposure to risk define what Slovic calls the "signal potential," or the anticipated risk exposure to a future event. Given a segregated information environment, signal potential may vary across polarized groups and influence their perceptions of risk exposure. Partisan media commentators routinely stoke the fear and anger of their audiences by painting political opponents as irresponsible, feckless, and deceitful. The desired ends of the pantomime—reminiscent of Orwell's "Two Minutes Hate" in *1984*—are outrage and ratings points. Perceived risk exposure in a polarized political and information environment is at the heart of the politics of insecurity and their policy consequences.

Security is also a primary concern of policy analysts who often link individual security to that of the state, whose reason for existence is to provide safety to those who live under its protection. Apart from different philosophical conceptions that define the desired extent of that protection (e.g., Locke vs. Hobbes), security means something very different to individuals than it does to states or to the international system that is composed of those states (Buzan, 1983; Rothschild, 1995).

Even in the field of international relations (IR), national security, a related concept, is "weakly conceptualized, ambiguously defined" (Buzan, 1983, p. 4; Paris, 2001). Tellingly, scholars began to use the concept of *human security* in the early 1990s, at about the same time that the concept of globalization had become current. The academic community, particularly IR scholars, began to rethink the concept of security as the end of the Cold War gradually increased the salience of less apocalyptic threats to well-being. After the threat of global nuclear war abated, attention turned to civil wars, failed states, famine, the environment, and a host of other issues that limited the life chances of individuals. Once a bipolar world with strong states, after the Cold War scholars reimagined the world picture as multipolar with states weakened by the emergence of transnational actors that included corporations, nongovernmental organizations (NGOs), and nonstate entities such as al-Qaeda.

The rise of these institutions and actors and a hypothesized weakening of states led to a view that saw individuals as persons rather than as citizens: "The individual has reached the status of a 'whole', a 'unit of account' in himself" (Tadjbakhsh & Chenoy, 2007, p. 13). It could not be otherwise, because if the state had been weakened, the guarantors of security must shift from states to international organizations such as the United Nations, NGOs, or to individuals themselves.* The expansion of the concept of security produced a range of normative and empirical definitions that reflected the differing levels of analysis and theoretical assumptions used by scholars to formulate their definitions. By 2001, a widely cited article (Paris, 2001) sought to clarify the definitions and the two dimensions that underlay them.

One dimension identifies the affected target—the state or those who fall under its protection: society, groups, and individuals. The second identifies the nature of the threat, military or other. Traditional definitions of national security fall into a type that intersects the state with military threats to its territorial integrity. Nonmilitary threats to the integrity of the state include international economic boycotts, threats to energy supplies, or the effects of long-term environmental change, such as reduced water supplies.

---

* A UN report (1994) identified "the legitimate concerns of ordinary people who sought security in their daily lives." Examples included hunger and disease, as well as the more vague disruptions "in the patterns of daily lives."

Turning to the social dimension, military threats subsume subnational conflicts such as civil wars and genocide, a type that has increased since the end of the Cold War. Finally, human security identifies those threats to society by global forces that readily cross national borders. They include such issues as unemployment due to corporate offshoring and illegal immigration, terror threats posed by suicide bombers, and local environmental disasters traceable to changes in the global ecosystem. Threats posed to human security test the capacity of weakened states to deal with them effectively. Environmental policy, for example, needs to be enacted at the state level to address the multiple problems that arise from global climate change. Because of inaction on the part of the US government, in part due to the politics of insecurity, threats to the environment have been taken up largely by local actors who have neither the resources nor the power to effect significant reductions in carbon emissions.

By contrast, 9/11 introduced the US population to the disquieting concept of a military threat posed by foreign nationals to individual citizens. The United States used a conventional national security rationale to deal with freelance acts of terror, invading two nation-states to thwart the actions of nonstate actors motivated by an ideology. Despite the absence of a clear political goal and a diffuse and a geographically dispersed enemy made up of guerilla fighters, the Bush administration used the widespread dread that followed 9/11 to launch a "war on terror." More than a decade after the start of the war, with victory still in doubt, Secretary of Defense Robert Gates told an audience of West Point cadets that "any future defense secretary who advises the president to again send a big American land army into Asia or into the Middle East or Africa should have his head examined." A categorical mismatch between the source of the security threat and an appropriate policy response reflected the unprecedented nature of the historical moment and the blind rush to familiar but inappropriate ways of thinking.

Perceived security is different for states and individuals, and among individuals different for experts and the general public. For the purposes of the book, I focus on the policy implications of perceived security, defined as protection from risks to physical safety and well-being that otherwise prevent citizens from leading stable, self-determined lives (Tadjbakhsh & Chenoy, 2007). King and Murray (2002) offered a qualification that reduces the scope of what might otherwise be an enormous range of potential issues: "include only those domains of well-being that have been important enough for human beings to fight over or to put their lives or property at great risk" (p. 593). How that importance is derived and whose interests it serves identifies the key issues in the politics of insecurity. In this book, I focus on globalization-related issues that have led to extended debate and political conflict that makes them even more difficult to resolve. They fall into three domains: economic, environmental, and existential.

Domains of Insecurity

Economic Insecurity

Economic integration, the most conspicuous and thriving dimension of globalization, has also led to disruption and uncertainty as Americans face chronic underemployment and increasing income inequality that is a feature of the US "brand" of capitalism (Hall & Soskice, 2001; Bartels, 2008). The financial crisis, the Great Recession, and the disconnect between employment and the stock market can be traced to global economic integration.* The contrast between "Main Street and Wall Street," a distinction that first surfaced in the mid-1990s, became a meme during the Great Recession of 2008 and is emblematic of the recognition of the disconnect.

Liberalized trade has led to impressive economic growth and to reduction of poverty in developing nations. At the same time, however, inequality measured by wage differences between skilled and unskilled workers has increased in high-income countries (Cornia et al., 2004). Economists' estimates of the increase in US income equality, as explained by outsourcing and growth in competition directly attributable to globalization, range from 15 to 33 percent (Lindert & Williamson, 2003). According to the US Commerce Department during the 2000s, multinational companies, who employ a fifth of all American workers, cut their workforces in the United States by 2.9 million while they increased them overseas by 2.4 million (Wessel, 2011). The shift in the distribution of jobs degraded employment opportunities and incomes for American workers despite the aggregate growth in the global economy, the result of the place-rootedness of labor and the economics of comparative advantage. The results of firms' investment in manufacturing offshore to seek low-cost labor lead to deindustrialization in the home country and the weakened bargaining power of labor (Alderson & Nielsen, 2002).

A dynamic globalized economy is the product of the evolution of national economies driven by the efficient geographic dispersion of corporate functions in a global supply chain: (1) labor-intensive, low value-added parts of the supply

---

* Paradoxically, the US recession would have been deeper had it not been for market integration with Chinese and Indian economies that grew during this period of economic globalization.

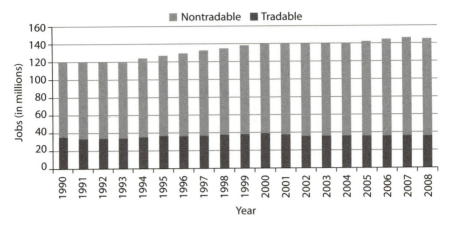

Figure 1.1. Nontradable and tradable jobs, 1990–2008. *Source:* Spence & Hlatshwayo, 2011, p. 11. Report available for download at http://www.cfr.org/industrial-policy/evolving -structure-american-economy-employment-challenge/p24366.

chain in emerging economies; (2) design and high-end manufacturing in high-middle-income or high-income countries such as South Korea; (3) and branding, marketing, and research as well as coordination of the supply chain in developed economies such as the United States (Spence & Hlatshwayo, 2011), and especially in its most globally connected cities. The latter has led to a dramatic shift in the profile of jobs available to Americans.

Economist Michael Spence points out that since 1990, nearly 98 percent of US job growth has occurred in the nontradable sector, goods and services that can only be produced and consumed domestically (e.g., legal and medical services, education, and food service). Tradable functions are those that can be off-shored to cheaper labor markets in the global supply chain. The sphere of tradable jobs has also moved beyond the confines of relatively low-wage manufacturing by way of technology that enables the offshoring of high-skill services in accounting, consulting, and IT servicing (Spence & Hlatshwayo, 2011). Figure 1.1 shows the trends from 1990 to 2008.

The freeing of time from space that characterizes globalization (Giddens, 1990; Held & McGrew, 2007) enables the dispersion of corporate functions and capital flows but not the place-rootedness of labor. Advocates of liberalized trade (e.g., Wolf, 2005) appeal to a Rawlsian sense of global justice for improving the lives of the world's poor. But there is little evidence for the support of this trade-off among vulnerable American workers who have been most negatively affected by technological advances and free-trade policy. The most visible signs of the weakened economy in the United States can be seen in cities such as Cleveland and Detroit, where reliance on manufacturing and an inability to develop a thriving service sector resulted in economic stagnation or collapse. By contrast, cities such as New York, Atlanta, Chicago, and San Francisco have such service sectors but also high income inequality.

Spence and Hlatshwayo (2011) found that over the past twenty years, the tradable sector in the US economy generated negligible incremental employment. But the United States did not have an unemployment problem until the Great Recession of 2008, an indication of a structural change in the economy that posed significant political problems:

> The expanding labor force was absorbed in the nontradable sector (roughly 26.7 out of a total of 27.3 million net new jobs), government and health care leading the growth (10.4 million incremental jobs between them). In our view, it is unlikely that this pattern will continue. Chances are good that the pace of employment generation on the nontradable side will slow. Fiscal conditions, the costs of the health-care sector, a resetting of real estate values, and the elimination of excess consumption all point to the potential for a longer-term structural employment problem. Expanding employment in the tradable sector almost certainly has to be part of the solution. Otherwise, the United States will have a longer-term employment problem. (pp. 31–32)

Six years after the onset of the Great Recession, moderate growth in the rate of job creation had reduced unemployment, but the recurring theme in news reports continued to be job growth with no increase in wages. Though the economy since the end of 2009 had grown by 12 percent, corporate profits risen by 46 percent and the stock market by 92 percent, median household income had decreased by 3.4 percent (Anonymous, 2014).

Changes in the US economy have not been uniform geographically. Research shows that between 2000 and 2007, US imports from low-income nations grew from 15 to 28 percent. China was responsible for 89 percent of that growth, the result of its admission into the World Trade Organization in December 2001. More importantly, local labor markets exposed to these imports resulted in increased unemployment, decreased labor-force participation, lowered wages, and increased reliance on disability and other income transfers. The most affected workers were those in manufacturing sectors, mostly those without college educations and least able to relocate. Black Americans have been disproportionately affected. The national unemployment rate among blacks in 2015 was more than double than that among whites. In Michigan and Ohio, states most affected by the Great Recession, black unemployment was triple that of white. The authors conclude, "The consequences of China trade for US employment, household income, and government benefit programs may contribute to public ambivalence toward globalization and specific anxiety about increasing trade with China" (Autor, Dorn, & Hanson, 2013).

Absent any short-term fixes to the employment and stagnant wage problems, expansion of the social safety net and redistributive policy provide alternative measures of security for affected workers. The United States has had difficulty making these adjustments. The importance of political culture for adapting to global economic integration is illustrated by Germany and other coordinated market economies in northern Europe where government expenditures as a percentage of GDP are far higher than in the liberal market economy of the United States (Tanzi & Schuknecht, 2000; Hall & Soskice, 2001).

Explanations for the differences between policy responses fall into structural and cultural categories, which are often interrelated. They include (1) greater beliefs among Americans for the possibility of social mobility than among northern Europeans, despite the absence of any actual differences (Bénabou & Tirole, 2006), perhaps because Europeans are nearly twice as likely as Americans to believe that luck explains differences in income (Alesina, Glaeser, & Sacerdote, 2001); (2) greater proportional representation in European political systems as well as higher ethnic homogeneity (Alesina & Glaeser, 2004); the latter may be related to (3) greater levels of social trust among northern Europeans and an associated increased willingness to pay higher taxes (Putnam, 2000; Algan, Cahuc, & Sangnier, 2011).

Some economists (Hall & Soskice, 2001) use the varieties of capitalism argument (Acemoglu, Robinson, & Verdier, 2012) to account for the differences. They argue that a globally integrated economy has created technological interdependences with one or a small subset of nations that contribute disproportionately to their mutual growth. Nations, such as the United States, with neoliberal market economies (e.g., deregulated labor markets and low-cost hiring and firing) work on the frontier of technological innovation. While these "cut-throat capitalism" nations strengthen their economic growth, they also weaken incentives for coordinated economies in Germany and other northern European states. In those states, industrial relations systems encourage employee cooperation and wage moderation. In short, they have few incentives to sacrifice their social safety nets and income equality to compete on the technological frontier.

Those states on the frontier, such as the United States, need to maintain high economic incentives for technological entrepreneurs (Acemoglu et al.,

2012).* The incentives exacerbate income inequality and poverty that characterize unrestricted capitalism. The authors' conclusion poses a conundrum for American political leadership: "Other nations free-ride on the cutthroat incentives of the leaders and choose a more 'cuddly' form of capitalism. . . . [T]hose that choose cuddly capitalism, though poorer, will be better off than those opting for cutthroat capitalism. Nevertheless, this configuration is an equilibrium because cutthroat capitalists cannot switch to cuddly capitalism without having a large impact on world growth, which would ultimately reduce their own welfare" (p. 36).

Taken together, the structural changes in the global economy and an unresolved debate on fiscal austerity have constrained the range of policy options and increased economic insecurity. Flattening incomes and an attending uncertainty about the future underlay one of the causes for the Tea Party and OWS movements that followed the Great Recession.

The principal driver of US economic growth in the 2000s was domestic consumption fueled by a housing bubble. Ever increasing housing prices provided Americans with a perception of rising wealth as middle incomes stagnated in the 1990s. The bubble was inflated by the purchase of US debt by China and Japan and low interest rates set by the Federal Reserve to hasten recovery from the 2001 recession. When the bubble burst, the US government lacked the tools and the political will to fuel job growth. Constrained by a high fiscal deficit and structural changes in a globally influenced job market, the 2008 Obama administration faced a lackluster recovery. Six years after the onset of the recession, polls revealed that citizens remained concerned about their future, despite lower unemployment (Pew Research Center, 2014).

Once optimistic about their chances for economic prosperity, Americans are now uncommonly pessimistic about their future. Aside from African Americans and Hispanics, every demographic group sees the United States as worse off than in the 1990s (Penn, 2011), and nearly four in ten see that decline as permanent (CBS News / *The New York Times*, 2011). Figure 1.2 plots aggregate public opinion data between 1981 and 2013 on how Americans feel about their children's future, a proxy for perceptions of insecurity regarding the long-term growth of the American economy.

Figure 1.3 plots aggregate data on the percentage of Americans who worry about meeting their future expenses.

---

* The problem may be compounded by a slowdown in technological innovation in general (Huebner, 2005), an added burden on economic growth for the United States.

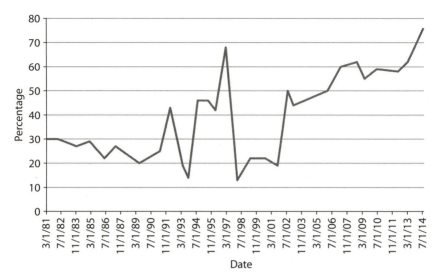

Figure 1.2. Americans who believe their children will grow up worse off, 1981–2013. *Source:* Asked by ten different survey organizations using variations of the question "Looking to the future, do you think most children in this country will grow up to be better off or worse off than their parents?" Retrieved from the iPOLL Databank, The Roper Center for Public Opinion Research, University of Connecticut.

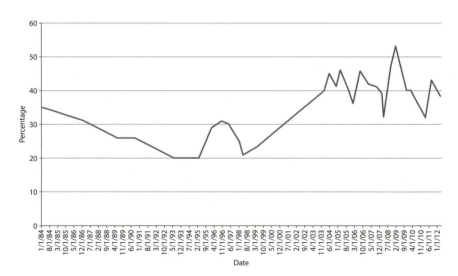

Figure 1.3. Americans who worry about meeting their expenses, 1981–2012. *Source:* Asked by four different survey organizations using variations of the question "How often do you worry that your total family income will not be enough to meet your family's expenses and bills?" Data reflect percentage who say "all or most of the time," "always," or "very concerned." Retrieved from the iPOLL Databank, The Roper Center for Public Opinion Research, University of Connecticut.

In both cases, there is a decline in concern through the 1980s, a brief rise and fall in the mid-1990s, and then a steady secular rise through the 2000s. What is notable is that the rise in economic insecurity precedes 9/11, evidence that structural changes in the economy explain the rise in insecurity rather than external events. In the case of concern for future generations, the line spikes after 9/11 and continues an uninterrupted climb despite the emergence of the housing bubble in 2001. In short, American economic security has become increasingly captive to global conditions. In the new world picture, employment is no longer a domestic issue. It is now, like the price of gasoline, *entrained in the flow of a globalized economy*. To think of it in terms of a traditional domestic–foreign dichotomy leads to imperfect diagnosis and ineffective policy.

The concept of *policy entrainment* also helps explain the relationship between what, on the surface, seem like disconnected issues. For example, the global justice movement ("antiglobalization"), or GJM, recognized the connection between US foreign policy with respect to trade agreements and the leverage of American labor. In the late 1990s, the GJM mounted a successful campaign to restrain Clinton's free-trade policy by raising awareness and media sympathy, particularly in the 1999 WTO demonstrations in Seattle (Rojecki, 2002).

The Tea Party arose after the financial panic of 2007, itself the joint result of foreign and domestic policy. Tea Party supporters blamed domestic deficit spending for risking their future financial security. They also blamed "unworthy" recipients of government largesse for squandering the nation's fiscal resources (Skocpol & Williamson, 2012). Parker and Barreto (2013) argued that Tea Party sympathizers were pseudo-conservative reactionaries to Barack Obama's presidency and especially to his person as an embodiment of change that threatened their economic security and social status. The latter signaled the symbolic, groupcentric politics symptomatic of the politics of insecurity.

While Parker and Barreto downplay the role of economic dislocation in favor of an explanation rooted in lost status for whites (they find only a weak association between sympathy for Tea Party beliefs and economic anxiety), it is difficult to dismiss the role of the Great Recession in undermining people's confidence in the viability of the social safety net (i.e., Social Security and Medicare). That the proximate target was Barack Obama in particular and minorities in general (e.g., Winter, 2006) does not factor out an anxiety for the future evident in the public opinion data cited in figures 1.2 and 1.3 and in studies that show much reduced economic mobility—regardless of race—in the Southeast and industrial Midwest (Chetty et al., 2013). Coincidentally, these were also areas of highest support for the Tea Party (Zernike & Thee-Brenan, 2010; Skocpol & Williamson, 2012), although it is hazardous to establish a direct causal link.

The perception of increased insecurity had political consequences. Because the Tea Party elected a number of representatives in the 2010 midterms, the movement limited the government's ability to use deficit spending to recover from the financial crisis and increase employment in the nontradable jobs sector. The Tea Party's resilience was demonstrated by the better-than-90-percent reelection of its candidates in the 2012 election. We examine the movement's success in chapter 7.

The OWS movement reacted to the same issues, but its membership was much younger than that of the Tea Party. OWS reflected the concerns of a generation facing a significantly dimmer future, even as developing economies like China recovered quickly and resumed strong growth. Weighed down by student debt and underwater mortgages, movement supporters blamed corporations, banks, and unresponsive politicians. Unlike the Tea Party, however, OWS avoided association with extant political institutions (Harcourt, 2012), opting instead to reframe politics entirely. For that reason, among others, OWS's influence was much less felt in the short term as compared to that of the Tea Party. We examine the movement, and in particular its interior dynamics, in chapter 8.

OWS had little effect on Obama's policy initiatives, stymied by an uncompromising GOP House and by a conservative trend in policy attitudes among Americans. One way of measuring the trend is by gauging "policy mood," a useful empirical indicator of mass public opinion.

Stimson (1991) defined policy mood as a general disposition among the public to favor policies on the right or left. At any given point in time, an asymmetric distribution of opinion (mood) represents a reference point for policy contemplated by political elites. The measure is calculated by aggregating the public's preferences for more or less government across 19 different policy areas (Atkinson et al., 2011). Figure 1.4 reveals its cyclical nature, a rise in liberal preferences during GOP presidencies and a fall during Democratic.

What is notable about the trend during the Obama administration is not so much the rightward turn but that it took place during the worst economic crisis since World War II, a period one would have expected to elicit high levels of support for increased government spending and income redistribution, key dimensions of liberalism.

Kelly and Enns (2010) noted this incongruity in their analysis of public preferences for income redistribution, especially between 1987 and 2010, the period that witnessed the greatest rise in inequality. They found that income groups at

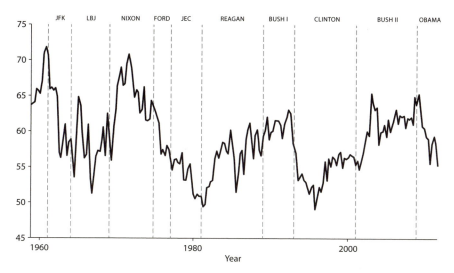

Figure 1.4. Liberalism of American public as measured by policy mood, 1958–2012. *Source:* A *Washington Post* blog written by John Sides, a professor at George Washington University, available at http://www.washingtonpost.com/blogs/wonkblog/wp/2013/03/31/no-the -2012-election-didnt-prove-the-republican-party-needs-a-reboot/. *Note:* The numbers in the vertical axis compose an index based on hundreds of survey questions. Their interpretive meaning is derived by comparing their relative values over time.

the top *and bottom* opposed tax policies that would reduce inequality. This violated not only a widely cited economic model that predicts that inequality leads to aggregate preferences for government spending (Meltzer & Richard, 1981) but also one that predicts opposition to income redistribution only among upper- and middle-income groups (Bénabou & Tirole, 2006).

Surprisingly, Kelly and Enns found that those at the bottom were no less aware of rising inequality. They also found that opposition to income redistribution was not confined to conservative presidential administrations when leadership cues could be responsible for opinion that runs contrary to the self-interest of those at the bottom. Exhausting alternative explanations, the economists speculated, "Media frames over this period may have increasingly emphasized stories of individualism, thus generating a negative link between rising inequality and public opinion liberalism." We see indirect evidence for their conclusion in an analysis of the mediated reaction to the New Orleans flood in chapter 5. Another explanation, pursued in greater detail in chapter 2, is the small role played by self-interest in explaining Americans' attitudes about various economic policies.

Evidence for the influence of a cultural component in the explanation comes from similar studies of British (Scheve & Slaughter, 2004) and Swiss (Walter, 2010) public opinion. Both studies show that economic globalization increases worker insecurity and that insecurity in turn increases support for government spending and provision of jobs. The absence of a similar reaction among Americans calls to mind studies cited earlier (e.g., Alesina et al., 2001) that indicate culture plays an important mediating effect in the politics of insecurity.

To summarize, major changes in the economy have altered the life opportunities for Americans and reduced the range of policy options available to government leaders. These changes are most evident during economic downturns, but for one class of problems—the environment—the changes are more gradual and only occasionally connected to attention-getting events. When those events take place, they shed light on the role of political culture and group identity in the politics of insecurity.

Environmental Insecurity

Environmental issues arguably pose the greatest collective threats to Americans as well as the globe at large, yet two features of those issues make them very difficult to address. One is the incremental pace of changes and the tendency of people to think in the short term and about local conditions. As Allenby (2000) put it, "Few people think beyond a time horizon of a few years, and a geographic range of miles. Many of the natural and human systems with which national security and environmental policy in the broadest sense must deal, however, lie far beyond these intuitive boundaries" (p. 6).

The second is more difficult to resolve because of the trade-offs between environmental and economic security. A global market capitalist system has raised expectations for material prosperity but also increased the risk of conflict and insecurity if those expectations are unmet. Growing economies require energy, much of it from fossil fuels. Increased use of these energy sources, however, contributes to environmental problems that readily cross national borders and convert the environmental tragedy of the commons to a global level.

The Intergovernmental Panel on Climate Change (2014), the leading international network of climate scientists, concluded that global warming is "unequivocal" and that there is a 90 percent probability that agriculture and fossil fuel have caused most of the rise in temperatures since 1950 (see also Oreskes, 2004). It also concluded that "surface temperature is projected to rise over the 21st century under all assessed emission scenarios. It is very likely that heat waves will occur more often and last longer, and that extreme precipitation events will become more intense and frequent in many regions. The ocean will continue to warm and acidify, and global mean sea level to rise" (p. 10).

Despite scientific consensus on this global problem, developing nations are unwilling to adapt a lean energy diet advocated by states with mature economies. The United States is also reluctant to trim its carbon consumption despite the apparent popular domestic support for doing so. In the United States, a majority believe global climate change is a serious problem and favors regulation of greenhouse gas emissions (Yeager et al., 2011) but have not yet been mobilized by a movement that puts serious pressure on Congress for reform.

At least a portion of the resistance can be explained by public misinterpretation of scientific opinion. Depending on how the questions are asked, Americans' belief that scientists have reached a consensus ranges from only one-third to a little over 60 percent (Nisbet & Myers, 2007).

Other explanations for the disparity between scientific and public opinion include: (1) political polarization on the issue, but with more unity among conservatives (McCright & Dunlap, 2011), an extension of the general polarizing trends in elite and public opinion to the scientific domain (Baldassarri & Gelman, 2008); (2) a systematic campaign by corporations and lobby groups to discredit scientific consensus, exaggerate the scope of scientific dissent, and intimidate opponents (Kolk & Levy, 2001; Dunlap & McCright, 2011; and (3) use of the balancing norm by the mass media to add undue weight to dissenting views—"fringe science"—on the role of humans in climate change (McCright & Dunlap, 2011; cf. Boykoff, 2007).

Social movements hold an important balancing force in the debate (Beck, 1994), but for a number of reasons they have not overcome conservative resistance to a systematic policy response to climate change. The environmental movement's individualized concept of the carbon footprint has been successfully publicized and recycling has become a routine activity, yet the absence of mobilization at the grassroots level has reduced the pressure on the United States to sign the Kyoto protocol, pass cap and trade legislation, or implement a carbon consumption tax.

Mol (2000) hypothesized that the environmental movement has been hampered by its suspicion of transnational institutions, as illustrated by its slogan, "Think globally, act locally." In this book, I argue that a key to understanding the movement's lack of progress is cultural resonance and an increasing emphasis on individualism, as evidenced by comparison of a response to an environmental crisis in an earlier period of US history when a vigorous right-wing movement similar to the Tea Party did not obstruct a large-scale federal solution.

In short, Americans have become inured to messages of alarm posed by environmental insecurity. The political culture for addressing the negative consequences of globalization on the environment has thus far failed to ignite the moral passion necessary for developing an effective response at the nation-state level. We examine the issue in detail in chapter 5, an analysis of the tardy and policy-free response to the catastrophic flood of New Orleans, an event that for a time signaled future risk exposure to the effects of the gradually rising temperatures of the oceans. By contrast, the public maintains a hair-trigger response to terrorism.

Existential Insecurity

The most obvious threats posed to the United States by globalization have been existential, comparable in some ways to the overhanging threat of nuclear war during the Cold War. What distinguished the two periods was an indelible image of an actual attack on US soil, the first since the War of 1812. For a time, 9/11 fused the cultural and political identities of most Americans and facilitated the nation's entry into two wars. The desire for security overrode the primary value of liberty, so much so that most citizens accepted the imposition of a massive security apparatus—most highly visible at airports but also that of pervasive electronic surveillance enabled by the Patriot Act—without complaint.

The imposition of this apparatus on perceived enemies was more severe. Reluctance of media elites to apply the term "torture" to what happened at Abu Ghraib (Bennett et al., 2006), the lack of urgency to close Guantanamo, and the tolerance for repeated incursions by pilotless drones into Pakistan and elsewhere to kill suspected terrorists indicated an increased tolerance for punishment of a new class of enemies whose motivations were diagnosed as beyond reason and therefore outside politics.

President Obama's assent to domestic counterterrorism measures, notably the National Security Administration's Prism program instituted by George W. Bush, indicated the scant difference between the two political parties on the effects of existential insecurity posed by terrorism. A poll taken after disclosure in June 2013 of the PRISM surveillance program revealed that over half of the population thought it was acceptable for the NSA to monitor domestic telephone records and were evenly divided on whether it was acceptable to monitor e-mail traffic to prevent terrorism. The numbers remained essentially unchanged from 2002, when Pew had conducted a similar poll (Pew Research Center, 2013).

The continued sacrifice of privacy for safety is an outward sign of the profound insecurity caused by 9/11 and the doubts it raised about the impregnability of fortress America. In an echo of the anxiety exploited by Richard Nixon and Joe McCarthy in the late 1940s and early 1950s after the Soviet Union tested an atomic bomb, 9/11 and the ensuing wars in Afghanistan and Iraq spawned controversies about the true identity of America and its citizens: Does the United States torture? Do terrorists deserve a fair trial? Is Barack Obama a Christian? The politics of insecurity were so potent that they helped sow doubts about 2004 presidential candidate John Kerry's military record in Vietnam. Kerry's attempts to present himself as a true American—"reporting for duty" in his acceptance speech at the Democratic convention—fell flat. Later in the campaign, a group known as the Swift Boat Veterans for Truth succeeded in raising public doubts about Kerry's Vietnam service record, even as George W. Bush escaped comparable media scrutiny of his own record in the Texas Air National Guard (Rojecki & Meraz, 2016).

Admiration for the military grew significantly after 9/11, an indirect measure of the increased concern for security among the US population. Figure 1.5 depicts the percentage of Americans who had a "great deal of confidence in people who run the military" in the 40-year period between 1973 and 2013.

Following the end of the Vietnam War, confidence averaged in the mid-30s, an indication of public fatigue and disappointment. The wars in the Middle East— first the Gulf War of 1991 and then the invasions of Afghanistan and Iraq in

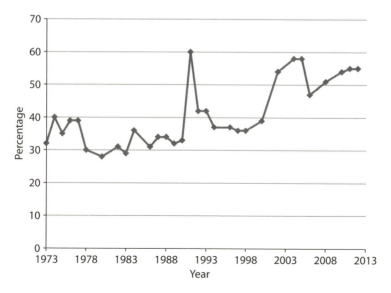

Figure 1.5. Americans who have a great deal of confidence in people who run the military. *Source:* Data from General Social Survey.

2001 and 2003—marked a dramatic rise in the public's confidence. While the Gulf War's influence was temporary, the rise in support since 9/11 was sustained for over a decade. To provide some contrasting context, while President Obama's level of support hovered in the upper 40s toward the end of his term in office and high confidence in congressional leaders and the mass media could be measured in the high single digits, confidence in the military averaged in the mid- to high 50s.

During Obama's first term, the most consistent and effective line of attack from the right centered on his identity and legitimacy as president. These questions folded readily into a parallel criticism of his alleged elitism based on his comment during the primaries on bitter, small-town Americans clinging to their guns and bibles and later in his presidency on his fondness for arugula. Accusations of elitism later morphed into attacks on Obama's loyalty to the nation itself. Cosmopolitanism came under effective attack from the right, a striking demonstration of the potency of fear in the politics of insecurity and of its provincial pull on identity. Although current campaigns are funded by well-heeled sponsors and broadcast by partisan media, they resonate with a political culture rooted in issues of vice and virtue. The culture wars illustrate the potency of morally inflected and inflexible issues that now play a prominent role in the politics of insecurity. In chapters 3 and 4, I examine the effect of 9/11 on elite opinion on economic and military policy, a debate influenced by both fear and self-interest.

Summary and Preview

The politics of insecurity are driven by insecurity caused by major changes in the political economy and increased vulnerability to the plate tectonic shifts that brought once abstract and remote problems onto the shores of America and into the daily lives of Americans. Because these conditions are at once unfamiliar and difficult to solve, political elites have incentives to trade on fear by raising issues that create a zero-sum game in which compromise is equivalent to submission. In these politics, the right has thus far been much more effective at framing and disseminating its policy positions and charging them with moral fervor. Not all areas of the United States are receptive to these appeals, but their influence is magnified by three factors:

1. The disproportionate, constitutionally granted power of the least populous states, whose citizens feel most vulnerable to the structural changes that result from a globalized (postindustrial) economy.
2. The marked influence of religion on the nation's political culture. Religious institutions have driven the nation's most influential reform move-

ments as well as reactions to federal implementation of those reforms (Morone, 2004; Noll, 2008). Paralleling fragmentation of the secular left on matters of identity (e.g., Gitlin, 1995; Rorty, 1998), a once vibrant movement of leftist evangelicals broke apart in the 1970s on issues of race and gender, and doctrinal differences on separation of church and state (Swartz, 2011). Disintegration of the evangelical left ceded majority influence to conservative evangelicals, which in turn have been growing in number, wealth, and political organization.

3. A balkanized media system that invites selective exposure and perception. Elements of that system are increasingly influenced by corporate power, as seen, for example, by the landmark ruling of the Supreme Court in *Citizens United v. Federal Election Commission*, in which the Court ruled that corporations and unions could not be restricted from funding political ads and broadcasts. Corporations have also increased their influence on everyday political discourse by funding a number of think tanks—for example, the Cato Institute and Heritage Foundation—that now routinely provide expert commentary to national media outlets. (Dolny, 2008)

The debates attending disparate but connected issues have been widely characterized as partisan, bitter, polarized, and ideological. For a nation known for its philosophical pragmatism and log-rolling politics, this marks an important disruption. The politics of insecurity, driven by processes on a global scale that entrain the domestic with the foreign, help explain the constraints and polarizing opportunities in this stage of the nation's history.

In summary, globalization has introduced new problems to the United States and exacerbated others already in existence. These have affected US politics, which have influenced or obstructed the formulation of American policy on globalization-related processes. The attending insecurity has increased the influence of symbolic politics that heighten the salience of group identities in the service of political discourse that obstructs rather than enables policy to address common problems. In this process, the American right has thus far been more effective at mainly obstructing legislation that responds to a new class of problems introduced by flows and processes of globalization. The obstructions create a feedback loop that influences the trajectory of globalization and American politics.

In the next chapter, I focus on the ideas that make up the ordinary discourses of mass media and trace their origins to group identity and the political culture from which these identities spring. I also describe the uncertainty model, the analytical model I use to examine the case studies that follow in chapters 3 through 8.

Chapters 3 and 4 focus on the high uncertainty conditions of 9/11 that created a keen sense of dread and insecurity in the population. Chapter 3 uses frame analysis to demonstrate the advantage held by elites in redefining the terms of debate on globalization as well as establishing a minor but intellectually respectable position for sociotropic politics—"the clash of civilizations." While the first reduced the differences between elites on the value of free trade, the second amplified the cultural resonance of the moral and institutional ideals of American exceptionalism that would legitimate the US invasions of Afghanistan and Iraq. I take up this topic in chapter 4, an analysis of the culturally influenced beliefs that political liberalism would trump religious sectarianism in the Middle East, an ironic expectation given the role played by religious sectarianism in the US politics of insecurity.

Chapter 5 examines the role of culture in the politics of insecurity via a historical comparison of reactions to two catastrophic floods that took place in the lower Mississippi River valley. Katrina was the first hurricane to stimulate a popular discourse that connected weather disasters to the issue of climate change. The polarized discourses on climate change were in stark contrast to near consensual scientific opinion on the issue, a demonstration of the gulf between popular and expert assessments of risk. Hidden elements that influenced the debate were resonant cultural assumptions that help explain the absence of popular support for policies that would address the underlying causes of climate change. In short, the perceived risk exposure to increasingly anomalous weather events (e.g., Hurricane Sandy, the "polar vortex" of 2013–2014) was diminished by resonant cultural beliefs as well as groupcentric politics.

Chapter 6 studies the long-standing debate on illegal immigration, the result of labor-market demands and second-order reactions to the insecurity caused by 9/11. Curiously, to the extent economic self-interest played a part in the mediated debate, it originated in cities most connected to the global economy. In other less connected locations, passionate opposition traded almost entirely on cultural fears. The fears led to a heated symbolic response that blocked policy reform.

Chapters 7 and 8 turn to the reactions of citizens to globalization-related insecurity and the absence of a meaningful difference between the parties on economic policy. The Tea Party movement followed the Great Recession of 2008 and reinforced the polarized politics in Congress that had been building since the Clinton administration. Chapter 7 studies the process by which the groups that made up the Tea Party maintained message discipline and solidarity and how these groups won mainstream media legitimation. By contrast, the OWS movement could not articulate a coherent political message or overcome infighting among the groups that made up its coalition. Chapter 8 analyzes an internal mediated dialogue among OWS organizers and participants. It provides a view of the ideas that supported the movement and how they failed to provide sufficient glue to keep the movement together. OWS nevertheless added a potentially important cultural anchor for future movements on the left to compete in the politics of insecurity, one of the topics I take up in the conclusion in chapter 9.

CHAPTER TWO

Uncertainty, Interests, and Identity

You know you're a "low information voter" when you blame Obama for the problems in Iraq. And it's obvious you're an idiot if you're going to ignore the fact that
Iraq asked us to leave. None of this would be happening now if it weren't for the
Republicans conning us into getting involved in Iraq in the first place. —*Comment
in* The Washington Post, *June 23, 2014*

All the result of the "cut and run" policy of Obama and Hillary Clinton who set up
this massive failure on a grand scale. They just pulled everyone out of there and
also totally disengaged from the Iraqi political power base, while overall leaving
the very vacuum being filled by these terrorist swarms. It's too late to do anything
now, as Americans are weary of wasting our blood and money on these Islamic
fanatics.—*Following comment in* The Washington Post, *June 23, 2014*

In this chapter, I lay the foundation for the uncertainty model, a model of political
communication on issues that disrupt citizens' expectations of a secure future.
The uncertainty model explains the dynamics of an increasingly polarized political and information environment that arose in the 1990s as *globalization*—a
generic term of reference in the public mind—and replaced Cold War Manichean
ideology for mapping the world. The disruptions created by globalization favor the
expansion of "position issues" that trade on emotion and moral judgment and lead
to uncompromising politics. These politics are driven in part by group identity,
whose strength is a function of beliefs reinforced in a feedback loop caused by an
increasingly polarized information system. The paradoxical result is that uncertainty in an interested-related domain of a citizen's life, such as job security, leads
to a grasp for certainty in an unrelated domain such as identity affirmation.

Collectively, this enhances the likelihood of symbolic politics, a misdirection
of attention from interests to assertions of identity that contribute to political
paralysis. The inaction serves the interests of those who benefit by the status
quo yet may also fuel citizen unrest. The success (or failure) of a political move-

Figure 2.1. An overview of the uncertainty model.

ment driven by insecurity tells us something about some of the dominant beliefs that insensibly influence politics. These appear in the ordinary political discourses that reflect and structure commonsense ways of thinking. By common
I do not mean inconsequential. They are, rather, critically unexamined ideas
and beliefs that are thereby all the more potent for influencing politics.

The uncertainty model explains the politics that arise from major changes in
the political economy and the emergence of a set of unique problems attributed to
globalization. The problems send signals of varying intensity to create insecurity
(perceived risk exposure) in the population. If citizens feel their exposure to risk
is excessive and unaddressed by elite policy response, they may mobilize their
dissent in the shape of a political movement. Alternatively, the insecurity may
simply lead to group-based antagonism that creates an obstacle to policy that
effectively addresses an authentic threat. Although the right has thus far enjoyed
a number of advantages by a number of psychological and historical factors,
both sides of the political spectrum are influenced by an information environment that has changed the partisan risk profile for news media and an increased
tendency for citizens, especially those who are most partisan, to seek one-sided
perspectives. These generate increased emotional, belief-driven energy, the fuel
for group solidarity.

Figure 2.1 summarizes key stages of the uncertainty model: A threatening
event creates uncertainty in the population. Perceived future exposure to the
threat leads to insecurity, which yields a political response of varying effectiveness.
The form of its expression and success depends on the support of like-minded
others. Each of these three stages may be conditioned by a number of variables.

I provide the details of the intervening variables and detail the model in the
final section of this chapter. Before doing so, I review several bodies of research
that support the main tenets and propositions of the model. The research includes the psychology of uncertainty, the cultural dynamics of identity politics,
and the current state of the information environment.

Discourses of Insecurity

As the comments from *The Washington Post* that open this chapter illustrate,
the arguments used by citizens in mediated exchanges amount to a discursive

gridlock that renders compromise all but impossible.* While there is no way to determine whether they represent the larger public, the posted comments of contributors follow a familiar pattern of assertion and counterassertion. It is a rare occasion when an opponent thanks a contributor for evidence or an insight that backs an opinion in conflict with that of his or her own, concedes a point, or admits to a change of mind. The usual pattern is an exchange that ignores claims made and evidence offered in earlier posts. Stories on rampage attacks by mentally ill killers, for example, unleash a ritualized interchange of opinions on the need for or the futility of gun control, with little or no acknowledged change in opinion. Similarly, extreme weather events bring down a rain of declarations, often laced with insult, on the reality of global warming and thoughts on the mental reserves of opponents who hold a contrary position.

It may be fanciful to think commentators expect concessions or a good-faith exchange with those who hold opposing points of view. Instead, contributors seem to be blowing off steam and seeking approval from like-minded others. One indication of the latter is that online news sites permit readers to endorse comments and rank them by "likes." Persuasion seems a lesser goal than approval from those who think alike, a sign of the group-based identification that drives a rancorous ersatz debate. The phenomenon is a miniature of present-day politics driven by sharply defined, polarized issue positions in which passion and group-centric affirmation rather than reason and respect are the marks of political value (Iyengar, Sood, & Leikes, 2012; Iyengar & Westwood, 2014). The debate that goes nowhere is reminiscent of Edelman's treatise on symbolic politics (1964), its most recent incarnation more extreme than anticipated in his work.

Founded in earnestly held belief, symbolic politics distract ordinary citizens from issues that, by default, advance those whose political and economic interests gain by the status quo. The paralysis accompanies an unfamiliar world untethered from the sure ideological moorings of the Cold War and the coinciding period of US world dominance of the economy, as opposed to the current globalized economy where the United States dominates little but the entertainment sector.

As I argued in chapter 1, globalization has created a new category of domestic issues entrained in the flow of global processes. The issues defy conventional

---

* Preliminary research (e.g., Ruiz et al., 2011) found that readers of *The New York Times* are respectful of one another's opinions (in contrast to newspaper readers in the polarized pluralist press of France, Italy, and Spain). The authors stipulate that *The New York Times* employs a moderator to maintain politeness. This is not the case for *The Washington Post* and other US media, where the debate is much like the intemperate exchanges in the European press.

distinctions between domestic and foreign policy and lower the threshold for the polarized discourses that typify the politics of insecurity. The entrainment of domestic issues in global flows partly explains the intractability of the debate that ensues. Their origin in remote and sometimes hidden causes contributes to the perception of loss of control. This is exacerbated by elite consensus on a given policy—for example, increased foreign trade, passive assent to Chinese monetary policies making US-made products more expensive—that may have second- and third-order effects, often outwardly disconnected from their origins.

To illustrate, the NAFTA treaty was intended, among other goals, to reduce wage differentials between the United States and Mexico, but a number of little known nontariff protectionist measures on behalf of US agriculture interest groups actually reduced Mexican wages (Stiglitz, 2007). This in turn increased the flow of Mexican labor into the United States and contributed to an emotional debate on illegal immigration that was arguably a prime factor in drawing white (non-Hispanic) voters to vote Republican. Vulnerability to future risk fuels the polarizing discourses around the issue of immigration reform as previously dependable paths to economic success, such as a college degree, have become less reliable. The resulting politics make governance of the United States increasingly difficult as group loyalty, partisanship, and narrowly based goals driven by fear, resentment, and moral judgment trump a consensual search for the greater good.

At times of rapid change and dislocation, as in the period following the Cold War, and especially following 9/11, polarizing discourses voice the anxiety that rises in times of uncertainty. Because globalization-related processes (e.g., mobile capital, structural unemployment) restrict the state's repertoire of policy alternatives, elites and political movements rely increasingly on value-driven moral discourses that underlie group identification to mobilize support for competing policy ends. In proposition form, the less the perceived resources available to citizens (or greater the risk they will lose existing resources), the greater the propensity for the rise of polarizing issues. The Wisconsin public-sector union controversy of 2011 is an example of competing moral publics trapped in a zero-sum game of anger and resentment. To illustrate the rapid polarization of politics in the state, in 1994 Wisconsin voters gave Republican governor Tommy Thompson and Democratic Senator Herb Kohl landslide victories. Eight years later, in 2012, less than 6 percent of voters split their votes between the two parties.

Because uncertainty is at the heart of the politics of insecurity, it helps to understand how individuals and groups react cognitively under that condition.

Recent advances in psychology help us contextualize the emergence, and significance, of ideas in political discourse in the mass media.

The Psychology of Uncertainty

How do people react when they or their beliefs are threatened? Multiple lines of research in subdisciplines of psychology have converged on the finding that individuals seek to reestablish well-being and coherence in their lives after exposure to unexpected and disconcerting anomalies. These forms of adjustment take multiple forms, including rumor, increased group cohesion, and polarization. Extreme versions of adaptation such as confrontations with mortality are explained by terror management theory (TMT) (Greenberg, Poole, & Pyszczynski, 2004). One of the most prolific sources of research in psychology, TMT scholars find consistent support for the theory's principal claims that once immediate fears of mortality are pushed aside, one's faith in a meaningful worldview and sense of self-worth are bolstered. The political consequences of this reaction are significant.

Reviewing a number of research studies, for example, Landau et al. (2004) found that, "taken together, these findings provide convergent support for the role of intimations of mortality in people's allegiance to and defense of the nationalistic aspects of their cultural worldviews" (p. 1139). TMT research thus helps explain the "rally round the flag" phenomenon—a short-term boost to the president's popularity—during foreign policy crises. Extending this line of research, Landau and his colleagues studied the effects of mortality salience on short-term political preferences. They found that mortality salience not only increased support for President Bush but also decreased liking for presidential candidate John Kerry and influenced voting intentions, with Kerry preferred over Bush in the control condition and Bush in the mortality salient condition. The experimenters noted that their results harmonized with findings from a number of other studies that indicated "political allegiances are not always based on the balanced, rational forces of self-interest suggested by the Jeffersonian notion of democracy but also on the operation of nonrational forces of which we are not always aware" (p. 1146).

Seeking to incorporate TMT research with other related lines, Heine et al. (2006) proposed a metatheoretical model—the meaning maintenance model—that integrates research, among other factors, in meaning-making and uncertainty reduction. Three propositions link the diverse literatures on this topic. First, meaning is relational (like a schema, a mental model) in that it links ideas, people, places, and objects in expected configurations, an unconscious activation of otherwise disconnected thoughts. Second, when deprived of meaning or otherwise confronted with meaninglessness, individuals seek to restore epistemic stability in their lives: the greater the disruption, the more urgent the need to restore meaning. Third, disruptions lead people to endorse alternative, intact frameworks in a process called "fluid compensation" (Steele, 1988). Individuals seek restoration of certainty in domains that are most easily called to mind, rather than in the domain under threat.

In a review of research on uncertainty reduction, the authors report that when subjects are made aware of a disruption in one domain of their lives, they respond by becoming more rigid in their beliefs in another. For example, if a highly religious individual loses her job and is unable to find work, she may become more committed to her religion. The rigidity that accompanies uncertainty compensation leads to increased identification with like-minded others and its attending "us versus them" consequences. Thus subjects faced with uncertainty are more likely to rely on stereotypes because they offer clear cognitive guidelines that also harden attitudes about social issues.

For example, Rosenblatt et al. (1989) found that increased mortality salience led to harsher treatment for accused prostitutes among those subjects who had negative attitudes toward prostitution. In a similar study, McGregor and his colleagues (2001) found that experimental subjects who were reminded of a personal dilemma were more likely to become more supportive of capital punishment. In the same paper, the authors report an experiment in which subjects who were reminded of their mortality showed greater intergroup bias than those in a control condition. Another study found that increased mortality salience among Christian subjects led to more positive evaluations of their in-group and a more negative evaluation of Jews, an effect especially pronounced among those who were high in authoritarianism (Greenberg et al., 1990).

The research on the cultural effects of uncertainty is similarly striking. Various studies have found that mortality salience increases reverence for the flag and the crucifix (Greenberg et al., 1995), supernatural beliefs, religious identification, belief in God, and faith in the efficacy of divine intervention (Norenzayan & Hanson, 2006).

Taking a slightly different metaphorical perspective, Hirsh et al. (2012) proposed a model of psychological entropy to explain behavior under uncertainty, a situation when individuals find it more difficult to distinguish signal from noise in what was once a familiar environment. A function of uncertainty, psychological entropy requires greater energy to restore the means by which we achieve our goals. As the authors put it: "Psychological entropy appears inversely related to the integrity of an individual's existence in the world, as reflected in his or her ability to successfully perform work and obtain rewards through goal-directed perception and action" (p. 316). This is another way of saying that under extreme uncertainty, interests become unattainable. When this happens, alternative systems of ideas, such as religion and ideology, provide a means for restoring a sense of control. Unless a new ideational core is available for achieving a political end, uncertainty reduction leads to emotional, symbolic assertions of identity. Highly religious individuals are especially advantaged in conditions of entropy because they have a clear explanatory framework that constrains their interpretation of the world and thereby reduces the experience of uncertainty (Hogg, Adelman, & Blagg, 2010). Not surprisingly, religious commitment is a powerful predictor of partisan polarization (Abramowitz & Saunders, 2008; Bafumi & Shapiro, 2009).

Hirsh et al. (2012) noted that the uncertainty-reducing effectiveness of such belief systems becomes even more pronounced when an individual lives within a community of like-minded others, who, because they are more predictable, are less likely to provoke ambiguity. In short, uncertainty primes individuals for group identification, purity of group opinion, and group conflict. The political relevance of this research is especially important in a polarized climate of opinion. Research in political psychology shows that ideologically committed individuals not only resist changing their opinion in response to corrective information but become even more committed to their positions in a process termed *motivated reasoning* (see, e.g., Nyhan & Reifler, 2010; Hetey & Eberhardt, 2014).

The group solidarity that arises under these conditions is a potent resource for mobilizing an effective political movement, especially one founded in religious beliefs. In the United States, religion has had a marked influence on the nation's political culture. Religious institutions have driven the nation's most influential reform movements as well as reactions to federal implementation of those reforms (Morone, 2004; Noll, 2008).

Because beliefs under conditions of uncertainty are resistant to new information, group identity has its dysfunctional limits, a dogmatism that makes it difficult to adapt to changing circumstances: "Attempts to minimize short-term entropy at all costs through the adoption of rigid cognitive structures and behavioral patterns (e.g., by willfully ignoring information that contradicts one's worldview or refusing to explore outside of one's familiar environment) may in fact result in long-term adaptive failure despite the short-term reduction in anxiety. Indeed, excessive rigidity and a reluctance to explore and confront uncertainty have been associated with a variety of pathological outcomes and the failure to adapt to changing circumstances" (Hirsh et al., 2012, p. 11). The researchers' concluding line identifies the functional limits of group solidarity at a point in which rigid belief may be overtaken by new ideas or paradigm that reconfigure worldviews and reset politics.

To summarize, uncertainty leads to decisions that violate the interest-based utility-maximizing assumptions of rational-actor models. The political consequences of uncertainty include uncritical support for state elites and appeals based on maintaining state security. As Murray Edelman (1964) theorized: "Under this kind of value patterning, mass responses are more manipulable . . . because responses are chiefly to threat perceptions and can be readily changed by making it appear that new threats are dominant" (p. 175). Edelman had in mind the threat of communism, today supplanted by the protean threat of terrorism that readily morphs into new forms and, unlike communism, is much less confined by national boundaries.

The ironic outcome of the politics of insecurity is that under certain conditions, the strength of public sentiment is inversely related to its efficacy for the nation as a whole. But because passion is the primary arbiter of political efficacy, marginal gains—primarily those that block effective solutions to large-scale problems such as income inequality—accrue to those who are most passionate. Edelman wrote at a time when American politics were more consensual (unimodal), less fraught, and more amenable to compromise through negotiation and log-rolling. In the current polarized (bimodal) climate, identity overtakes common ends and the struggle for incompatible goals defines political undertaking. The paralysis that ensues accrues to those who have benefited the most by ongoing trends (i.e., by increased religiosity, neoliberalism, and globalization and its attendant inequality).

One issue illustrating the insecurity that drives group-based politics is immigration reform. For over two decades, immigration reform remained moribund, as the right was able to control the debate on issues of security, economic costs, and law and order. Only after the 2012 presidential election, when 71 percent of the fast-growing Latino population voted for President Obama, did the GOP briefly consider changing its issue position. The more interesting question is why the left could not rally public opinion in favor of reform earlier. In chapter 6, I argue that economic self-interest, especially in those US cities most connected to the global economy, played a part in the immigration controversy, lessening the passion needed to compete successfully in the politics of insecurity.

Controversial issues such as immigration reform enter a feedback loop that contributes to increasingly dysfunctional governance. One result is an increase in a class of issues conceptualized by Carmines and Stimson (1980) as "position issues" that make it much more difficult than in the 1940s–1970s to achieve policy consensus in times other than those of extreme crisis.

Position Issues and Partisanship

Position or "easy issues" are those focused on a controversial policy end rather than a path used to reach it. Symbolic and readily communicated, position issues appeal to values and intuition rather than sustained analysis (Leege et al., 2002). By contrast, a valence ("hard") issue such as high unemployment requires effort to analyze the evidence used to support competing paths to a consensually desired end. Easy issues are symbolic in the sense that they are rooted in abstract values that define membership in a group. Readily communicated, they are not easily resolved and often are lodged in long-standing conflicts and associated with (or "owned" by) specific political parties and candidates (p. 28). No issue is intrinsically "easy," but it can become such by being framed that way. The key is to establish a pattern of talking about an issue in rigid terms that maximizes the distance between supporters and opponents, us and them. The result of this divisive process is frozen politics that benefit those who gain by the status quo. For example, a rigidly opposed position to immigration reform lowers the bargaining power of low-wage service workers.

Because position issues are rooted in values and moral judgment, the argumentation used to advance them is uncompromising. Competing parties in the debate on income inequality, for example, use incompatible emphasis frames—"big business" versus "big government"—that make compromise all but impossible. As opposing groups engage in ostensibly reasoned debate, mutually exclusive positions lead to a zero-sum game. The process is exacerbated by an expectation that each side's perception (what they see, but what might not actually be) of logic and reason will be the neutral arbiters of the outcome.

As Hume pointed out in his *Treatise of Human Nature*: "Morals excite passions, and produce or prevent actions. Reason itself is utterly impotent in this particular." Facts may be piled up to little effect, a phenomenon psychologist Jonathan Haidt (2001) called the "wag the other dog's tail illusion," the expectation that wagging a dog's tail will make it happy. Nor is it realistic to expect individuals to defend their values. As Carmines and Stimson (1980) put it: "Normative premises are not by definition informed; neither do they need to be articulated" (p. 80). Indeed, they may be incapable of being articulated because they arise from emotion and identity that may disconnect them from the drive for utility-maximizing self-interest.

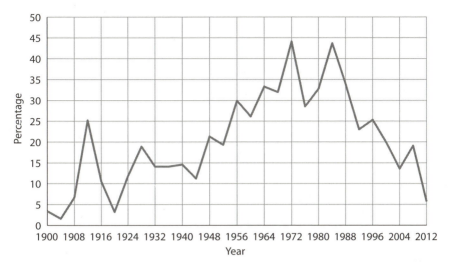

Figure 2.2. Ticket splitters between presidential and House candidates, 1900–2012. *Source:* Ornstein, Mann, Malbin, & Rugg, 2013.

Contemporary research on political polarization documents the increasing role of emotion and group identity in American politics. In the first decade of the twenty-first century, polarization reached historically high levels. While political scientists differed on the extent of the policy divide among Americans (e.g., Fiorina, Abrams, & Pope, 2011; Abramowitz, 2010), by 2012 ticket splitting had fallen to a 92-year, all-time low as well as widespread lack of tolerance among Americans for those who held political views different than those of their own. The line graph in figure 2.2 shows present levels of partisan voting not seen since the Gilded Age, not coincidentally the earlier high-water mark of globalization and inequality. The partisan voting patterns explain the intransigence of Congress as House members have little incentive to cooperate with a president of the opposing party.[*]

Echoing the absence of comity in government, Iyengar and his colleagues (2012) found high levels of what they call *affective polarization* among American citizens: "Democrats and Republicans not only increasingly dislike the opposing party, but also impute negative traits to the rank-and-file of the out-party" (p. 407). In follow-up research, Iyengar and Westwood (2014) found that partisans demonized one another to a degree that exceeded prejudice based on race, the animus

---

[*] I am not claiming symmetry in obstructionism. Where the Democrats voted in favor of the Iraq War and granted George W. Bush two tax cuts, the GOP was much less generous to the Obama administration.

strongest among highly partisan Republicans. Iyengar et al. hypothesized that exposure to political campaigns and selective exposure to partisan media contributes to polarization. To these causes, I would also add increased insecurity among Americans about their future prosperity, group-defining beliefs that pose obstacles to policy remedies for globalization-related problems, and the political and economic interests who gain by the current largely paralyzed policy regime.

When I use the term *group*, I refer to those who identify with a common set of interests and perceive these interests to be in conflict with those of another. Long-standing social cleavages (e.g., class and race) provide the grounds for interests and conflict, but only if they are salient and find expression in institutional forms such as party representation. The nature of the two-party system in the United States requires assembling disparate groups into coalitions large enough to win elections. The salience of interest-specific issues and long-standing conflicts among voters (Lipset & Rokkan, 1967; Manza & Brooks, 1999) as well as the stability of a coalition determine the outcome of political competition.

The origins of partisanship combine issues and value orientations aligned with ideological and party identification. Bafumi and Shapiro (2009) found that "partisanship has voters more strongly anchored than ever before by left/right ideological thinking" (p. 3). Economic issues expectedly predict party identification, but the authors also found partisanship to be strongly influenced by social issues (e.g., abortion, homosexuality, and family values), religious values, and race. Similarly, Jacoby (2014) found that different value orientations predict political identification—morality, patriotism, and social order for conservatives and economic security and equality for liberals—thus his conclusion that a culture war is at the foundation of fundamental divisions in American politics.

Because the most knowledgeable and active citizens are also the most partisan (Layman & Carsey, 2002; Abramowitz & Saunders, 2008), they have an outsized influence on political elites and on the marketing strategies of partisan media. Their influence derives from their active participation in the earliest stages of electoral campaigns when party elites are most sensitive to their preferences and when conflict-seeking media are most likely to draw attention to the most extreme candidates. As Bafumi and Shapiro (2009) declared: "These voters, once created, may contribute to the increasingly visible partisan conflict that occurs at the elite level. On the other hand, the large number of voters who have not sorted themselves into the extremes remain the decisive, ostensibly centrist, voters in elections. The level of partisan conflict that the contemporary mass media thrive on and magnify will only change if the parties put forth candidates to appeal to these moderate voters" (p. 20).

In their wide-ranging sociological study of the social cleavages that express American politics, Manza and Brooks (1999) pointed to the increased importance of issues for group identification, the foundation for symbolic politics. In their analysis of the four enduring social cleavages that have defined group-based interests—race, religion, class, and gender—the authors found that only race has provided the most stable source for group identification and institutional expression, an indication that new issues are overtaking traditional social cleavages and increasing tension in traditional party coalitions. For example, Miller and Schofield (2008) reported that in the Republican coalition, social conservatives have found themselves at odds with economic liberals on such issues as stem cell research. Meanwhile, economic conservatives in the Democratic coalition feel pressures from New Deal progressives who oppose free-trade policy such as the Trans-Pacific Partnership. Increased income inequality and the severity of the Great Recession would seem to have advantaged groups on the left, but the right has more than held its own despite crosscurrents in its coalition. One explanation for this counterintuitive finding may be found in the cultural foundations of the values and beliefs that influence political thinking.

Interests and Beliefs

In chapter 1, we reviewed some reasons for the sparse social safety net in the United States compared to other nations with similarly advanced economies. These included structural differences between American and European political and economic systems as well as differences in beliefs about the role of luck and hard work in social mobility. Before we explore the cultural foundations for the latter in greater detail, I now briefly review one of the principal reasons for the uncertainty of Americans' future prosperity and research on the scant influence of public opinion on policy that would offer a remedy.

The principal reason for Americans' sense of a dim economic future is wage stagnation, despite the robust growth of wealth among top income groups and of productivity that in the past was shared among top and middle (Piketty, 2014). Thus the top one percent of the wealthiest Americans saw their share of total income double from 10 percent in the 1950s to 22 percent in the mid-2000s. The top tier also recovered much more quickly from the ravages of the first Great Recession of globalization. Their income grew by 31 percent compared to less than one half of one percent among the bottom 99. By 2013, the top one percent had nearly recovered, while the bottom 99 had "hardly started" (Saez, 2013, p. 1). As we found in chapter 1, the reasons for the growth of inequality include the increased uses of automation, the off-shoring of tradable labor, and resistance to redistributive policy (cf. Piketty, 2014).

As for the US political system, scholarship shows that the principal obstacle to a redistributive policy that would reduce inequality and strengthen the social safety net (i.e., taxes and the minimum wage) is contributions to political campaigns (Bartels, 2008). Other research shows that neither majority public opinion nor a pluralistic model of interest group influence predicts policy change. In their analysis of 1,779 issues that were affected by legislation passed between 1981 and 2002, Gilens and Page (2014) found that economic elites and a narrow range of business interest groups had the most influence on policy outcomes. The authors also found that the preferences of ordinary citizens are highly correlated with those of economic elites, a possible instance of what Lukes (1974) called the "third face of power," the influence of elites on public opinion. Their conclusion echoes Bartels's (2008) finding that lower income groups support policies that undercut their self-interest (e.g., repeal of the estate tax). Bartels explains the paradox in the domain of economic policy as a reflection of the ambivalence Americans express about equality: in favor of equal opportunity but against redistributive policy that would reduce the inequality of outcomes (Hochschild, 1981). The influence of this belief points to a prominent role for culture and the circulation of ideas in the politics of insecurity.

Culture and Political Communication

Like ideology, culture is a notably challenging concept to define. Scholars have revised definitions of the concept numerous times, most recently into two broad categories: as a semiotic system and as a practice.

Culture as a system takes language and symbols as the foundation of human action. Geertz's (1973) definition of symbols as "tangible formulations, notions, abstractions from experience fixed in perceptible forms, concrete embodiments of ideas, attitudes, judgments, longings, or beliefs" (p. 91) is representative of the semiotic view of culture. Because of its static qualities—the tangible, fixed, and concrete—the concept of culture as a stable system was questioned by poststructural critics who argued for an agency-centered perspective.

Culture as practice, the "performative" view, relates to a more recent turn in the social sciences that foregrounds the interpretation and use of symbols. The repertoire of concepts used by practice theorists emphasize the dynamic qualities of culture: openness, indeterminacy, and resistance. Swidler's (1986) metaphorically revealing concept of "cultural toolkit" is representative of the performative view of culture.

To resolve the tension between these two perspectives, Sewell (1999) proposed a dynamic dialectical relation between them. Thus a symbol may have one meaning at one time as it is put in the service of a political goal and its political leverage imperceptibly reduced by changes in its meaning that may have occurred in the interim. In this respect, a symbol's meaning may also become a constraint, a burden that impedes political action. I argue in chapter 6 that such a change occurred in the meaning of nature when used in the political context of the issue of global warming.

In using a symbol to some purpose, individuals reproduce a structure of power relations, a reminder that culture is often embedded in domains of action. Laitin (1988), for example, does not grant culture a primary role in political action but acknowledges its power as an efficient surrogate for interests: "Once a cultural group organizes politically, the common symbolic system makes for efficient collective action. Tamils in Sri Lanka, French speakers in Quebec, and Jews in the Soviet Union can be easily maintained as groups not because culture is more real than class but because organizational costs are relatively low when common and powerful symbols are readily available and rules of exclusion easily formulated" (p. 591).

Such a symbol system may have obscure historical roots but can nevertheless be used effectively to achieve a political end. In a history of the circumstances leading to World War I, for example, Clark (2014) illustrated the use of a symbol by Serb irredentists, a 14th-century battle with the Turks, to justify a vision of a Greater Serbia: "Embroidered over the centuries, this rather indecisive medieval battle burgeoned into a symbolic set-piece between Serbdom and its infidel foe. Around it twined a chronicle peopled not only with shining heroes who had united Serbs in their time of trouble, but also by treacherous villains who had withheld their support from the common cause, or had betrayed the Serbs to their enemies" (p. 23). In 1989 Serbian president Slobodan Milošević invoked the same obscure battle to stir Serbian nationalist sentiment to support the "ethnic cleansing" of Kosovo Albanians. In both cases, the state used the battle—part of the Serbian "mythscape"—to heighten the salience of a symbol that played in Christian–Muslim tensions to justify a land grab. The appeal was successful because its contextual meaning remained consistent with its intended political use.

As the example illustrates, a dialectical view of culture does not exist apart from action. Beliefs and symbols that evoke them interact with politics through the concept of cultural resonance, a property of a symbol that indicates the strength of its force multiplication in political persuasion. What is culturally resonant strengthens the beliefs that define group identification and solidarity and thereby amplifies the reach and political leverage of a discourse. Symbols can thus be conceptualized as doing work (Schudson, 1989). In the politics of insecurity, symbols act as ground wires for tapping off uncertainty.

In an uncertain environment, the natural impulse to restore cognitive order leads to phenomena such as rumor, the content of which may also tell us something about how groups differentiate themselves from others. Research in social psychology, for example, provides empirical evidence for the role of uncertainty and anxiety in rumor transmission (DiFonzo et al., 2013; cf. Rojecki & Meraz, 2016). In this context, rumor reflects group sense-making, which often trades on beliefs that define group identity. For example, rumors passed through African American social networks include beliefs that the US military deliberately spread the AIDS virus in black neighborhoods and that the KKK owned Church's Chicken (Turner, 1993). The content of the rumors not only reflected the vulnerability of African Americans but also delineated a boundary defined by the ill will of their enemies, perceived and real.

Because beliefs are potent delineators of group identity, they also incorporate a high potential for political action driven by outrage and passion. If that action is based on a dispute regarding the social appraisal of a group category, symbolic politics founded on group identity may result. The outcome of those politics depends on the makeup of the coalition that composes the groups and the extent to which their interests in a particular issue or ideology are perceived as more important than their identification with any particular group.

A discussion of identity politics joins the long-standing controversy on whether identity trumps presumably more important economic interests. One exemplar is the book *What's the Matter with Kansas?*, in which Thomas Frank argues that working-class Kansans vote against their economic interests by what he regards as the distractions of cultural issues such as abortion and the degradation of popular culture (cf. Bartels, 2006; Fiorina, Abrams, & Pope, 2011). In the politics of insecurity, identity may often trump interests, real or imagined.

To cite one example, white support for affirmative action varies depending on the way survey questions are phrased. The highest levels of support result when questions are phrased in theoretical terms but lowest when phrased in operational forms as, for example, "preferences for blacks." The drop in support is taken by some scholars (e.g., Jackman, 1994) as a veiled expression of self-interest coded as support for abstract principles of racial equality but opposition to policies that would implement them. Jackman cites evidence that whites supportive of racial equality in principle are opposed to school busing and other measures that might threaten their self-interest. But how does one explain white resistance to affirmative action on issues that have no tangible effect on their interests? For example, what explains opposition to the preferences for black applicants to police departments or to law schools among those whites who do not have children, relatives, or friends aspiring to either profession?

The answer is that group identification rather than *immediate* interests drives opinion. We see the same pattern in public support for science-related policies such as reduction of fossil fuel consumption, fracking, and the teaching of evolution. A number of studies (e.g., Brulle, Carmichael, & Jenkins, 2012) show that information itself has no bearing on opinion. Rather, as Kahan (2012) pointed out, identification with a group trumps knowledge: "Positions on climate change have come to signify the kind of person one is. People whose beliefs are at odds with those of the people with whom they share their basic cultural commitments risk being labelled as weird and obnoxious in the eyes of those on whom they depend for social and financial support" (p. 255). Here Kahan identified the difficulty of distinguishing the social from the material, an especially difficult task under conditions of uncertainty.

Since Hobbes, economists and political scientists have invoked interests to explain economic and political preferences. The definition from neoclassical economics of utility maximizing by individuals who rank choice alternatives is also an assumption of the rational actor model in political science. Although Adam Smith credited self-interest in producing wealth, he also argued for the role of the regard by others (sympathy) in moderating self-interest, chiefly through such virtues as prudence and justice. He saw self-interest and sympathy as complementary rather than as antithetical (McCloskey, 2006).

Research shows that self-interest does predict economic policy attitudes if the benefits are tangible, relatively immediate, and personal or family directed (Chong, Citrin, & Conley, 2001). Absent these specific attributes in media coverage of economic policy, citizens rely on their perceptions of how the United States is doing as a whole ("sociotropic politics") or, in the case of movements like the Tea Party, on beliefs, values, and out-group anxiety (Mansfield & Mutz, 2009). In fact, a broad range of research finds numerous exceptions to self-interest as the principal explanation for individual preferences and choice (see, e.g., Mansbridge, 1980; Sears et al., 1980), which are also determined by justice, commitment to selfless ideals, empathy, cognitive limitations (Kahneman, 2011), but also compensatory reactions to uncertainty.* Under conditions of uncertainty, a clear path to pursuing one's interests, however defined, becomes unavailable. What happens when one is unable to estimate a risk profile—no matter how imperfectly it may be assessed—for a course of action? To answer the question, we first need to underline the difference between risk and uncertainty.

Uncertainty is qualitatively different from risk because for the latter, individuals can estimate the probability of an event or course of action, whereas for the former, no such path is available because the situation has no precedent. A "black swan" event (Taleb, 2004) creates maximum uncertainty because it renders useless once productive paths to goals. In his analysis of the two economic transformations in the United States in the 20th century (the Great Depression and the period of stagflation in the 1970s), Blyth (2002) clarified the distinction: "Because the situation is 'in a high degree unique,' agents can have no conception as to what possible outcomes are likely, and hence what their interests in such a situation in fact are. As agents are unable to form a series of instances of like-type events and thus project probabilities, agents' interests in such an environment cannot be given by either assumption or structural location and can only be defined in terms of the ideas that agents themselves have about the causes of uncertainty" (p. 32).

Blyth established the grounds for explaining how deregulated market capitalism (known variously as monetarism, supply-side economics, and neoliberalism) came to replace Keynesian policy in the 1970s and 1980s. He traced the development and synthesis of a set of ideas and assumptions that gradually supplanted the institutions of embedded liberalism. When the economic crises of the late 1970s and early 1980s created doubts about the effectiveness of Keynesian policy, no credible alternative was available other than a set of ideas that had been gradually advanced by monetarist economists, corporate actors, and conservative think tanks funded by high wealth individuals such as Richard Scaife. The editorial page of the *Wall Street Journal* provided a public forum for ideas

---

* Social constructionists (e.g., Berger & Luckman, 1966; Gergen, 1973) further pointed out that concepts such as self-interest lead to research agendas that can reify what may be a historically contingent and situational component of a more nuanced picture of human behavior. Others (e.g., Miller, 1999) argued that self-interest is institutionalized in workplaces and governments where a presumption of the importance of self-interest as principal motivator leads to norms that invite that behavior. The result is a feedback loop that exaggerates the importance of only one of many potential contributors to human action. As Miller argued, "The theory of self-interest has spawned a norm of self-interest, the consequence of which is that people often act and speak in accordance with their perceived self-interest solely because they believe to do otherwise is to violate a powerful descriptive and prescriptive expectation" (p. 1053). Rodrik (2012) put it more compactly: "Our interests are in fact hostage to our ideas."

declared by Ronald Reagan's Office of Management Budget director, David Stock-man, to be based on numbers no one in the administration understood. Stock-man also admitted that a key piece of legislation aimed at implementing the economic policies of trickle down was no more than a Trojan horse intended to reduce the tax rates of the wealthiest Americans (Greider, 1981). The policy was in fact a political project that sought to reduce the size of the welfare state and therefore to reduce redistributionist tax rates.

Aside from Robert Reich's mercantilist proposal to provide federal support to new industries that would fill the void left by those who sought cheaper labor markets overseas (the idea failed to gain political support), the left had no answer. Bill Clinton would continue the policies of financial deregulation, succumb to monetarist calls for the elimination of the federal deficit, and "end welfare as we know it." After the Great Recession, Barack Obama continued to be constrained by the same ideas (and his Wall Street supporters) that had been institutional-ized into policy buttressed by an uncompromising GOP voting bloc in Congress. The debt ceiling crisis of 2013 was an outward manifestation of an economic doctrine that made government debt a bogeyman in popular discourse and the political muscle of the Tea Party movement. That there was no such reaction when the deficit grew under a Republican president, 2001–2009, points to the political effectiveness of the right, a function in part of the strength of right-leaning groups' greater unity and solidarity.

Blyth's point is that under conditions of high uncertainty, ideas matter because interests cannot be determined. When an economic crisis developed in the 1970s, the ideas supporting supply-side economics had become part of the received issue culture. As important, the wholesale substitution of a cognitive framework for structuring the public's view of the economy also imported a set of values that established a moral discourse that justified the framework. Because the left had failed to revise Keynesian ideas, the only plausible alternative to what was perceived as a failed economic theory became resonant by default, a cultural force multiplier for the political campaign of Ronald Reagan. As supply-side economic theory became institutionalized in the anti-inflation policies of the Federal Reserve, a po-litical campaign followed to deregulate banking and to erode support for regula-tory bodies such as the EPA and OSHA. These policies constrained the economic prerogatives of following administrations. George H. W. Bush arguably lost his second term of office because of his broken promise not to raise taxes, a violation of what had become the doctrine of supply-side economics (cf. Vavreck, 2009).

This explains the importance of group-defining beliefs for a low-information public. The key is the accretion of ideas into a cultural matrix that becomes relevant when events disrupt expectations. Risk profiles are available to those who experience disruptions but not insurmountable obstacles to their interests. But for those groups whose future is clouded with uncertainty, beliefs rather than interests become foundational. The answer to the question "What do we do if we do not know what is best to do?" (Blyth, 2002) is either new ideas or a default to beliefs and comfort positions (symbolic politics) that redirect paths away from effective solutions.

The turn to the right in economic policy illustrates that thus far in the politics of insecurity, groups on the right have maintained greater ideological solidarity than those on the left, a phenomenon found in such diverse contexts as motivated reasoning (Nyhan & Reifler, 2010), rumor control (Garrett & Danziger, 2011), partisan information exposure (Sides & Farrell, 2010; Stroud, 2011), distrust of mainstream media (Ladd, 2012), and in-group loyalty as a foundation for moral reasoning (Graham, Haidt, & Nosek, 2009). The decline of unions is a crucial factor in undermining in-group solidarity on the left, intimately related to the rise of globalization and the neoliberal economic policies that support it. We review these in chapter 7 on the rise and success of the Tea Party movement.

Group Identity and the Information System

Perceptions among scholars about the autonomy of the social sciences sometimes leads to an unproductive debate on the relative importance of a discipline's concept or theory in an explanation of some phenomenon. One such debate is on the primacy of culture in explaining the outcome of a political issue (e.g., Laitin, 1988). One way of resolving the matter is to regard culture as an essential variable interlocked with others in an indivisible explanatory system. As Sewell (1999) put it, "When a given symbol is taken by its users to be unambiguous and highly constraining, these qualities cannot be accounted for by their semiotic qualities alone but must result from the way their semiotic structures are interlocked with other structures—economic, political, social, spatial, and so on" (pp. 50–51).

The interlocking is necessary because symbolic systems merely offer what Sewell refers to as "thin coherence." Because meaning may be disputed and unstable, groups and larger institutions are needed for stabilizing and reinforcing group identity. Political and religious movements provide bottom-up sources of coherent and stable group identity for potential adherents, while sites of "concentrated cultural practice" such as the institutions of religion, the state, and the media serve as top-down nodes of cultural meaning. The institutions do not impose uniformity; rather, they organize meaning that makes an otherwise incoherent mass of information intelligible. The results are "official cultural maps," which even though susceptible to criticism and resistance, as received matrices of meaning, they cannot be ignored.

On the supply side, the current information system provides a rich source for political identity information, but its fragmented nature and partisan incentives currently favor the right. In this respect, the news media have entered an era of uncertainty not unlike the population that it serves.

Compared to the decade preceding the end of the Cold War, the media today are far more numerous and more diverse. A new information system that has developed since then has disturbed traditional sources of news, so much so that since 2000, four new academic journals dedicated to the study of journalism came into being. A number of factors have reorganized the system of information distribution once commanded by newspapers and broadcast television, referred to variously as legacy media, mainstream media, and the broadcast news regime. The latter is Williams and Delli Carpini's (2011) term for the mid-century configuration and dominant influence of broadcast TV news and traditional newspapers. The eclipse of that regime began with the development of cable TV in the late 1970s, the rise of talk radio stimulated by the FCC's elimination of the fairness doctrine in 1985, and the explosive growth of the World Wide Web at the turn of the 21st century.

The result has been summarized by the Tow Center for Digital Journalism as "news from everywhere" (Grueskin, Seave, & Graves, 2014). In addition to an order of magnitude increase in information sources, the development of Web 2.0 has also empowered citizens to call attention to a story or issue—unnoticed or given low prominence by conventional broadcast and print sources—by using Twitter, Facebook, and other social media. One concept used to describe citizen-driven agenda-setting is called "going viral," a telling metaphor that speaks to the ambivalence about mass audience preferences that include a wide spectrum that subsumes serious issues, showbiz gossip, rumors, and what Goffman once called "unusual doings" illustrated by videos of compassionate, comedic, or trained animals.

In their conceptually rich account of the new information environment, Williams and Delli Carpini (2011) referred to Baudrillard's concept of "hyperreality" created by stories that gain attention despite their being bypassed by mainstream media gatekeepers. Now a "multiaxial" information environment exists, which is made up of legacy media and entertainment programs such as late night comedy shows, talk radio, and numerous internet-based information and opinion sources that have reduced the influence of the broadcast news regime.

One of the cases analyzed by Williams and Delli Carpini is the Clinton-Lewinsky scandal, set in motion by a variety of nonelite actors on the far right that included interest groups, media aggregators such as Matt Drudge, and alternative internet-based information sites. They remark that the new media environment—now made up of a wider variety of politically relevant media sources—has especially empowered extreme groups, making it more difficult for political parties to assemble ideologically diverse coalitions (p. 165).

The empowerment of citizens has not benefitted both sides of the ideological spectrum equally. To illustrate, Williams and Delli Carpini (2011) analyzed the issue of climate change and found that because of inattention to the mundane, incremental nature of the issue and the use of a balancing norm by reporters, mainstream media have not provided the kind of coverage needed to energize public opinion or stimulate an effective political movement as an alternative mechanism for political influence. They contrast the success of the environmental movement of the 1970s to pressure the federal government for environmental regulations with the failure thus far of a movement to materialize on climate change. In the new media environment and the politics of insecurity, the availability of information by itself is insufficient for political effectiveness. The absence of a unified broadcast regime makes it more difficult to find a broad-based audience for a political movement, but it does reveal the advantage held by more narrowly targeted movements, especially those driven by conservative causes.

Jonathan Ladd (2012) found in his analysis of public trust of mainstream media that citizens who distrust mainstream media have significantly different opinions on issues from those who trust them. For example, American National Election Study data from 2000 show that low-trusting Republicans were less likely than high-trusting Republicans to agree that the deficit had decreased and the economy improved during the Clinton presidency. In fact, both had occurred. Moreover, panel survey data from the 2000–2001 General Social Survey show that citizens who do not trust mainstream media are more likely to seek information about the government from the internet. Ladd concludes that "Americans tend to choose news sources and interpret messages consistent with their political predispositions" (p. 168).

As we saw earlier, because research on partisanship across a number of disciplines points to greater fidelity to beliefs on the right as compared to the left, it is reasonable to assume that right-leaning media sources have fewer incentives to cover issues in a balanced fashion. Thus my hypothesis that the current information environment is a greater asset for the right than the left.

There is, in addition, evidence for a stronger market orientation for media due to a decreased audience for news and the increased opportunities reporters have to gain a more refined sense of what Herbert Gans (1979) termed the *imagined audience*. Today, nearly all news media have an online presence that invites a robust feedback system from audiences. It is not unusual for *The Washington Post* and *The New York Times* to get upward of 1,000 comments for certain stories. Those comments together with the content of social media like Facebook and Twitter and audience analytics data available from marketing organizations such as Omniture form an efficient market-based feedback system heretofore unavailable to journalism. In turn, groups use the information system to structure their perceptions of political life and to advance their political goals.

The evidence for the erosion of the distinction between audience as public and audience as market is more suggestive than definitive, yet it is worth considering. Fox News is perhaps the best known example of a media source that caters to the conservative views of its viewers (Aday, 2010). At Fox News, the cable network's self-consciously ironic slogan "fair and balanced" summarizes the result of the tension between professional detachment and conservative market incentives. Similarly market oriented, MSNBC's slogan "lean forward" acknowledges the network's left-leaning audience. Traditional media such as newspapers are also coming under market pressures as their readership has decreased from 62 million to 49 million between the late 1980s and the late 2000s (cited in Ladd, 2012, p. 72). Gentzkow and Shapiro's (2010) study pointed to the role of consumer demand on a newspaper's slant and the ideology of its readers and thus to the pressure to retain an audience under increased competition for advertising revenue.

Successful newspapers such as *The New York Times* retain a formal commitment to professional detachment, but an ethnographic study of the influence of the Web on reporting at the *Times* (Usher, 2014) showed a journalistic culture in transition. Reporters are encouraged to be mindful of the concept of interactivity for the paper's online website, though management is unclear what that means. Editors continue to subscribe to the values of independence and objectivity yet commonly use expressions such as "clicks for dollars" and a "sticky" website. The latter refers to the value of keeping readers on the paper's website for as long as possible in an effort to generate advertising revenue. These concepts and readily accessible metrics such as most e-mailed articles and reader comments (moderated) provide abundant data for refining one's picture of the audience, once imagined at the *Times* and now precisely measured.

Other studies (e.g., Anderson, 2011; Bright & Nicholls, 2014) found online versions of news sources increasingly sensitive to reader preferences. Bright and Nicholls found that most-read articles—entertainment and political—on online versions of British news sources were more likely to stay on the front page, an effect that was especially pronounced for quality sources such as the BBC, *Daily Telegraph*, and *Guardian*. The abundance of audience feedback mechanisms—online tools for tracking media audiences, clicks, and page visits, coupled with "likes" and "shares" that identify like-minded demographics—are kin to the sophisticated tools available to pollsters for conducting political campaigns.

To summarize the implications of these findings in propositional form, the more targeted the media audience, the more coherent and exclusionary its symbol system and the more available it is for creating group-defined identity. One example is the development of program content intended to put off undesirable audiences for advertisers, as in the early history of MTV (Turow, 1997). Put in a positive way, media outlets, especially those that wish to reduce their risk exposure by narrow casting to a partisan audience, organize and purify a system of symbols thought to appeal to a given group of like-minded people (a market). While this is obvious for partisan sources such as Fox News and MSNBC, research shows that this is also the case to a lesser extent for traditional media such as newspapers, which are often local monopolies and thus have economic incentives to cater to the political beliefs of their audiences. For example, using zip code demographics that include share of political donations and common phrases used by Democrats and Republicans in the Congressional Record, economists Gentzkow and Shapiro (2010) found that the news content of US newspapers is slanted to the ideological beliefs of local readers: "Consumer demand responds strongly to the fit between a newspaper's slant and the ideology of potential readers, implying an economic incentive for newspapers to tailor their slant to the ideological predispositions of consumers. We document such an effect and show that variation in consumer preferences accounts for roughly one-fifth of the variation in measured slant in our sample" (p. 64). Interestingly the researchers found no relationship between the political beliefs of the newspaper's publisher and content, suggesting that competition for audience share overrides incentives for ideological recruitment. Thus my second hypothesis, more tentative than the first, that increased competition and decreasing audiences make local media sources more sensitive to the political sensibilities within their markets.

From the demand side, two trends have transformed the consumption of information: (1) selective exposure and (2) reduced audiences for news. Though not yet definitive, experimental and survey research shows that those interested in the news are less likely to seek points of view at odds with those of their own, especially among conservatives (Iyengar & Hahn, 2009; Lawrence, Sides, & Farrell, 2010; Stroud, 2011; cf. Gentzkow & Shapiro, 2011). A Pew Research Center study (2014) found information polarization on both ends of the liberal-conservative spectrum but considerably less trust of mainstream and liberal media among conservatives than of conservative media among liberals. Nearly half of "consistent conservatives" rely on Fox News as their principle news source. Contrast this with consistent liberals who rely more or less in equal proportions on CNN (15 percent), NPR (12 percent), and MSNBC (12 percent).* Although committed liberals and conservatives represent only 20 percent of their respective groups, they are much more politically influential because they vote in greater numbers, donate money, and talk politics with others.

There is stronger evidence for reduced news consumption in general because of the much broader media content choices available (cf. Williams & Delli Carpini, 2011). Whereas from the 1950s through the 1970s viewers were exposed to news in the flow of television content, today most opt out of news in favor of entertainment (see Ladd, 2012). The result for information-seeking audiences is an interaction with selective exposure that increases political polarization (Prior, 2007).

Although the news audience is reduced, citizens nevertheless continue to hold opinions. And because opinion does not arrive from nowhere, information seekers pass their views to low-knowledge individuals in their friendship networks. As opinions are formed in the exchange of selective information, opinions become entangled with and inseparable from social identity. Wildavsky (1987) pointed out that though citizens are not especially informed about current events or the structures of government, they may have strong feelings about issues nonetheless. Opinions arise from affect and moral judgment and end in post hoc rationalization, a process aphoristically described by Wildavsky as the origin of miles of preferences from inches of facts: "The ability of people to know what they prefer without knowing much else lies at the crux of understanding preference formation" (p. 8).† The key process, Wildavsky says, is cultural conflict, in which differences and distances from others define one's own cultural identity and thereby one's preferences.

---

* Although the latter three sources are thought to be consistently liberal equivalents to Fox, their content is less ideologically consistent than Fox's. MSNBC's *Morning Joe*, for example, features a host who is a former Republican congressman.

  † Jonathan Haidt (2001) supported Wildavsky's (1987) claim with evidence from experiments on the post hoc rationalizations given by individuals who have difficulty explaining the foundations of their moral judgments.

Under conditions of extreme uncertainty, especially disorienting events like 9/11, elites hold dominant power because of the difficulty of rapid formulation of novel ways of thinking among a low-information public. If elites fail to offer effective policy—either by way of consensus or gridlock—group-linked beliefs become important by default. If they are misaligned on a large scale with elite interests, emotionally laden group beliefs can be the foundation for political movements. Examples include the Tea Party and Occupy Wall Street movements that followed the Great Recession. The degree to which such movements succeed depends on their resources, the degree to which they connect with the larger population, the strategic deployment of their symbols, and the strength of their group solidarity. Sociological theory on social movements (e.g., Melucci, 1989; Klandermans, 1997) connects group identity to group interests via the concept of collective identity—shared representations of a group based on common interests and experiences. In sum, the more developed the collective identity (group solidarity), the lower the threshold for the diffusion of a discourse that embodies a preference associated with that group, the greater the probability of a polarizing and energy-providing "us and them" frame of reference, and the higher the probability of success. Movements are, or course, dependent on the information system for disseminating their messages. Models of political communication guide our understanding of how movement and elite messages may be received, processed, and disseminated.

Models of Political Communication

The most widely cited models in political communication—propaganda, indexing, and cascading activation—explain media content largely on the basis of elite interests. The propaganda model uses class interest as the chief explanatory variable. It assumes that media content indoctrinates and defends "the economic, social, and political agenda of privileged groups that dominate the domestic society and the state" (Herman & Chomsky, 2002, p. 298). Accordingly, the model would predict that the economics of free trade that enrich elites would receive little critical analysis in the press. The media would also fail to address employment insecurity and the environmental degradation that results from the opportunistic exploitation by transnational companies of nations that have poor or nonexistent environment protection legislation.

The indexing hypothesis relies on elite dissent, a Gramscian concession to differences of opinion among Washington politicians that protect the foreign policy prerogatives of the state. The indexing model would predict critical coverage of these issues in harmony with elite dissent, a top-down perspective that discounts the autonomous power of political movements. This makes sense given that the indexing model is aimed mainly at coverage of foreign policy where, in the absence of a military draft, the immediate self-interest of citizens is no longer a factor as it was in the Vietnam War.*

Of the three, only Entman's (2003) cascading activation model includes media, public opinion, and culture as important elements among several others in its account of what explains the content of the news. The model takes (a degree of) press autonomy and public opinion into account in those instances where the White House is unable to achieve frame dominance. For example, "Strategically maladroit administrations, such as the Carter and Clinton White Houses, often found news frames spinning out of their control. Poor strategy creates a power vacuum that opposing elites and journalists may enter with their own interpretations" (p. 422). In the case of the Carter administration, it may have been the dreary economy and the failure of his advisers to formulate an alternative economic policy that led to the cascade of problems that made Carter a one-term president. Such was also the case for George H. W. Bush, whose "no new taxes" pledge ran against the grain of a new economic paradigm. In Carter's case, it was the absence of resonant ideas that inevitably led to a failed communication strategy, in Bush's case the collision with a set of a beliefs that had been instilled in the population. In the first instances, the message had become moribund; in the second, the message had become incompatible with what Bush himself had mocked as "voodoo economics."

Entman's (2003) cascading activation model addresses the influence of culture: an idea that is widely accepted (congruent) is much more likely to be accepted uncritically, while an idea that is incongruent is unlikely to gain any traction. The latter would include the claim that the 9/11 terrorists were courageous believers in their cause, willing to die to hasten the arrival of global jihad. While the first two models consider culture to be epiphenomenal, secondary in importance to more tangible interests—be they money or power—the third grants its influence but does not explain why some ideas are widely accepted while others summarily rejected. "Framing of such ambiguous matters depends more heavily on motivation, power, and strategy" (pp. 422–23). The uncertainty

---

* A fourth and more recent model (Niven, 2005) explained media content as a function of utility-maximizing on the part of journalists. In so doing, Niven provided theoretical detail that explains why indexing sometimes works and when it does not.

model focuses on those three as well as other elements that explain political communication in the politics of insecurity.

The Uncertainty Model

While the three models each have value for explaining media content for certain classes of issues under certain circumstances, they do not address the cultural dimension of political communication and the unique constraints of uncertainty and their influence on identity politics in a polarized political environment. They also take a largely top-down perspective that misses the turmoil felt by citizens faced with a unique set of problems, those that have threatened the nation's chief claim that defines its exceptionalism—the American Dream. The cascading activation model does take citizen influence into account but largely as a function of perceived public opinion gleaned by elites from media content. The model I propose takes both elites and citizens into account. It includes a bottom-up approach by examining the beliefs and solidarity of rival groups in issue disputes, an important consideration given the broadened partisan scope of the current information system. It also recognizes the role of self-interest on the part of elites as well as citizens.

Notable variables in the model include the level of uncertainty created by a given globalization-related issue, elite consensus on (or a gridlock obstacle to) a solution, the alignment of elite and citizen self-interest, the coherence and consistency of ideas and beliefs that define group identity, and, relatedly, the degree and quality of group solidarity.

In the case of uncertainty, it may be of the extreme outlier variety, such as the suicide attacks of 9/11, the punctuated uncertainty of economic crises and catastrophic events such as major hurricanes and other extreme weather events linked to global warming, or the chronic uncertainty attending issues such as illegal immigration. Each of these cases has a political signal potential—anticipated future risk—that establishes a threshold for the passion needed to succeed in a polarized political environment.

Elite consensus influence on media discourse varies depending on the degree to which events destabilize citizens' sense of well-being and certainty. Their power is near absolute for black swan events, less so for events that may be interpreted as uncertain for some groups but either merely risky or quietly aligned with material interests for others. As we move to reactions—citizen and elite— we take note of relevant assumptions and beliefs that dovetail with public issues and ask how they are depicted by the media with respect to the problem at hand.

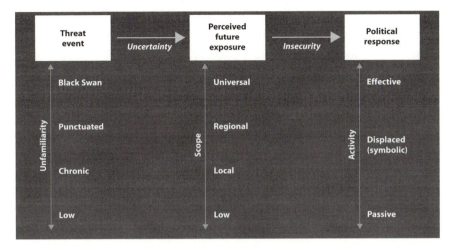

Figure 2.3. The uncertainty model.

Effectiveness is a product of coherence and consistency but also of strategy and cultural resonance. The latter may be a force multiplier for citizen-led movements but may also act as a constraint. Because group beliefs are intimately related to group solidarity, I consider them in tandem; however, I also add historical context to examine the dynamics of group coalitions. I now turn to the details of the uncertainty model, illustrated in figure 2.3.

The model has three phases. The first identifies an event or a salient condition that creates a degree of *uncertainty* in the population. The second is the degree of *insecurity* created by the event or condition, exposure to a future threat perceived by the scope of the population to be at risk. Perceived risk exposure is a joint function of information and control, subjective states of mind influenced by mediated discourses. The third is the *political response* of one or more segments of the population provoked into action by their risk exposure. Absent an organized movement, citizen responses may also be measured by public opinion polls. An effective response—either pressured by a political movement or an aroused public opinion—leads to a policy change perceived to address the threat posed by the event. A displaced, or symbolic response defeats an effective policy response either by substituting one that fails to address the true origins of a threat or by failing to promote one successfully. A passive response simply accepts the status quo.

Each stage is conditioned by intervening variables: (1) uncertainty may not be universally felt because globalization affects some geographic locations more than others; (2) insecurity may be conditioned by the self-interest of those who gain by what others perceive as a threat; and (3) the nature of a political expression may be conditioned by elite consensus, group solidarity (and belief coherence), and the cultural matrix that includes politically potent (resonant) assumptions and beliefs that can either enhance or impede political effectiveness. Beliefs build group solidarity—a key component of an effective political movement—but group identity must not override the primacy of a belief if the group is part of a coalition.

The uncertainty model yields a number of propositions:

1. Under conditions of high (i.e., unknown) uncertainty, political elites will have dominant influence on issue frames.
2. Elite consensus on policy (e.g., free trade) or partisan gridlock that creates insecurity among the public leads to belief-driven political discourses. Amplified by the unresponsiveness of elites to respond to insecurity experienced by citizens, these beliefs create a structural opportunity for the rise of a political movement.
3. Those groups whose beliefs are consistent and coherent (and thereby strengthen solidarity) are more likely to be politically successful. Their success will be enhanced if the self-interest of other citizens gains from an existing state of affairs. The absence of ardor in those who benefit by the status quo increases the political success of those who feel insecure and angry.
4. Except for high-uncertainty events, news media are more likely to be influenced by the group beliefs dominant in their specific markets.
5. Cultural resonance is a potential force multiplier for beliefs, but for those beliefs to be politically effective, they must align with proposed policy aims.

Preview

We now turn to the case studies that illustrate the central argument of the book and the value of the uncertainty model for making sense of the relationships in the politics of insecurity. The case studies follow chronologically through a series of globalization-related crises and events that took place in the first decade of the 2000s. I use a chronological organization because each crisis or event is embedded in a historical flow that is influenced by what preceded it and influences what follows. I thus take what historians have called an ecological approach (e.g., Gaddis, 2002), which highlights the unique relationships among and between a set of events that occurred in a particular phase of the nation's history. While I define and apply a model for analyzing these events, I also use it to highlight what I regard as the most important factors for making sense of what may be an exceptional set of circumstances, for which existing models fail to provide a complete account. In the flow of events, the most notable was the 9/11 black swan.

CHAPTER THREE

Unknown Unknowns

9/11 and the Dark Side of Globalization

In today's globalized world, if you don't visit a bad neighborhood, it will visit you.
—T. Friedman, "Thinking about Iraq," The New York Times, January 22, 2003, p. A21.

In 1991, two years after the demise of the Soviet Union, the doomsday clock of the Bulletin of Atomic Scientists was pushed back to 17 minutes before midnight, a metaphorical summary of the judgment of 18 Nobel laureates on the prospects for the destruction of the human race. The scholars had pushed back the clock because of post–Cold War reductions in nuclear arms that removed an over-hanging threat of a Russian missile attack. Americans gradually came to feel secure as the spans of the Atlantic and Pacific once again subjectively afforded them protection from conflict abroad. In the decade that followed, only a small group of intelligence officials contemplated the outlandish possibility of asym-metric warfare launched by cells of stateless terrorists against the United States. Advised in July 2001 by CIA officials that such an attack using commercial air-liners as weapons could occur (Bush, 2010), Secretary of State Condoleezza Rice discounted the warnings and President Bush dismissed action against al-Qaeda as "swatting at flies" (Clarke, 2004).

While critics held the administration accountable for its inattention and even negligence, it's fair to say that the president and his cabinet experienced the same shock as most Americans. 9/11 was a quintessential black swan event that combined vanishingly small predictability and high risk exposure to create max-imum dread in the population of a future attack and, as the uncertainty model predicts, receptiveness by the public to elite framing. The imprint of the event would be registered in a cultural matrix that would influence the grounds of argument for a number of issues, some immediate and others (e.g., illegal im-migration) more remote. One of the short-term consequences was that in 2002, the laureates set the doomsday clock forward to seven minutes before midnight. The time change reflected increased concerns for the increased risk of terrorist attacks using unsecured nuclear materials and an aggressive US foreign policy that spurned arms reduction, a topic that is discussed in chapter 4.

Because of the scale of uncertainty created by 9/11, the event upended convention, expectations, and customary politics. The disruptions created a vacuum of confidence as disoriented citizens sought comfort, answers, and action from political and media elites. Most proximate were the establishment of a Department of Homeland Security and passage of the Patriot Act to meet the possibility of future threats. The more subtle effects of elite framing of 9/11 would register on more distant issues. One was globalization itself. Some theorists pointed out that the same communication and transportation infrastructures that had brought increased prosperity and democratic reform had also been used by al-Qaeda to hatch and execute their plot.

New York Times columnist Thomas Friedman's comment that opened this chapter was an example of the increased connections made in public discourse between globalization and the importation of the world's ills to American shores. The metaphor of a borderless world became increasingly salient in public discourse and a resonant part of a reconfigured cultural matrix for US foreign and economic policy. Because opinion under extreme uncertainty is crystallized or led by elites (Zaller, 1992), how they came to understand the world after 9/11 became a vitally important component of the Bush administration's strategy for influencing public perceptions of a suddenly changed world.

In this chapter, I use the uncertainty model to analyze the reactions of media and political elites to establish the terms of the globalization debate and how it would influence post-9/11 US economic and foreign policy. In summary, dominant elite opinion would uphold and add moral luster to the circulation of trade and capital for reducing terrorism but would restrict the flow of people, particularly those who posed a civilizational threat to the West. These ideas became part of a largely insensible cultural matrix that would influence public understanding of an ever-riskier environment.

Spooky Action at a Distance

Citizens rarely attribute changes in their lives to the multiple flows of causes and effects of global-scale phenomena. They depend instead on mediated discourses and information for their understanding of a process whose causal chains are often long and complex. Anthony Giddens (1990) coined the term *time-space distanciation* to describe the action-at-a-distance attribute of the phenomenon. As outlined in chapter 1, public opinion reflected the lack of an elite consensus on the meaning and desirability of globalization. As late as the mid-1990s, for example, polls indicated that only slightly more than half of the US population knew enough about globalization to offer an opinion about it. By 1999, 70 percent of Americans said they had heard of the term, but a poll in 2000 revealed that only 57 percent understood the phrase "globalization of the American economy." In these polls, patterns of support depended on the issue at hand. Majorities thought globalization had contributed significantly to the stability of the American economy—a sentiment positively correlated with education and income— but half had trepidations about unfair labor competition from overseas labor markets (Hart and Teeter Research, 1997). Other polls showed that although two-thirds of Americans thought globalization would have a positive effect on consumer prices and on the US economy, they were divided on the influence of globalization on domestic job creation and degradation of the environment (Conlin, 1999).* In short, prior to 9/11, state power and security were not salient dimensions in the public's understanding of the phenomenon.

Terrorism and its relation to globalization touch on a number of issues, but I limit my analysis in this chapter to three: (1) elite understanding of the role played by globalization in leading to the terror attacks, (2) policy that would reduce future exposure to another attack, and (3) how the diagnosis and recommended course of treatment helped create an issue culture that provided a policy and moral rationale for increased free trade as well as a traditional notion of the concept of national security that would justify a war against a state. A less noticed outcome was the effect of a suppression of a vigorous public debate on the role played by religion in the 9/11 attacks. This effect contributed to public ignorance of sectarianism in Islamic religion, its political significance in states such as Iraq, and the potential consequences of a military invasion that would unleash violent sectarian conflict.

Media Frames and Issue Cultures

Frame analysis has joined content analysis as a productive technique for analyzing media texts. Unlike content analysis, which examines the overt elements of a text (e.g., the number of references to violence), frame analysis brings to light the hidden assumptions that organize textual content (e.g., the implied causes of violence). A frame is a structured, coherent way of thinking about an issue. In

---

* By 2007 (but before the financial crisis), majorities felt the United States had lost more than it had gained from globalization. Those with the least education made up the largest group (CBS/*New York Times*, 2007).

this sense, a frame differs little from a theory that emphasizes some aspects of reality as more important than others in explaining a phenomenon (Druckman, 2001). What differentiates a frame from a formal theory is that a frame is not always recognized formally as a theory needing clear specification and formal testing. To a degree, a frame's success depends on its not being recognized as one; absent active critical examination, a discourse dominated by a frame may construct a stable worldview (i.e., an ideology), even one that contains contradictions but that reduces uncertainties nonetheless.

Although the concept of framing has resulted in a number of insightful and productive studies, a definitive theory, let alone a widely accepted research paradigm, remains to be developed (Entman, 1993; Reese, 2001; D'Angelo, 2002). Gamson (2001) characterized the field of frame analysis as more of an assemblage of exemplars and techniques rather than a unified theory. The complexity arises from shifts in analytical emphasis as scholars turn their attention from the study of the production and reproduction of frames, to analysis of frames in text, to the interaction of frames and audiences. While the distribution of social and political power influences the prominence and power of issue frames (Carragee & Roefs, 2004), so does uncertainty.

For the analysis in this chapter, I examine the discourse of elites who have a clear advantage in setting the terms of public debate for a deeply unsettling event. Because 9/11 involved the juxtaposition of a new concept with an event that had no modern precedent (the United States was last attacked on its own soil during the War of 1812), it offers a unique opportunity to see how opinion leaders reconfigured the coordinates of a world picture that complied with their view of a radically changed set of circumstances.

Analysis of elites' diagnoses of globalization's role in leading to the terror attacks also reveals heretofore hidden dimensions of support for policies that influence globalization. I ground my analysis on this assumption: frames that clearly specify a policy intended to correct a carefully defined problem are more likely to develop a settled policy discourse, an *issue culture*. I define an issue culture as the taken-for-granted knowledge around a given topic, the set of common frames used to structure an analysis of an issue and the symbols, metaphors, and images that refer to and evoke those frames (Gamson & Modigliani, 1989; Entman & Rojecki, 2000). Analysis of those issue frames provides a useful guide for analysis of public opinion and thereby for guidance on the arguments likely to shape public policy.

For the framing analysis, I use two concepts that I regard as most useful for examining political issues under conditions of uncertainty, *probative value* and *salience.* Probative value refers to the clarity and specificity of the diagnosis of an issue and a proposed resolution: the greater the clarity and specificity of a frame, the greater its potential political influence. For this dimension, I use Entman's (1993) definition of a frame because it identifies those textual components that offer a path to a policy outcome: (1) problem definition, (2) diagnosis of its causes, (3) moral evaluation, (4) and solution.

Probative value allows a distinction between *politically functional* and *nonfunctional* frames. I regard a frame as politically functional if it offers a clear statement of cause and suggests a productive remedy. This is vital for establishing a sense of control for citizens under conditions of uncertainty and dread. In contrast, a nonfunctional frame is one where no clear policy remedy is evident, either because the cause is so abstract that a policy does not easily suggest itself or where the cause is identified as an ineluctable force, such as an unfolding historical process, that makes an outcome all but inevitable and any action opposed to it futile (see, e.g., Hirschman, 1991).

Salience identifies those factors that assess the staying power of a particular frame, the likelihood that it will take root in or produce its own issue culture. Gamson and Modigliani (1989) hypothesized that every issue is contested in a symbolic arena of metaphors, catchphrases, and other condensing symbols that reproduce and make salient a way of thinking about an issue, a "package" (one such example during the Cold War was "domino"). They argue that the production of a salient issue culture depends on cultural resonance, the depth of a package's identification with a recognized cultural value; sponsor activities, the energy invested in the promotion of a particular package by institutions or organized groups (see Pan & Kosicki, 2001); and media practices, how well a package comports with the working norms and practices of journalism.

Because of the novelty of the concept of globalization in the early 2000s as well as of the event that provided a new context for it, my primary emphasis here is to map the discourse—the set of most available and politically functional frames that linked globalization with terrorism. Establishing a set of analytical categories and then assessing the potential political influence and staying power of a given frame helps us see the origins of a new issue culture forged in a period of high uncertainty and of the remedies that would reduce citizens' perceptions of future risk exposure.

I analyzed all stories, columns, and editorials that included the terms *globalization* and *terror* (and its cognates such as terrorism and terrorist) for the six-month period following 9/11. The sources covered included the prestige press (*New York Times, Washington Post, Los Angeles Times*), national newspapers (*Chris-*

tian Science Monitor, USA Today), and prominent regional newspapers, such as the *Atlanta Journal and Constitution, Boston Globe, Denver Post, Saint Louis Post-Dispatch*, and *Seattle Times*. The sources represented the most influential newspapers as judged at the time by newspaper editors themselves (Anonymous, 1999).* I excluded those items that merely mentioned the search targets without offering either an explicit or implicit substantive connection between them and repeated stories from syndicated columns. Using these criteria, the search yielded 92 stories.

Uncertainty and the Issue Culture of Globalization

The importance of the issue of terrorism for globalization is revealed by a comparison of its linkage in the press pre- and post-9/11. In the nine-month period prior to September 11, 2001, less than 2 percent of the stories on globalization in *The New York Times* included references to terrorism. By contrast, in the three-month period following the attacks, one-third of the stories on globalization included such references. The risk of terrorism had become after 9/11 a significant part of the issue culture of globalization.

Figure 3.1 shows the frequency of three master frames that made explicit connections between globalization and the terror attacks: (1) the dark side of globalization (half the coverage); (2) American hegemony (a little over one-third); and (3) clash of civilizations (about a tenth).

The remainder fell outside these categories but also didn't warrant separate categories because of their infrequency. These included (1) regarding the attacks as the hopelessness of divining the meaning of anything as abstract as globalization (Vitello, 2002), (2) the inadequacy of US government efforts in promoting the fundamental goodness of the nation to the rest of the world, and (3) linking the attacks to Americans' ignorance of international politics: "Though it is the engine of globalization around the world, the nation has never been more inward looking, less worldly" (Klein, 2001).

The three dominant frames appeared as singular organizing frameworks for about one-third of the coverage, mainly in editorials, op-eds, and news analyses that offered the opportunity for an author (columnist, invited commentator, or expert) to explore a single thesis. For example, an op-ed piece in *The Los Angeles Times* traced the origins of the terror attacks to a reaction by religious fundamentalists to corrupting cosmopolitanism brought to light by globalization (Balzar,

---

* Methodological details on coding and reliability appear in the appendix.

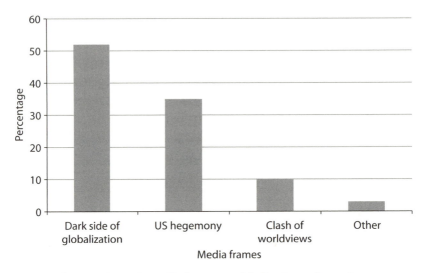

Figure 3.1. Post-9/11 media frames on globalization and terrorism.

2001). News articles were more likely to offer several frames in the form of analyses and opinions offered by two or more experts. More often, however, seemingly unrelated themes represented different facets of a common frame. Thus a *Minneapolis Star Tribune* piece on the origins of the terror attacks (Black, 2001) bore this subtitle: "Hatred of America has many complex roots; Anti-U.S. attitudes involve religion, economics, military power and often the globalization of American culture." Note here that although four separate themes are mentioned, all are common facets of a single, master frame. We now turn to an analysis of the frames.

US Hegemony

Although by the numbers American hegemony was the second most common frame, one could regard it as the most dominant because of its concentration in the news and editorial sections of the press. The most numerous frame, the *dark side of globalization*, appeared in two versions split between the news/editorial and the business sections.

The American hegemony frame addressed the role of United States responsibility for the terrorist attacks. Given the negative reaction to Susan Sontag's (2001) essay in *The New Yorker*, in which she traced a line from the attacks to Washington policy ("Where is the acknowledgement that this was not a 'cowardly' attack on 'civilization' or 'liberty' or 'humanity' or 'the free world' but an attack on the world's self-proclaimed super-power, undertaken as a consequence of specific American alliances and actions?"), it is surprising to find that this is the dominant frame in news coverage and editorial reaction. There are, however, important qualifications that complicate and, in due course, reverse this interpretation.

Coverage included three versions of a frame that highlighted the primacy of American influence in one or more of the economic, political, or cultural domains of globalization. The general assumption was that the United States inspired envy and resentment because of its powerful economy and the political and cultural influence that resulted. From an economic standpoint, because capitalism spread inequality in and between nations, the United States was perceived to have benefited the most by the system. In the political domain, globalization was a cover for reinforcing American dominance with the UN as a fig leaf, most notably in the Middle East where the US supports corrupt regimes that routinely violate human rights. Perceptions of US one-sided support of Israel by the "Arab street" increased the bitterness of those oppressed by their governments. Finally, in the cultural domain, globalization spread American popular culture, which displaced cherished tradition and sacred belief (similar to Thomas Frank's diagnosis of the culture wars in Kansas). This excerpt from an op-ed in the *Boston Globe* is a characteristic example:

> Fouad Ajami of Johns Hopkins University wrote years ago that since the 1920s, 'Muslim cults . . . have looked at the defiled world around them—wild cities, shocking cultural trends, foreigners with alien ways, subjugation to the outsiders, a world that seems to be perpetually in crisis, young men and women who have strayed from time-honored ways—and have felt at one time or another the urge to destroy or the urge to withdraw and escape.' Since the end of the Cold War and the beginning of globalization, America has emerged as the symbol of everything that has gone wrong for them.

Note that in this (common) example, the frame is not an assertion of American hegemony but rather a claim of the perception by others that such is the case. In fact, these perceptions may have been exaggerated or entirely mistaken. As the op-ed concluded, "And who is responsible for their misfortune? Those in power in their individual countries, often. But who has corrupted their leaders? What is the font of everything they half envy and half fear? The United States of America, or so they believe" (Greenway, 2001, p. A15).

A second way the coverage weakened the equation of American hegemony with globalization was to attribute the supposition to generic foreign others who, in their desperation, appeared less than fully rational:

They live where globalization is not working or not working well enough. They believe, or can be led to believe, that America—or their pro-America government, if they live under one—is to blame for their misery. Many are adrift, cut off from their social foundations. Perhaps they moved into the city from dying villages, or were driven there by war or famine. There is no going back for them, yet in the city there is not much going forward; the movement tends to be downward. As they fall, they grab hold of whatever they can, and sometimes it is the violent ideas of religious extremists. (Maas, 2001, p. 48)

The following example does not impugn the rationality of the impoverished but nevertheless weakens the connection between their poverty and American responsibility by attributing it to the understandable but perhaps unreliable perceptions of the afflicted: "Perhaps we should not have been surprised that the success of capitalism should have also created violent hostility among those who've been left out—people with no power in the world of international diplomacy. They feel that the squalor and poverty of their lives is something being done to them by those who do have the power" (Holstein, 2001, sec 3, p. 7).

Of the 30 instances in coverage that implicated the role of US influence (however indirect), 17 made a substantive connection between the terrorism and America's role in (or as a majority beneficiary of) globalization. While this sounds impressively self-critical, only six quoted American sources, and two of these were representatives of the "antiglobalization" movement, whose claims are questioned within the body of the text itself. Thus only four of the 30 were assertions by noncontroversial American sources. One such example: "We should listen to the grievances of the Islamic peoples, stop propping up repressive regimes in the area, protect Israel's security but denounce its apartheid practices in Palestinian areas and reform our 'globalization' policies so that they no longer mean that the rich are getting richer and the poor poorer" (Johnson, 2001, part M, p. 1).

One of the few highly critical domestic views of American Middle Eastern policy cited these examples: "U.S. foreign policy operates as a political shield as well, for the rulers of Saudi Arabia and of Egypt and other Arab states. Arab media, which are threatened with criminal action if they criticize these rulers, are allowed to denounce the United States government in the vilest terms for opposing Iraq, supporting Israel or promoting globalization" (Hoagland, 2001, p. A25). The other 11 instances quoted foreign sources or highlighted perceptions rather than assertions of American culpability.

Coverage using the frame of the United States as global hegemon often invoked the "Arab street," a metonymic reference to the frustration felt by Arab

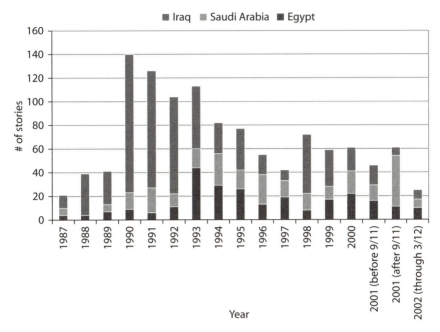

Figure 3.2. Stories mentioning corruption or human rights abuses, *The New York Times*, 1987–2002.

populations of authoritarian states whose leaders use Israel and its relationship with the United States to bleed off the frustration and anger that might otherwise be turned on the regimes themselves. We have seen how its being put forth by non-American sources weakens the probative value of this frame. Nevertheless, press discourse did use the frame. What is the likelihood that this claim would resonate nevertheless with a common set of beliefs? Put another way, to what extent did Americans have routine access to information that would persuasively link terrorism to frustration with Washington support of corrupt regimes in the Middle East? To determine this, I searched the Nexis database for stories in *The New York Times* since 1989 that included any mention of government corruption or human rights abuses in Egypt, Saudi Arabia, and Iraq. The graph in figure 3.2 summarizes the coverage.

In the post–Cold War era, more than half of the 1104 stories that mentioned corruption or human rights abuses were targeted at Iraq, and the two years 1990 and 1991 (during the buildup to and the actual Gulf War) contained nearly one-quarter of all the stories that linked these states to corruption and human rights abuses. Saudi Arabia and Egypt were not ignored in this respect; they shared the spotlight for corruption now and then, particularly after 9/11. Saudi

Arabia (in particular the conservative Wahabi movement and its support of al-Qaeda and the Taliban) became the focal point for these stories in the three-month period after 9/11, but there was a drop-off in attention during the first three months of 2002 and a rebound in this period to matters Iraqi.

The shift away from a focus on possible Saudi complicity in the attacks was largely due to the combination of Bush's claim of an axis of evil that identified Iraq, Iran, and North Korea but not Saudi Arabia as potential sources of weapons of mass destruction to terrorist groups; the administration's repeated calls for a regime change in Iraq; and the Saudi announcement of a comprehensive peace proposal at the height of the Israeli invasion of the West Bank in the spring of 2002. Egypt, meanwhile, suffered comparatively little critical attention despite its repressive regime, its Islamic movements such as the Egyptian Brotherhood (linked to al-Qaeda and the first World Trade Center bombing), and the $2 billion in annual United States foreign aid the nation received, in part to contain the Islamic groups that threatened its government.

In short, the potential cultural resonance of a theory that cast the United States as a global hegemon that therefore bore responsibility for the terror attacks, however indirect, was weakened on several dimensions: lack of sponsorship by domestic interest groups, lack of credibility afforded to foreign news sources (Page & Shapiro, 1992), and a lack of resonance for a claim of US culpability due to the absence of a factual foundation for establishing its credibility. In this context, it is therefore not surprising that the editorial board of *The New York Times* offered this advice to the White House: "Washington must guard against the perception abroad that the war against terrorism is simply another form of American arrogance or even the enforced expansion of globalization to nations that already resent the spread of Western culture and commerce" ("Calibrating the use of force," 2001, p. A24).

The Dark Side of Globalization

The dark side frame has two variants—one political, one economic—that compose functioning parts of the same structure of understanding, weighing the short-term risks of globalization against long-term benefits. Illustrated by the Friedman quote that opened this chapter, the political frame invokes previously unimaginable consequences of globalization: the world is brought closer together but must now confront problems that at one time seemed at a comfortable distance (Fortress America). Nearly all of the instances of the political frame appeared in news/editorial pages. The economic version also spoke to the short-term risks posed by terrorism but placed a greater emphasis on the long-term benefits of an expanding market economy. The economic frame structured coverage in the business sections of the paper; when it appeared in the editorial section, an economist or an official of a regulatory body such as the WTO advanced it.

The most common metaphor used to evoke the political frame was the "dark side," "underbelly," or "downside" of globalization. The dark side frame conceded the inescapability of the underlying technological dynamics of globalization but also of the importation of the world's ills along the same communication and transportation networks that enlarge and accelerate markets. The frame complicates the end of history thesis of the 1990s with the dark realities of continuing social and political dislocations that intrude on the states of the West, particularly the United States. The lesson to be drawn is that, *pace* Fukuyama (1992), history continues apace:

> We have been lulled by the disappearance of the menace of the Cold War, and the indisputable erosion of the national security state by the cultural and economic forces of globalization. Open borders were inevitable, markets were never wrong and there was an irreversible dependence by all on vast easy flows of goods, capital and people among nations. Why worry? Those are compelling ideas with solid veins of truth. But even they need to be put in perspective by looking realistically at the chances for evil that such freedom from control offers. Globalization is a circle that pumps poison as well as benefit through the system. (Hoagland, 2001, p. A25)

In short, terrorism draws upon the same global circuits of trade, finance, and information that drive beneficial economic development. The same circuits, however, support the highly leveraged form of power by which nonstate actors gain an asymmetrical power advantage over nation-states. Because terrorists are beyond the control of a democratically empowered people, finding a means of accountability or responsibility is not possible. As such, the actions of terrorists present a brazen challenge to state sovereignty, and the state is encouraged to reply with due force:

> Now, American president George W. Bush and Russian president Vladimir Putin trade horses and roll logs as if they had never heard of globalization. They take their playbook not from the theorist of the moment but from Metternich and Thucydides. Last week's summit in Washington and Texas marked a return to the bad old days of power politics, secret diplomacy and backroom deals. And it's about time. International institutions, regional associations and non-governmental

organizations all have important roles to play in today's world. Only states, however, can mobilize the resources, popular will and territorial base to fight terrorist organizations like al-Qaeda—which in turn relies on state support in places such as the Taliban's Afghanistan or Saddam Hussein's Iraq. (Strauss, 2001, p. B4)

In those articles and editorials that proposed an explicit remedy to the "dark side" theory of globalization and its facilitation of terrorism (14 of 28), all recommended the reinvigoration of state power as the most effective solution. Of the remaining 14, 8 highlight the increased vulnerability to a globally dispersed economy, potentially tainted food supplies from foreign sources, opportunities for laundering money intended for terrorist cells, and to the asymmetries of power created by terrorists who strike and then melt away. Although there is no explicit call for increased state intervention, the implication is inescapable. The remaining six pieces simply used the metaphor in broader analyses that range from the death of globalization to that of civilization to itself. One colorful example of the latter included an instructive quote from Gibbon: "'The present is always a fleeting moment, the past is no more; and our prospect of futurity is dark and doubtful.' It has always been thus. That we belong to the cycle of history—not, as Mr. Fukuyama would have us believe, to its 'endpoint,' but caught within its motion of rise and fall—is a profoundly disquieting thought; who really believes that nothing is eternal?" (Atlas, 2001, sec. 4, p. 5). On the whole, the political rhetoric in this framework defines a critical area of vulnerability and cedes power to the state for a security-restoring program of increased vigilance and regulation. Popular support for an invigorated state during a national emergency is a deeply embedded feature of US political culture, and as psychological research finds a deeply resonant base of support for this perspective. The "rally round the flag effect" was much in evidence after the 9/11 attacks, a surge of patriotic pride in the United States (Smith, Rasinski, & Toce, 2001) and near-unanimous levels of approval for a war on terror that would begin with an attack on Afghanistan. As we saw in chapter 2, this was an expected psychological response to future risk exposure represented by 9/11 and the dread that followed the anthrax attacks. Critically, however, this solution did not warrant isolation from global economic interdependence. In short, the economic benefits of globalization outweighed the security dangers that would otherwise justify isolation.

To the extent that terror required state intervention and added security measures, however, both were regarded as frictions that would impede the efficient operation of the engine of global prosperity. State intervention connected the political short-term frame to the economic frame of the long-term benefits of free

trade. Through this connection, the dark side frame smuggled in the broad principles of free-market capitalism: the prosperity of a nation depended on its openness to the global economy and on the reform of institutions that restricted free
trade. The dark side frame did not undermine globalization of the economy, for
it was held as the long-range solution to the problems of poverty and underde-
velopment that were the source of the anger and frustration. The clearest statement of this appeared in an op-ed written by the US trade representative to
the WTO:

> Open markets are vital for developing nations, many of them fragile democracies
> that rely on the international economy to overcome poverty and create opportu-
> nity; we need answers for those who ask for economic hope to counter internal
> threats to our common values. . . . We need to infuse our global leadership with a
> new sense of purpose and lasting resolve. Congress, working with the Bush admin-
> istration, has an opportunity to shape history by raising the flag of American eco-
> nomic leadership. The terrorists deliberately chose the World Trade towers as their
> target. While their blow toppled the towers, it cannot and will not shake the foun-
> dation of world trade and freedom. (Zoellick, 2001, p. A35)

In short, a consensus developed among elites on the left and right that the free
movement of capital and information would create a tide of wealth that would
lift all boats, including those of frustrated Islamists who might otherwise be re-
cruited by al-Qaeda. Ordinary American citizens also shared this view. A number
of pre-2007 recession opinion polls revealed solid majority support for free trade
as a solution to global poverty (e.g., Pew Research Center for the People and the
Press, 2003).

The prosperity interpretation was at odds with the view that globalization,
understood as unregulated free-market capitalism, resulted in the inequalities
that led to terrorism in the first place. Inequality understood as a system-specific
negative outcome of capitalism in general was a relatively minor frame, related
to the American hegemony frame. Notably, those who made this claim were
representatives of the global justice ("antiglobalization") movement who suffered
some loss of credibility in accounts that called attention to their eclectic political
agenda and exotic dress (see, e.g., Pinkerton, 2001a). This was rarely the case for
other frames of reference. The greater part of the inequality discourse took place
within the American hegemony frame, where, as we noted earlier, the claims were
only weakly supported and contested vigorously by the discourses on the inevitability of globalization and the prosperity it would bring to the globe.

To summarize, the dark side frame found the source of terrorist power in the infrastructures of globalization itself, the same networks that increased the chances for global prosperity. Because of the asymmetry of power that provides terrorists with a formidable advantage over sovereign states, the clearly articulated solution was an increase in state power. State intervention undermined globalization only to the extent that increased regulation would create a drag on the efficiencies of a growing global market, which was regarded as the long-term solution. Thus the difference between this frame and the American hegemony frame is that the dark side frame focused mainly on the universally applicable economics of free trade. Whereas American hegemony was responsible for terrorism in the first instance, the space-time compression of globalization itself was responsible for the latter. The short-term risk weighed favorably against the more desirable long-term benefits of a global market, however, a position heavily sponsored by recent presidential administrations and the greater majority of American think tanks (Rojecki, 2003).

Clash of Civilizations

The Huntington hypothesis (1996)—culture, and especially religion, as the major source of resistance to globalization and thus the instigator of the terror attacks— received comparatively little support in press framing, perhaps because of the Bush administration's strenuous efforts to divide the extreme Islamic ideology of al-Qaeda from Islam in general. This excerpt is characteristic of the press's rejection of a singular view of Islam: "The notion of a monolithic Islam defies reality and common sense. It is shared by roughly a billion believers, spans several continents and dozens of societies. It encompasses a wide range of different, often contradictory, at times incompatible theories and practices. As a religious belief system, it enjoys more than enough latitude to justify openness to the outside world and seclusion from it; political conservatism and militancy; jihad as an effort to redeem oneself and jihad as a war against others" (Malley, 2001, p. A33).

Nonetheless, a significant minority view upheld the Huntington hypothesis. The most common metaphor for terror was evil, and it appeared in two of the frames on globalization: The *dark side* frame represented the worldly variant where aggression was borne of frustration with economic disadvantage, political repression, or cultural homogenization. The *clash of civilizations* traced the origins of terrorism to unbridgeable worldview differences due to either religious fundamentalism or to irreconcilable philosophical outlooks: "It is the epistemological nature of Bin Laden's type of terrorism that makes it so insidious. . . . Unlike other terrorists who can be denoted, the new enemy is a way of thinking. And because this enemy is mythos, a non-rational way of knowing, one cannot negotiate or reason with its proponents. Indeed, the seeming irrationality of the terror, the randomness of it and its disconnection from any goal, is precisely why it is so unsettling. It doesn't make any sense" (Gabler, 2001, part M, p. 6). Globalization remains at the heart of this explanation because through modern systems of communication, groups with insular views become aware of foreign outlooks that contradict or offend their own (i.e., the Huntington hypothesis). In this respect, all fundamentalisms are the same, no matter their origins: "Christian fundamentalists and Islamic fundamentalists worship different deities but they both live in dread of the anything-goes, individualized and expanding culture of the United States. They believe that America brought upon itself the wrath from the heavens" (Balzar, 2001, part 2, p. 9). Writing in *The New York Times Magazine*, conservative columnist Andrew Sullivan (2001) made a similar point: "This war even has far gentler echoes in America's own religious conflicts—between newer, more virulent strands of Christian fundamentalism and mainstream Protestantism and Catholicism" (p. 44).

Although commentators attributed the reaction to corrupt culture rather than a difference in worldview, their diagnosis of the cause as unreasoning absolutist thought was the same. In general terms, elites framed the conflict as a clash between modernity (broadly conceived as faith in science and technology and the prosperity it brings) and an atavism founded in a backward species of parochial, absolutist religious faith. The caves in which the caftan-clad, bearded Taliban and al-Qaeda sought shelter from American bombers (the most common image in editorial cartoons) provided the central metaphor for a retreat to an earlier age of intolerance and poverty, inversions of the openness and prosperity that are the fruits of liberal democracy and capitalism.

Thus the clash of civilizations is more accurately a clash of faiths: faith in the institutions and practices supporting modernity defined as expansion of capital growth and, to a lesser degree, governments responsive to popular will, versus faith in tradition founded in a theological understanding of the world. To the extent that this perspective offered a remedy to terror, it was an implied rejection of the fundamentalism that underlay it. In this light, the clash of worldviews frame provided the moral suasion for whatever actions were seen fit for eradicating the evils of fundamentalism and intolerance. Far from the ambiguities of cultural relativism, however, cosmopolitanism requires an active defense. As Giddens (2000) put it: "All of us need moral commitments that stand above the petty concerns and squabbles of everyday life. We should be prepared to mount an active defence of these values wherever they are poorly developed, or threatened. Cosmopolitan morality itself needs to be driven by passion. None of us would have anything to live for if we didn't have something worth dying for" (p. 68). Strictly speaking, the clash of civilizations frame is not politically functional because it fails to offer a clear path to policy that would remedy the problem. It does, however, raise the moral stakes and create an urgency to implement whatever policy would become part of the issue culture. Lodged in the cultural matrix of terrorism, despite the entreaties of Bush and Obama, the term *Muslim* would become a resonant source of othering for political enemies.

The Breeding Grounds of Insecurity

In a speech to Chicago airline employees two weeks after 9/11, George W. Bush sounded two themes that would define his presidency: (1) a new kind of war against people "who knew no borders." The war would target not only jihadists but also those who supported them or provided sanctuary. The latter would come to include Afghanistan and Iraq. (2) The imposition of a security net that abridged rights to privacy established in the Fourth Amendment. Significantly, Bush did not make a moral appeal for sacrifice on the part of American citizens, no draft to spare American troops of repeated tours of duty in the wars to come, nor an increase in taxes to pay for them. Bush relied instead on the Federal Reserve to stimulate the economy and restore confidence in Americans to resume their lives: "When they struck, they wanted to create an atmosphere of fear. And one of the great goals of this Nation's war is to restore public confidence in the airline industry. It's to tell the traveling public: Get on board; do your business around the country; fly and enjoy America's great destination spots; get down to Disney World in Florida; take your families and enjoy life the way we want it to be enjoyed." Bush's message was that if the object of the al-Qaeda was to instill fear in Americans, Americans' moral duty was to resume their normal lives, to travel and consume, a domestic variant of the nation's free-trade policy.

Bush's call for the resumption of travel despite the imposition of a chokepoint at US airports was emblematic of a two-track approach to global terrorism, enlargement of the state in the form of a domestic security apparatus (e.g., Department of Homeland Security, Patriot Act), and continued expansion of the movement of capital and trade; in short, a borderless world for consumption, trade, and capital flows but not for the free movement of people.

While it is difficult to establish a direct connection between elite discourse and citizen attitudes, it is instructive to compare free-trade policy pre- and post-9/11. When George W. Bush entered office, the United States had free-trade agreements with only Canada, Mexico, and Israel. During his two terms, Bush signed legislation to reduce tariffs with 14 additional states—including Jordan, Morocco, and Oman—part of what he called his freedom agenda: "I believed over time that freedom inherent in the market would lead people to demand liberty in the public square" (Bush, 2010, p. 427). As we saw in the analysis, this was also a dominant frame promoted by media elites.

Barack Obama continued the policy, his biggest accomplishment signing an agreement with Korea in 2011 that removed duties on American farm exports and that would phase out tariffs on nearly all industrial and consumer exports by 2016. Obama also sought fast-track approval for the Trans-Pacific Trade Agreement and the Transatlantic Trade and Investment Partnership (TPP). The agreements were opposed by many Democrats who echoed the concerns of the global justice movement on free trade's exacerbation of income inequality and degradation of the environment by corporations who sought locations with favorable (or nonexistent) antipollution laws. Meanwhile, some House Republicans opposed giving Obama fast-track authority not so much on the merits of the agreements but on his exercise of executive authority. The public remained largely detached. In a poll taken at one peak of news coverage (CBS/*The New York Times*, 2015), over three-quarters said they knew little or nothing about TPP.

In short, free-trade policy assented to by Clinton, accelerated by Bush, and continued by Obama showed there was little daylight between political elites on this issue. The absence of meaningful differentiation would deprive Democrats of the moral resources to energize its base and would also contribute to a recurring GOP theme that Democratic presidents and candidates such as Hillary Clinton (who had supported TPP while Secretary of State but demurred when running for office) were inauthentic.

To summarize, dominant press frames linking globalization and 9/11 were primarily political and economic. The notion of an unbridgeable cultural gulf or a clash of civilizations failed to gain much traction in the overt issue culture because the frame was not sufficiently probative (no remedies were offered) and because political elites resolutely avoided claims that Islam was to blame for 9/11.

In some respects, this reflected a successful campaign on the part of the White House to avoid the diplomatic nightmare of offending states that encompassed the world's population of one billion Muslims. But just as norms have largely eliminated racist talk from public discourse but not private conversations or thoughts, information without control contributed to private uncertainty about the role of Islam in terror and sociotropic politics. The Huntington clash of civilization thesis was rejected by mainstream elite opinion but became a staple of conservative talk show radio as it took the form of an "Islamo-fascist" threat. Being soft on Islamo-fascists became a point of differentiation between conservative and liberal candidates for office. Barack Obama took the brunt of the attack as Rush Limbaugh frequently emphasized the president's middle name, Hussein, in his routine critiques of the president. Numerous polls showed significant differences between self-identified Democrats and Republicans on perceptions of Muslims. For example, nearly seven in ten Republicans viewed Muslims mostly or very unfavorably compared to three in ten Democrats (Program on International Policy Attitudes, 2012).

With regard to information, the public remained largely ignorant about Islamic beliefs and the significant division among adherents that had been concealed by secret post–World War I divisions of territorial spoils between England and France. The latter included arbitrary territorial lines that ignored sectarian differences between Sunni and Shia Muslims, the signature example being the state of Iraq. The American public knew little about the significance of these divisions or the composition of the Islamic population in Iraq. As late as 2007, for example, only one-third of Americans knew that Shiites made up the majority in Iraq (CBS/*The New York Times*, 2007).

By contrast, the political frames that linked terror to globalization did advance remedies. The political frames were, however, driven by opposing theories of international relations and thus offered two different directions for policy. From a liberal international relations perspective, elites declared that the US was obliged to act as an exemplar on the world stage because it had benefited the most from a global expansion of market capitalism. In this domain, elites downplayed the connections between US policy and the nation's strategic interests that inhibited the spread of democracy, key (according to liberal international relations theory) to the maintenance of a peaceful world. One assumption of this view is that the state is not a political actor but "a representative institution constantly subject to capture and recapture, construction and reconstruction by coalitions of social actors" (Moravcsik, 1997, p. 518).

As we observed in analysis of elite media discourse, however, democratic reform as part of a strategy for reducing the breeding grounds for terror was not high on the policy agenda. The reason for this is because of the more common view that US intentions in the Middle East were not self-interested so much as misunderstood, perhaps the result of inadequate self-promotion. Indeed, in response to this widely reported perception, the Bush White House funded a program for the United States to better market itself to the Arab world. In March 2002 the Broadcasting Board of Governors (BBG), a government-supported, international broadcasting service, established the Middle East Radio Network, also known as Radio Sawa. A pilot project of the Voice of America, the network broadcasts around the clock a mix of Arabic and Western popular music interspersed with news with a "subtly pro-American spin" (Tough, 2002). This was the sole tangible policy response by the Bush administration to the view that US policy bore any relation to 9/11.[*]

By contrast, the assumptions of realpolitik underlay a number of stories that called for the alliances of convenience promoted by the Bush administration in the War on Terror. Prior to 9/11, the Bush administration had been much less receptive to the globalist model championed by Bill Clinton. George W. Bush took unilateralist positions on such issues as AIDS, global warming, and defense, and pulled back from the position that the United States would make aid to governments contingent on upholding human rights and fighting corruption in their own regimes. After 9/11, the world appeared to have become bifurcated, as during the Cold War, when Bush asserted that "you're either with us or against us in the fight against terror." Bush appeared to be reaching out to build a coalition of states to fight the al-Qaeda network, but he was not building a coalition of states to meet the challenge of another. Rather, he reasserted the primacy of state sovereignty for meeting the challenge of a power network that transcended state borders.

An asymmetrical power advantage was to be rebalanced in favor of sovereign states threatened by terror. State interests, particularly those of the United States, became preeminent. States' internal institutions and human rights policies became irrelevant. Russia would no longer be taken to task for its Chechnya policy, and China would not be criticized by Washington for violating human rights in pursuit of purportedly bin Laden–supported gunmen operating in Eastern Turkestan (Xinjiang province). Human rights and the promotion of democratic institutions became part of the Bush administration's argument for going to war in Iraq in 2003, but this did not occur until well after the war started, when weapons of mass destruction (whose eradication was the major reason for the war) failed to turn up.

Elites' analyses of the economic dimensions of globalization and their relation to terrorism focused on economic inequality and the political unrest this provoked. Unlike the political frame that invited state intervention for securing

---

[*] The results of the Radio Sawa innovation are thus far inconclusive. One study (el-Nawawy, 2006) found that Arab students' attitudes toward US foreign policy had actually worsened after they started listening to Radio Sawa.

borders as a remedy, no specific role for state policy was present in economic frames of analysis. There was no clear policy path for reducing income inequality, such as making foreign aid contingent on the establishment of property rights; widely available, high quality primary and secondary education; and other redistributive measures (Kapstein, 2001). Thus the economic coverage either explicitly favored or defaulted to the assumptions of unregulated free-market capitalism. Prosperity would depend on the establishment and maintenance of a deregulated super-efficient market that operated at an ever-increasing rate of velocity. Security measures were the cost of doing business, a necessary but burdensome weight on global prosperity.

What, then, were the implications of these responses for globalization itself? Elites did not discredit modernity or the economic dimension of globalization but also did not favor the development of the institutions that (according to proponents of liberal international relations theory) would simultaneously hasten global interdependence and improve the political conditions that breed terror. Thus, although editorial cartoons of Osama bin Laden and the Taliban ridiculed their rudimentary living conditions and their oppression of women, press coverage did not place great emphasis on constructive policies such as those that would reduce income inequality or promote democratic rule. As we shall see in chapter 4, these would be invoked in a ritual manner to justify US military action, but they took a backseat to national security interests.

To summarize, 9/11 sent a shockwave of uncertainty through the entire population and established an issue culture that would influence Americans' reception of economic and foreign policy. When Barack Obama took office, he was constrained by the issue culture that had been initiated by his Democratic predecessor and cemented by Bush. On free trade policies that had eroded the base of tradable jobs, American citizens had little reason to favor the all but identical views of either political party. With elite consensus that was unresponsive to these economic anxieties, according to the uncertainty model, this gave a foothold for a populist reaction that would begin to materialize during the Great Recession. Well before that economic downturn, the Bush administration would use the heightened sense of vulnerability among Americans to fuel elite support for the invasion of two nation-states.

Appendix to Chapter Three

To catalog the frames, I noted each author's assessment of the principal causes of terrorism as it related to globalization. Thus the unit of analysis was a causal connection made in text between globalization and terrorism. To avoid problems with reliability, I first sought explicit connections to establish a preliminary set of coding categories.

There were a total of 127 causal connections made between globalization and terrorism in the 92 articles analyzed for this book. These fell into eight categories: global interdependence (N=28), inequality (N=26), evil (N=25), the United States as global hegemon (N=24), religious fundamentalism (N=10), American popular culture (N=6), clash of worldviews (N=5), and the ignorance of the American public (N=3).

After a thorough analysis of the coverage, it became clear that several of the aforementioned themes functioned as parts of broader frames of analysis—master frames. The inequality theme, for example, proved to be part of two larger frames: (1) inequality resulted from the dynamics of market capitalism that either had not yet had a chance to work effectively (by far the most common view) or because of the inherent tendencies of capitalism to widen inequality, or (2) because the United States was the most prosperous and therefore the most militarily powerful, others suffered by and were resentful of comparisons of relative wealth. Thus the inequality theme was subsumed under two broader frames of the dark side of globalization or the United States as a global hegemon. Reaction to American popular culture also fell under the global hegemon frame because of the connection between United States economic power and its ability to disseminate American values through widely distributed media products. The evil theme was subsumed under the dark side frame because of its frequent pairing with the communication and transportation infrastructures underpinning globalization. Increased interdependence, the "small globe" hypothesis, also supported the importation of evil along the networks of globalization; this, too, was subsumed under the dark side of globalization frame. The connection made between religious fundamentalism and terrorism was mainly associated with the global hegemon frame (reaction to United States cultural and political power), but several instances were associated with a conflict in worldviews. I combined these latter instances of fundamentalism with the clash of civilizations. I now turn to a more detailed analysis of the three principal frames that subsumed these themes and those catchphrases, slogans, or words that indicated the presence of these frames.

The hegemony frame emerged from the frequent mention of United States political, economic, or cultural influence and the resentment and frustration it bred in the homelands of the terrorists. A story was cataloged as including this frame if it mentioned the role of United States political, economic, or cultural power, real or perceived, as playing a part in the attacks. In this excerpt, for example, the connection is explicit: " 'Most of the time the face of globalization is an American face, and they feel helpless to defeat it,' Hayes said. 'Out of this sense of helplessness comes a rage that takes great satisfaction in striking an icon of American culture' " (Black, 2001, p. 6A). In the following excerpt, it is less direct but still discernible: "With the end of the Cold War America went too quickly from declinism to triumphalism. All the trends of globalization and the information age favor the growing power of the United States, 'but only if we avoid stepping on our own message' " (Greenway, 2002b, p. A23). Several words and phrases indicate the presence of this frame, the most explicit being "global hegemon." More subtle but no less recognizable indicators were words and phrases such as "American unilateralism," "supporter of corrupt regimes," and, in the cultural realm, "Starbucks," "McDonalds," and "Hollywood."

The "dark side of globalization" emerged initially from the most common metaphor used in press coverage. The phrase itself (or related ones such as the "underbelly," "downside," or "flip-side" of globalization) signaled the pairing of terror with the economic and technological infrastructures of globalization. When the phrase did not occur explicitly, the frame was easily discerned by examples that illustrated the ready use of these benign networks for evildoing: "Because while transnational yuppies doing deals are fun to read about, it's now evident that bin Laden used many of the same techniques—satellite communications, sneaky cash flows, virtual networks—in his dealings, and that's not as much fun" (Pinkerton, 2001b, p. A39). While this pairing most often lead to the short-term remedy of increased state power, it also led to the long-term remedies afforded by globalization itself. The promise of neoliberal policy was evidenced primarily by the remedies advanced for terrorism: open markets and reduced state regulation. While the explicit examples were obvious, those that were implicit employed the same logic, even when reversed: "Nothing so captured American confidence in the wake of Communism's collapse as the expansion of global trade and the flood of United States investment into developing nations in the '90s. And nothing may dry up so quickly in the wake of the attacks" (Gosselin & Shiver, 2001, p. 1).

Finally, the "clash of worldviews" frame emerged from claims of the irreconcilability of worldviews attributed either to religious fundamentalism or to profound philosophical differences: "Terrorism arises not from fundamentalism but from extreme fundamentalists who fight for the only order that makes sense to them" (Balzar, 2001, p. 9). Most often the term fundamentalism signaled the use of this frame.

Two coders were trained to recognize the frames defined in the iterative process described previously. They each coded 20 percent of a randomly selected sample of the coded stories. Percentage agreements were as follows on each of the frame types: US hegemony (.91), dark side of globalization (.88), clash of worldviews (.95).

CHAPTER FOUR

American Exceptionalism
and Post-9/11 Foreign Policy

International opinion matters, but America should never ask permission to protect our people, our homeland or our way of life . . . I believe in American exceptionalism with every fiber of my being. But what makes us exceptional is not our
ability to flout international norms and the rule of law; it is our willingness to af-
firm them through our actions.—*Barack Obama, speech at West Point, May 28, 2014*

Barack Obama's speech to graduating cadets at West Point embodies the contradictions in American foreign policy. His embrace of American exceptionalism—
the idea that the United States is a model of high moral purpose to the world—
does not rule out unilateral action if its interests are at stake. A striking example
of this win-win principle in action was the Abu Ghraib prison scandal of 2004.
Other than the most partisan Republicans and conservative media commentators,
most elites seemed genuinely shocked by pictures of Iraqi prisoners arranged
in sexual poses or otherwise humiliated and threatened in order to "soften them
up." The photos and characterization of what they revealed as torture were incompatible with an image of the United States as a somewhat naïve but nevertheless well-intentioned moral exemplar to the world, the familiar frame used
by *New York Times* columnist David Brooks (2004) on the eve of the Iraq War:
"There's something about our venture into Iraq that is inspiringly, painfully,
embarrassingly and quintessentially American. No other nation would have
been hopeful enough to try to evangelize for democracy across the Middle East.
No other nation would have been naïve enough to do it this badly. No other nation
would be adaptable enough to recover from its own innocence and muddle its
way to success, as I suspect we are about to do" (p. A23). Such reactions and jus-
tifications arose from a matrix of culturally resonant uncritical assumptions—
refreshed by the attacks on 9/11—that reinforced support for unilateral US
foreign policy, and thereby US primacy, at a time globalization had ostensibly
reduced the power of the state.

Support for the military policy of a GOP president from an elite center-right columnist is neither surprising nor interesting, but support from the elite liberal press is. In this chapter, I argue that the high uncertainty created by 9/11 induced media elites to fall back on value-based beliefs rather than dispassionate analysis in order to support two conventional land wars against groups of stateless actors. Although the specific rationales differed for the approval of the invasions of Afghanistan and Iraq, they were both married to a set of beliefs that set the United States apart from other states. The same beliefs also contributed to the media's tempered reactions to Abu Ghraib, Obama's resistance to releasing a Senate Intelligence Committee report on the use of torture by the CIA during the Bush administration, and a controversy expressed in as an unlikely context as the Academy Awards.

Globalization and Liberal Internationalism

As we reviewed in chapter 1, Fukuyama's *The End of History and the Last Man* (1992) provided a template for mapping the post–Cold War world. The merging of the world into a cosmopolitan unity, a universal and homogenous state, was the logical end state of history's fulfillment. Fukuyama's thesis spawned a number of successful popularizations (e.g., Friedman, 2000; Mickelthwait & Wooldridge, 2000) that declared a new economic and political order, a realization of Woodrow Wilson's liberal internationalist vision. One version of this argument set the foundations of stability on a shared desire among states to take part in increased prosperity and thus to reduce the incentives for war. As we saw in chapter 3, this was a dominant elite prescription for avoiding future terror attacks. Another version claimed that the increased power of markets and capital flows would weaken states.

Critics of the weak-state hypothesis declared that multinational corporations remained tied to specific locations (e.g., Mann, 1997) and that strong states would continue to bend international law and markets to suit their interests (Barber, 1996). Realist critics pointed to an analogous economic interdependence in Europe that did little to prevent World War I (Mearsheimer, 2001).

From an international realist's perspective, the sheer economic and military power of the United States (Brooks & Wohlforth, 2002) was an advantage to be safeguarded given the absence of a governing authority over the international environment. Paul Wolfowitz developed a doctrine that would assure US primacy. As undersecretary of defense for the George H. W. Bush administration, Wolfowitz leaked a document to *The New York Times* that articulated a military policy that formed the nucleus of George W. Bush's War on Terror: "First, the U.S. must show the leadership necessary to establish and protect a new order that holds the promise of convincing potential competitors that they need not aspire to a greater role or pursue a more aggressive posture to protect their legitimate interests. Second, in the non-defense areas, we must account sufficiently for the interests of the advanced industrial nations to discourage them from challenging our leadership or seeking to overturn the established political and economic order. Finally, we must maintain the mechanisms for deterring potential competitors from even aspiring to a larger regional or global role" ("Excerpts from Pentagon's plan," 1992, sec. 1, p. 14). The issue for this chapter is not whether nations strive for power but whether the uncertainties following 9/11 yielded a political culture that provided the United States a moral cover for its actions and thereby a potent influence on public opinion. The Bush administration would use the uncertainty that followed 9/11 to argue its case for land invasions of Afghanistan and Iraq to avert future terror attacks but also to demonstrate the "shock and awe" of American military power. To convince skeptical media elites and public opinion, especially for an invasion of Iraq, the administration would rely on the tenets of American exceptionalism to fortify US military action with high moral purpose.

American Exceptionalism and Its Critics

Aside from the former Soviet Union, the United States is uniquely distinguished from other nations by its ideological origins. The values that define American political culture are not distinctive individually but collectively define what some (e.g., Cherry, 1971; Lipset, 1996) have called American exceptionalism. These values find their origin in an uneasy marriage of Enlightenment ideals and Protestant sectarianism that promotes individual rights and the exercise of reason in the service of the improvement of the human condition. An amalgam of beliefs and values—faith in progress, optimism, antistatism, and an unusually religious outlook—creates a foundation for American exceptionalism's influence on foreign policy. The route to such influence begins in the antistatist and moral components of American political culture.

Some theorists argue that the antistatist component of American political culture impedes development of the solidarity necessary for achieving political goals, a remedy for which is a polarizing "us and them" frame of reference (Ellis, 1993). An inclination to find external sources of evil—Manicheanism—is assisted by religious beliefs that seek the reform of nonbelievers and their corrupt practices. The post-9/11 shift in American foreign policy ("you're either with us or against us") was significant in a political culture strongly influenced by religious beliefs.

Despite their faith in reason, Americans are more likely than citizens of other Western nations to believe in God, the soul, the devil, and life after death. They are also much more likely to assign great importance to the role of God in their lives (World Values Survey, 1995–1997). Notwithstanding the nonestablishment clause in the Constitution (see Perry, 2003), studies of trends in public opinion data show that Americans are of two minds on the issue of the role of religion in government: split on the desirability of the influence of Judeo-Christian principles on political life and, in recent years, increased support for the expression of views on social issues by religious leaders (Servín-González & Torres-Reyna, 1999; Pew Research Center, 2014). The Pew study shows a growing divide between believers and nonbelievers on the issue.

The trends were accompanied by the rise in the visibility and the political influence of the evangelical Christian movement (Domke, 2004), itself fueled by the increasing numbers of Americans who regarded themselves as born-agains (one-third of Americans who attended religious services, according to the 2000 NES). A numerical minority, the Christian Right is highly organized and politically influential but more significantly had sympathetic allies in the Bush White House who regarded the group as a key electoral constituency. George W. Bush was a born-again Christian, as were Attorney General John Ashcroft and Michael Gerson, Bush's senior speechwriter. This excerpt from a 2004 press conference reveals the imprint of an evangelizing religious faith on Bush foreign policy:

> So long as I'm the president, I will press for freedom. I believe so strongly in the power of freedom. You know why I do? Because I've seen freedom work right here in our own country. I also have this belief, strong belief, that freedom is not this country's gift to the world. Freedom is the Almighty's gift to every man and woman in this world. And as the greatest power on the face of the earth, we have an obligation to help the spread of freedom. . . . That's our obligation. That is what we have been called to do, as far as I'm concerned. (George W. Bush, news conference, April 13, 2004)

The concept of American exceptionalism is not without controversy; critiques come from two directions. From a macro-comparative view, Wilson (1998) argued that Western European states differ less ideologically from the United

States today than they did when they embraced organic conservatism and social democracy. Whatever differences continue to distinguish the United States, Wilson argued, these are insufficient to support an exceptionalist status for the nation.

American Exceptionalism, Public Opinion, and Foreign Policy

A moralizing discourse was used to justify foreign policy during the Cold War, but it supported a multilateral approach that reduced the cost of US involvement (Gaddis, 2004). The Vietnam War fractured the veneer of the cold war consensus (Hallin, 1992) as controversies emerged on the use of US military force abroad and, if this were to take place, whether the nation should act unilaterally (Wittkopf, 1994; Sobel, 2001). In the 1990s Americans remained committed to internationalism but were divided over its form—unilateral or multilateral—and were more likely to be isolationist than opinion leaders and elites. Sobel's (2001) analysis of three post-Vietnam foreign policy debates found that public opinion constrained policy makers and thus played a role in their formulation of strategies that advocated the use of military force. But what about the period following 9/11?

As the uncertainty model would predict, a disquieting and wholly unfamiliar event such as 9/11 would stimulate both information seeking and a need for control, components used to judge future risk exposure. A Chicago Council on Foreign Relations (2002) survey of attitudes on foreign policy found that after 9/11, Americans became more interested in foreign news, were much more supportive of increases in defense spending (44 percent vs. 30 percent in 1998, the highest increase in 30 years), and were nearly unanimous (more than eight of ten) in their preference for the United States exerting "strong leadership" in world affairs.

One might think that the 9/11 attacks would also have created support for a US-centric, realist approach to foreign policy. Not so. Americans remained highly supportive of multilateral action: nearly two-thirds opposed the United States playing the role of world policeman, more than half opposed US intervention were the nation to "take the lead responsibility and supply most of the forces," and less than one-third thought the United States should act alone in solving an international problem (though this represented a 10 percent increase over 1998). On the specific issue of Iraq, two-thirds said that the United States should invade only with UN approval and the support of allies.*

---

* One study found majority support for multilateralism but also that Americans thought the majority favored unilateralism and thus perceived greater support for Bush foreign policy (Todorov & Mandisodza, 2004).

Al-Qaeda's attacks made Americans more supportive of military force, but they remained committed to multilateralism and the approval of the UN. If the Bush administration were to contemplate a unilateralist approach, it would need to depend on a resonant cultural matrix of beliefs that would legitimize its foreign policy to a skeptical public and the liberal media.

American Exceptionalism and Bush Foreign Policy

The phrase "axis of evil" first appeared in George Bush's State of the Union address in January 2002. Its significance was not limited to what on the surface appeared to be an echo of Reagan's foreign policy rhetoric. During the 1980s, the Reagan administration cast its foreign policy in a moralistic tone but maintained close ties with its Western European allies despite mass demonstrations against US deployment of intermediate range and cruise missiles. By contrast, the European allies first learned of the axis of evil from news reports (Mann, 2004).

The George W. Bush administration's foreign policy presented an anomaly to a conventional realist-liberal analytic scheme, criteria used to evaluate the purpose and effectiveness of military intervention. To cite one familiar contrast, liberal internationalists claim that democratic states are much less likely to go to war with each other and that international cooperation with rules that govern state behavior enhance the prospects for peaceful coexistence (see, e.g., Brown, Lynn-Jones, & Miller, 1999). By contrast, realists are indifferent to the internal political systems of nation-states and have little faith in the efficacy of rules promulgated by international institutions such as the UN. Realists contend that the environment, not rules, has a decisive influence over a state's behavior (Mearsheimer, 2001). US foreign policy post-9/11 blurred these distinctions.

Bush's foreign policy team[*] developed a policy whose central aim was to safeguard American primacy through military power, a view made more conspicuous after 9/11. What distinguished this conventionally realist approach is that it did not subscribe to the "billiard ball" tenet that the internal political institutions of a state make little difference to its foreign policy; on the contrary, a Straussian perspective[†] regarded totalitarian states a threat to freedom. National Security

---

[*] Calling themselves the "Vulcans" (Mann, 2004), the Bush foreign policy team came from the Project for a New America (PNAC), a conservative Washington think tank. Dick Cheney, Donald Rumsfeld (both founders), Paul Wolfowitz, Richard Armitage, and twelve other members were appointed to key positions within the Bush administration.

[†] A number of the Vulcans admired Leo Strauss, an enigmatic figure whose political philosophy has inspired a lively debate on his presumptive justification of an elite-led state (see, e.g., Drury,

Advisor Condoleezza Rice (2000) borrowed freely from the political culture of American exceptionalism (here tilted toward material rather than moral progress) to justify US primacy but also to check what she regarded as a "reflexive" instinct to bend to "notions of international law and norms": "The belief that the United States is exercising power legitimately only when it is doing so on behalf of someone or something else was deeply rooted in Wilsonian thought, and there are some echoes of it in the Clinton administration. To be sure, there is nothing wrong with doing something that benefits all humanity, but that is, in a sense, a second-order effect. America's pursuit of the national interest will create conditions that promote freedom, markets, and peace" (p. 47). Note here the equation of US good with that of the rest of the globe, a classically exceptionalist view married to a justification of US unilateralism.

It is important to note that US unilateralism was not strictly attributable to partisan differences. The 9/11 attacks on New York and Washington crystallized a unilateralist tendency that had begun to steer Clinton foreign policy: Clinton opposed an international treaty banning land mines, refused to put US troops under UN command, and did not join the International Criminal Court (Woollacott, 2000). Similarly, Barack Obama withdrew US troops from Iraq because the Iraqi parliament would not grant US soldiers immunity from prosecution. After a group of Sunni jihadists seized chunks of territory in western Iraq in 2014 and threatened what Obama claimed were US national security interests, Obama sent military advisers to stop their advance. The retreat and counterattack illustrated how American exceptionalism served as an all-purpose post-9/11 security rationale that would not inflame domestic public opinion.

The Bush administration also made unilateralism a keystone of its foreign policy in its National Security Strategy (2002). The policy declared the right to preemptive war but also the promotion of democratic values, "a balance of power that favors human freedom" (p. 2). The concept of "balance of power" is a component of realist theory and the strategic aim of Bush foreign policy, but the administration's use of the phrase "favors human freedom" previewed the rhetoric

---

1997; Smith, 1997). Strauss was a friendly but vigorous intellectual opponent of Alexandre Kojève, who reconfigured Hegelian analysis from an ideational foundation to one of active human agency. Strauss (1991) argued that a homogenous cosmopolitan state, the telos of Kojève's analysis, would yield a society that would fail to provide recognition, a deep human need, and would inevitably lead to an oppressive state led by a universal tyrant. Ironically, Fukuyama adapted Kojève's analysis for his end of history thesis but concluded that such a state would deny human nature its Nietzschean will to power. Fukuyama later became associated with the neoconservatives in the Bush cabinet but disapproved of the invasion of Iraq.

that would be used to imbue the strategic goal of US primacy with an aura of moral purpose.

The formulation would account for the promotion of democracy in hostile states such as Iraq and Iran, but not Pakistan, Saudi Arabia, or Egypt (as we learned in chapter 3, reflected in media coverage as well). The eclectic synthesis of realism and liberal internationalism would also be consistent with Donald Rumsfeld's dismissal of France and Germany as "Old Europe" after these Cold War allies rejected a US-sponsored UN resolution to invade Iraq. The policy also explained the use of the redundantly qualified concept of the "coalition of the willing": the United States would pursue what it saw as its vital interests, with allies if possible, but would not hesitate to act alone "if necessary" (National Security Strategy, 2002), a formulation not unlike the one declared by Obama at West Point.

After 9/11, the moral tone of the administration's foreign policy rhetoric became steeped in resolve and righteous indignation (Mann, 2004). The subtleties of pre-9/11 foreign policy were eliminated with a stroke and returned the world to the familiarity of cold war Manichaeism, this time under a unilateralist banner of strength sanctioned by virtue: a textbook example of the psychological process of fluid compensation that takes place under conditions of high uncertainty.

To what extent did a progressive/exceptionalist vision of the United States—a "city on a hill," a beacon of morality and progress—inflect the discourse on foreign policy? Did liberal media elites accept the union of American exceptionalism with US unilateralism? An analysis of elite liberal media commentary on the two wars of the first George W. Bush administration offers some clues.

Method and Data

As in chapter 3, I use frame analysis to examine the beliefs underlying the opinions of elites of post-9/11 US foreign policy, to see whether any assumptions were smuggled into favored policy arguments and whether they were more or less compatible with certain policy stands than others—specifically whether the values of American exceptionalism favored the ideals of a cosmopolitan, cooperative globalism or whether they served the interests of US primacy. I also examine whether post-9/11 foreign policy was supported by uncertainty-driven beliefs rather than dispassionate analysis.

I analyzed the editorial and op-ed pages of the nation's two most influential liberal newspapers whose columnists are syndicated in papers across the United States: *The New York Times* and *The Washington Post*. The selection criteria for the

Nexis database included all op-eds and editorials that included the term *Afghan-istan* for the two-month period that began on September 12, 2001, and ended on October 17, 2001, the run-up to the war to topple the Taliban regime in Afghan-istan. Similarly for Iraq, the time period begins January 1, 2003, and ends on February 28, 2003, two weeks prior to the start of the invasion. The range includes a key date—February 5, 2003—the day on which Colin Powell addressed the UN on "what the United States knows about Iraq's weapons of mass destruction, as well as Iraq's involvement in terrorism." Articles on the Afghan crisis numbered 92, on Iraq 133.

Coders were asked simply to note whether a particular theme appeared in a column or editorial.* The themes signaled the presence of three principal frames:

1. The United States as a political and economic exemplar to the world— *American exceptionalism*. Example themes included emulation of the United States as a solution to political and economic injustice and explicit moral judgment of US enemies and of uncooperative (and thereby), morally bankrupt allies.
2. The United States as part of an emerging, interdependent global order— *globalism*—an advance on Wilsonian internationalism. Here the themes centered on concerted, multilateral action (generally through the UN) on a problem with implications for the world as a whole.
3. The United States as an actor on the international stage with interests no different from any other power—*realism*. Example themes included approval of alliances of convenience with nations once held in disrepute and the punishment of states that harbor terrorists.

It should be noted that the themes that emerged in coding did not always strictly adhere to the tenets of these frames. For example, the punishment of states that harbor terrorists need not be a strictly realist theme. In fact, a number of IR realist theorists signed and published a letter in *The New York Times* advising against an invasion of Iraq because the regime was already contained and did not pose a threat to US strategic interests (see, e.g., Mearsheimer & Walt, 2003). The theme was coded as a realist theme, nonetheless, because the administration claimed Iraq posed such a threat.

Tables 4.1 and 4.2 summarize the most general findings: exceptionalist and internationalist/global themes appeared in slightly more than half of the edito-

---

* A separate coder examined 20 percent of the coding and found over 90 percent agreement on the detection of the themes.

Table 4.1. Rank order of frames by crisis

	Combined (N=225)	Afghanistan (N=92)	Iraq (N=133)
Exceptionalism	54.7%	54.3%	54.8%
International/globalism	51.1	31.5	64.7
Realism	27.5	45.6	25.6

Table 4.2. Rank order of themes by crisis

	Combined (N=225)	Afghanistan (N=92)	Iraq (N=133)
Multilateralism (international/globalism)	33.3% (75)	25.0% [1] (23)	39.1% [1] (52)
Evil enemies (exceptionalism)	19.1 (43)	22.8 [2] (21)	16.5 [3] (22)
US virtue (exceptionalism)	18.2 (41)	22.8 [2] (21)	15.0 [5] (20)
UN (international/ globalism)	17.8 (40)	6.5 [4] (6)	25.6 [2] (34)
Alliances of convenience (realism)	16.4 (37)	22.8 [2] (21)	12.0 [6] (16)
US as model of success (exceptionalism)	11.6 (26)	5.4 [5] (5)	15.8 [4] (21)
Punish state-sponsored terrorism (realism)	11.1 (25)	22.8 [2] (21)	3.0 [8] (4)
Corrupt European allies (exceptionalism)	5.8 (13)	3.3 [6] (3)	7.5 [7] (10)

Note: Ns in parentheses; numbers in square brackets indicate rank order of the theme for that crisis.

rial/op-ed content for the two cases combined. Realist themes structured slightly over one-quarter of the pieces overall, but they were much more dominant in the Afghanistan case: nearly half compared to only one-quarter for Iraq. Internationalist/globalist themes dominated the Iraqi case, nearly two-thirds compared to slightly less than one-third of the commentary preceding the War on Afghanistan. At this general level of findings, exceptionalism was the most stable frame of the post-9/11 issue culture, its partner frames changing depending on the specific nature of the crisis.

The most general patterns show that the Afghanistan case more closely followed the contours of the Bush foreign policy linking American exceptionalism to realism and American primacy, while exceptionalism was more closely linked to globalism in the Iraqi case. Clues as to the reasons for this variance appear in an analysis of the specific themes.

Post-9/11 Foreign Policy Frames

Although exceptionalist frames appeared in nearly the same proportion in both cases, they supported different political ends. The most common exceptionalist themes for Afghanistan made moral judgments that either condemned enemies or praised American virtue. The Iraqi case shared with Afghanistan the relative prominence of the condemnation of evil and proclamation of US virtue, though both appeared slightly less often than in elite opinion on Afghanistan. In the Iraq case, the exceptionalist frame appeared in the guise of the United States as a model for the restructuring of Iraq's political and economic institutions. Commentators cited this three times more frequently for Iraq than for Afghanistan.

Multilateral-globalist themes were twice more likely to appear in analysis of the Iraqi crisis than in the case of Afghanistan. Pleas for multilateral action and deference to the UN—either for continuation of the weapons inspections regime or UN sanction for a US military attack—were the most common themes. The latter issue may have exaggerated the importance of an internationalist/globalization frame for the Iraqi case, however, because the United States did not consult with the UN prior to its invasion of Afghanistan. Bush rejected requests for Security Council approval for an attack, and much of the diplomacy in organizing basing arrangements in countries such as Turkey, Uzbekistan, and Oman was conducted quietly so as not to arouse the presumed ire of their populations (Sciolino & Myers, 2001). In the Iraqi case, commentaries and editorials called for UN endorsement of US action and counseled patience with the UN inspections regime.

Realist themes also differed for the two cases. Alliances of convenience and the punishment of state-sponsored terrorism appear in equal measure for Afghanistan. By contrast, in the Iraqi case, alliances of convenience appeared half as often—12 percent of the opinion versus 25 percent for Afghanistan—while punishment of state-sponsored terrorism was nearly a nonissue. It appeared in just a few op-ed pieces written by William Safire, who tried to establish a link between an al-Qaeda operative and an Iraqi diplomat. Media elites simply did not accept the Bush administration's linkage of Iraq with 9/11.

I explore the relationship of these patterns in greater depth in a later stage of the analysis. I now turn to a brief analysis of each of the themes.

Multilateralism

A call for cooperative action among states was somewhat more prominent in the Iraqi case. Much of the opinion reacted to the Bush administration's willingness to go it alone: "The United States should not engage in tit-for-tat polemics directed at its most important allies. That is as demeaning as it is destructive. There is an urgent need for a reaffirmation at the highest level of the priority of the Atlantic alliance as the anchor point of America's engagement in the world" (Brzezinski, 2003). Here, as in other examples, a call for multilateralism had less to do with burden sharing than with external validation of the correctness of the Bush administration's diagnosis of the case for the invasion. Evidence for this interpretation comes from an analysis of the Afghanistan crisis; here the case for multilateralism was less urgent because there was more sympathy across the globe for the United States after the 9/11 attacks, consensus on the identity of the attackers, and a recognition that this brand of terrorism was not only an assault on the United States but on the nation-state system itself. The calls for concerted action had perhaps less to do with a zeitgeist of global cooperation than with pragmatic necessity, but a sense of global purpose drove the coverage nevertheless: "The administration has reached out to many prospective partners, including NATO members, Russia, China and India. Wisely, it has recognized the importance of enlisting major Muslim nations like Pakistan, Indonesia and Saudi Arabia in the antiterrorist coalition. Osama bin Laden's network is active in 60 countries, most of them with large Muslim populations. Cooperation with the governments of these nations will be crucial in locating and arresting terrorists and disrupting their communications and financing" ("Calibrating the use of force," 2001, p. A24).

Exceptionalism: US Virtue and Moral Judgment

A key theme of exceptionalism invokes the unique political culture and history of the United States and thus its exemplary status for the world. Thomas Friedman of *The New York Times*, a strong supporter of economic globalization, invoked this theme on a regular basis: "It pits us—the world's only superpower and quintessential symbol of liberal, free-market, Western values—against all the super-empowered angry men and women out there. . . . [M]any in this part of the world crave the best of America, and we cannot forget that we are their ray of hope" (2001, p. A27).

Another version of the same frame was used to caution against an excessively violent response that might arouse a backlash in the Islamic world but that would also tarnish American principles: " 'I ask you to uphold the values of America,' President Bush said to Congress and the nation. That will be a fair test of his policy for dealing with terrorism as the policy unfolds: Does it uphold the values of America? . . . But right now we need to make sure that we do not forget ourselves in our immediate response to the terrorists' criminal assault. President

Bush used three words repeatedly in his speech: 'freedom,' 'patience,' 'justice.' "
They are the right words (Lewis, 2001b).

A derivative theme was moral judgment of US enemies (use of terms such as evil, corruption, perversion, darkness, backwardness) and thus a clear demarcation of a virtuous us from an evil them. Plentiful examples occurred in both cases. For Afghanistan: "There is no way to reason with people who think they will go directly to heaven if they kill Americans. . . . But here on earth, as President Kennedy suggested, we human beings are responsible—and must act to prevent evil" (Lewis, 2001a, p. A23). An op-ed on the Iraq crisis invoked a religious theme: "[The] Christian Gospel is not only about 'the law of love,' as war opponents like to put it. It's also about the fact that people violate that law. That's why Jesus talked a great deal about punishment, and the moral obligation to oppose evil with a strong and swift hand. Human evil must be confronted, he said, not merely contained. Depending on the threat, a kind of 'pre-emptive strike' or judgment against evil might even be required: 'Be afraid of the one who can destroy both soul and body in hell'" (Laconte, 2003, p. A21).

Colin Powell's February 5, 2003, speech to the UN marked an important moment in the debate on Iraq. Powell's perceived moderation* coupled with the dubious intelligence on Iraqi WMD had a marginal influence on US public sentiment in favor of an invasion. Figure 4.1 shows a partisan divide with large majorities of self-identified Republicans approving an invasion as early as September 2002 and majority support among Democrats after the speech.

As table 4.3 shows, Powell's testimony altered patterns of elite media discourse. Although Powell's speech came three-fifths of the way through the time period studied, it neatly divided the number of published editorials and op-eds on the issue. There was little change in calls for a multilateral approach to crisis, the most frequent theme before and after the speech, but there was a significant drop in the theme of soliciting UN support for US military action and a corresponding increase in the use of a moralist discourse to characterize Saddam Hussein and the venality of "old Europe." Commentaries and editorials that called for deference to UN inspections or its approval for a US invasion fell by nearly 40 percent (13 items vs. 21 prior to the Powell speech). Meanwhile, references to evil increased by twofold (15 items vs. 7), and references to corrupt European allies increased by fourfold (eight items vs. two prior to the speech).

---

* According to Mann (2004), Colin Powell's moderate views were confined to social issues, not defense policy. Powell shared Caspar Weinberger's hawkish views on foreign policy—a strong US military and avoidance of conflict unless it is based on overwhelming force and clear political objectives.

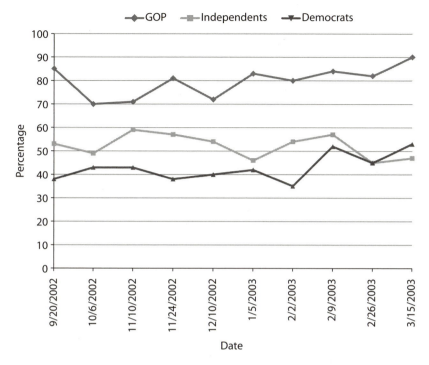

Figure 4.1. Americans favoring invading Iraq with US ground troops to remove Saddam Hussein from power, by party ID. *Source:* Gallup/CNN/USA Today Polls.

Table 4.3. Rank order of Iraq themes by crisis before and after Powell speech

	Before (*N* = 66)	After (*N* = 67)	Combined (*N* = 133)
Multilateralism (international/globalism)	36.4% [1] (24)	41.8% [1] (28)	39.1% [1] (52)
UN (international/globalism)	31.8 [2] (21)	19.4 [3] (13)	25.6 [2] (34)
Evil enemies (exceptionalism)	10.6 [5] (7)	22.4 [2] (15)	16.5[3] (22)
US as model of success (exceptionalism)	16.7 [3] (11)	14.9 [4 (10)	15.8 [4] (21)
US virtue (exceptionalism)	15.2 [4] (10)	14.9[4] (10)	15.0 [5] (20)
Alliances of convenience (realism)	10.6 [5] (7)	13.4 [5] (9)	12.0 [6] (16)
Corrupt European allies (exceptionalism)	3.0 [7] (2)	11.9 [6] (8)	7.5 [7] (10)
Punish state-sponsored terrorism (realism)	2.0 [8] (1)	4.5 [7] (3)	3.0 [8] (4)

Note: *N*s in parentheses.

Put in more general terms, prior to Powell's speech, a globalist frame of reference dominated American exceptionalism by a ratio of about 1.6 to one (68 percent vs. 42 percent). After Powell's testimony, the frame of American exceptionalism in support of the war (now including open criticism of European allies, 12 percent of the total) had overtaken globalist themes (64 percent vs. 61 percent). The difference was attributable to a shaken belief in the legitimacy of the UN, primarily because of the unwillingness of European allies to approve US military action. Here commentators opined that financial or political advantage for France and Germany had corrupted their moral vision, which the United States was now obliged to restore with its coalition of the willing: "France and Russia insist on U.N. inspections. But in the 1990s, France and Russia weakened the economic sanctions designed to make inspections work. China and Russia urge multilateralism—but when the United States asks for their help in dealing with North Korea's nuclear threat, it's absent. Germany is entitled to oppose U.S. military action. But Gerhard Schroeder didn't have to resort to anti-Americanism to rescue his faltering election campaign. He and French President Jacques Chirac have not merely disagreed with U.S. policy; they have stoked anti-Americanism" (Samuelson, 2003, p. A23).

Major differences between the two cases include the near absence of UN-related themes in the Afghanistan crisis—less than one-tenth of the coverage as opposed to nearly one-quarter for Iraq. Elite media discourse on the Iraq crisis cautioned against hasty, unilateral action. One thread of the opinion showed a preference for the UN inspections regime, and another noted that the UN had failed to find weapons of mass destruction and, thus, undermined the Bush administration's principal reason for going to war. A *New York Times* editorial included both of these themes: "There can be no wavering from the goal of disarming Iraq, but all chances of doing so peacefully should be explored before the world is asked to decide on war. Before that point is reached, Washington should share its evidence with the public" ("Iraq dossier," 2003, p. A22).

Realism

A realist theme of support for alliances of convenience appeared in over one-fifth of the Afghanistan coverage. Columnists and commentators sometimes recognized the risks of sullying US exceptionalism, but pragmatic necessity tilted the decision in favor of pragmatic alliance: "Keeping Pakistan from plunging over the precipice will be a difficult task, complicated by the fact that the Pakistani intelligence service itself has supported jihadists in Kashmir and Afghanistan. But despite such complexities, the United States needs to work with Gen. Pervez

Musharraf—whose concern about radicalism appears genuine—to bring his country back into America's orbit by lifting some sanctions, extending economic assistance and even providing limited military cooperation" (Benjamin & Simon, 2001, p. A37).

The punishment theme asserted that states harboring terrorists were fair game for US military action, an imperfect but lone available remedy for a political force that transcended the nation-state system itself: "No longer can any nervous Arab ruler pretend to doubt bin Laden's direct culpability for the hijack attacks. And because the interests of Middle Eastern terrorists are clearly the same, no longer can the world separate his Al Qaeda cult, the terrorists of Hamas and Hezbollah and the P.L.O. warring on Israel, and the center of world terror in Baghdad run by Saddam Hussein" (Safire, 2001, p. A17). Another: "The objective of this war must be to make it impossible or intolerable for any state to harbor, protect or aid and abet terrorists. The point is not to swat every mosquito but to drain the swamp. The campaign, however, cannot stop there. Nor with bin Laden. (Although when the Taliban government falls, finding bin Laden and his associates will be that much easier.) Afghanistan is just stage one" (Krauthammer, 2001, p. A39).

The hybrid concept of "state-sponsored terrorism" was applied to Afghanistan coverage but rarely to Iraq (4 of 133 items). Public perception of a link between al-Qaeda and Iraq grew from the Bush administration's repeated assertions in speeches and news accounts rather than the opinion in op-eds and editorials. The case for an invasion of Iraq would ultimately rest on the Bush administration's claims of WMD in Iraq, a claim whose credibility would be underpinned by the resonant appeal of American virtue.

Dimensions Underlying the Themes and Their Compatibility

Factor analysis permits an analysis of the dimensions underlying the themes, an indirect test of whether they are derived from the same frame and the compatibility of the themes. To preview the findings, media elites reflected majority opinion preference for internationalism but also regarded the United States as endowed with uniquely admirable qualities. Expressed pragmatically, these beliefs and values set the nation apart as a political and economic model for emulation; expressed in moral terms, the values perceived to animate US foreign policy were regarded as an expression of the nation's founding virtues. The latter expression restrained a frank declaration of realist-based preferences on the one hand but also facilitated moral judgment of enemies and those states who disagreed with US policy. The discourse thus became open to a critique of multilateralism and the UN, and thus justified US unilateralism on moral grounds. The Bush administration fortified its rhetorical justification for war with the values of American exceptionalism to overcome the conventional frames used by the press to judge foreign policy.

Using factor analysis on the entire set of opinions and op-eds combined yielded a three-factor solution that explains a relatively low 47 percent of the variance; this means that the two cases warrant separate analyses.

As shown in table 4.4, factor analysis of the opinion on Afghanistan yields a four-component solution that explains 62 percent of the variance. The first cleanly captures the two most prominent exceptionalist themes—the United States as a model to the world (.81) and as a paragon of virtue (.76). In effect, this dimension embodies the American exceptionalist frame for the war on the Taliban and acts as an independent test of the frame's validity.

The second dimension includes multilateral action (.75) but also the realist themes of alliances of convenience (.55) and punishment of states that harbor terrorists (.52). In short, this dimension establishes the discursive foundations for the Bush administration's eclectic foreign policy that would draw key support during the Iraq crisis: it melds an internationalist principle with a realist principle and thereby confers legitimacy for the concept of the coalition of the willing, even as it simultaneously draws attention away from the absence of international approval.

The third dimension establishes the tensions between moralism and internationalism as it pits cooperation with the UN (−.81) against judgment of the

Table 4.4. Factor analysis of themes, Afghanistan: Rotated component matrix

Themes	Component			
	1	2	3	4
Multilateralism	.022	.751	−.001	.007
Alliances of convenience	−.226	.552	.004	−.534
Evil	.164	−.356	.684	.042
Punish state-sponsored terrorism	.248	.518	.035	.435
US virtue	.761	.066	.064	.018
UN*	.022	−.263	−.813	−.034
US as a model*	.810	−.041	.036	−.038
Corrupt European allies*	−.137	.047	.054	.796

Note: Themes arranged in order of frequency (four tied for second). Extraction method: principal component analysis. Rotation method: Varimax with Kaiser normalization. Rotation converged in seven iterations.

*$N \leq 6$

enemy as evil (.68). Although few commentators advocated cooperating with the UN, we begin to see the origins of the success of the Bush administration's argument for a policy of unilateralism predicated on moral condemnation of the enemy, a strategy that would facilitate dismissal of arguments by allies who might oppose US action.

The fourth dimension is logically related to the third in that it establishes a moral predicate for the realist policy of establishing alliances of convenience in the face of the moral bankruptcy of now former allies. The latter theme is comparatively rare, however, appearing in less than 4 percent of the coverage.

Table 4.5 shows results of a factor analysis of the Iraqi crisis discourse. It also yields a four-factor solution and once again explains 62 percent of the variance. The first two dimensions establish a moral rationale for unilateralism and US primacy.

The first component is predicated on the moral component of American exceptionalism: characterization of enemies as evil (.83) and its negative relationship to multilateralism (−.61). The second dimension is significant: it captures a predicate for US primacy first by linking US virtue (.61) with approval of alliances of convenience (.68) and second by its negative relationship with appeals for cooperation with the UN (−.46). This dimension echoes and reinforces the Bush administration's eclectic appeal established during the Afghanistan crisis. Here, too, it legitimates the coalition of the willing by its linkage with American exceptionalism, but it now adds rejection of cooperation with the UN as a bolstering theme for US primacy.

Table 4.5. Factor analysis of themes, Iraq: Rotated component matrix

	Component			
Themes	1	2	3	4
Multilateralism	−.495	−.095	−.446	−.071
UN	−.259	−.458	.002	−.631
Evil	.652	.290	.140	−.122
US as a model	−.167	−.204	.044	.852
US virtue	.019	.612	.345	−.065
Alliances of convenience	−.007	.675	−.406	.010
Corrupt European allies	−.012	−.014	.794	.022
Punish state sponsors of terrorism*	.778	−.301	−.223	.043

Note: Themes arranged in order of frequency. Extraction method: principal component analysis. Rotation method: Varimax with Kaiser normalization. Rotation converged in six iterations.

*N = four cases

The third dimension is a variation of the second, but it reestablishes the tensions between internationalism and moral judgment. A claim of the moral bankruptcy of European allies loads positively on this dimension (.79), while multilateralism loads negatively (−.45). Revealingly, alliances of convenience also load negatively on this component (−.41), suggesting the success of the Bush administration in investing realist necessity with virtue.

Like the third, the fourth dimension reveals the role of American exceptionalism in supporting US primacy. Here the elevation of the United States to exemplar status (.85) contrasts inimically to engagement with the UN (−.63).

To summarize, the themes of American exceptionalism provided a potent rhetorical tool for unilateralism and US primacy in the case for war with Iraq and left a permanent imprint on political culture that limited the scope of Barack Obama's foreign policy options.

Discussion and Conclusion

The Bush administration used the ostensibly high moral standing of the United States to privilege its judgments over those of foreign bodies. In so doing, it also spun up a dynamic that obliged the nation to act once such a judgment had been made: "The president [cannot] turn back politically. He began the march on Iraq with his State of the Union address a year ago. He identified the axis of evil as the single greatest threat to America and the world. To now admit that he can and will do nothing to meet that very threat would not just leave him without a foreign policy, it would destroy his credibility as a leader" (Krauthammer, 2003, p. A27).

The Iraq case pitted moral judgment against multilateralism—condemnation of the enemy was associated with unilateralism, however reluctant and even if delivered in high-ironic style: "Everyone knows Saddam is lying; the question is whether it's worth a war. . . . With or without the fussy Frenchies, we're going to war. For this White House, pulling back when all our forces are poised for battle would be, to use the Bush family's least favorite word, wimpy" (Dowd, 2003, p. 11). Although not addressed in this chapter, the primary objections to the war were less based on its necessity than on the absence of a plan for its aftermath.

What linked these two cases was the prominence of a compelling discourse among media elites that set the United States apart from the rest of the globe at a time when globalization was ostensibly bringing the world closer together. American exceptionalism in its moral and pragmatic guises was a primary part of the post-9/11 discourse, but it performed different functions in the two cases. In Afghanistan, it served as a potent support for a realist argument that rationalized US action and excused alliances with states of dubious moral character. Media elites applied American idealism selectively to punish those states on the wrong side in the War on Terror; states with dictatorial regimes, such as Saudi Arabia, that had strategic value for US interests were spared this moral judgment. As we observed in chapter 3, coverage of Middle East foreign policy in *The New York Times* that spared US allies of judgment regarding their authoritarian regimes has long supported this myopia and thereby promoted an exceptionalist reading of US foreign policy.

The Bush administration tried with little success to link Iraq with the attacks of 9/11, making assertions of such a linkage rather than providing definitive evidence. This war, too, was fought against a discursive field of American exceptionalism. Here, however, it was used to overcome a potent appeal by media elites for multilateral approval and aid. The Bush administration finally relied on insecurity by presenting its dubious case for the existence of WMD in Iraq. This discredited "Old Europe" and undermined its moral authority, thereby enabling the overthrow of Saddam's regime.

Realism was the least frequent frame brought to bear on post-9/11 US foreign policy. This is not entirely unexpected either from the perspective of uncertainty or from elite exploitation of uncertainty to craft emotional appeals. From this view, realists may be viewed as experts whose views are discounted by citizens whose judgments are clouded by the kind of compensatory reactions observed in terror management and meaning maintenance research. At a cultural level of analysis, proponents of realist IR theory point out that the moral and optimistic components of American political culture are either inimical to the ostensibly cynical self-interested components of realism (Mearsheimer, 2001) or that moralism in international relations is a mere veneer that conceals a more authentic (and sensible) self-interest at the core (Kaplan, 2000).

What is curious about the lesser position of discourse acknowledging the cause of American primacy is that it formed the core of Bush foreign policy. Its linkage to American exceptionalist themes obscured its prominence. To this end, one study (Todorov & Mandisodza, 2004) found that Americans were more likely to be supportive of unilateral US action if they overestimated the number of citizens in favor of this policy, which also made them more supportive of the Bush administration's decision to go it alone in Iraq. It is not clear whether this represented a form of pluralistic ignorance (and thus a foundation for a spiral of silence effect) or a surge of nationalist feeling founded in a discourse freighted with the resonant values of American exceptionalism. That this was advanced by liberal media elites spoke to the resonant power of beliefs that become salient under conditions of high uncertainty.

Little more than a year after the invasion of Iraq, *The New York Times* buried an apology for the paper's credulous coverage of the WMD controversy ("The Times and Iraq," 2004). The anonymous author (the byline cited "The Editors") blamed reliance on self-interested sources and the eagerness of reporters to scoop the competition for the paper's uncritical reporting. Taken together, these reasons describe a collective process driven by confirmation bias that increased perceived risk exposure to an imaginary threat. According to prospect theory, individuals are more willing to undertake a risky line of action to avoid a loss rather than to achieve a gain (see Perla, 2011). This finding is also supported by an extensive analysis of public opinion that shows Americans have greater tolerance of casualties in support of war that defends American allies or combats global terrorist organizations than war that promotes democracy in other nations or defends human rights (Gelpi, Feaver, & Reifler, 2009).

The eclectic formulation of the Bush administration's foreign policy unraveled as its contradictory components failed to offer clear guidance for action or for its justification. Over the course of the Iraqi crisis, loss-avoiding realism (the case for weapons of mass destruction) gave way to gain-seeking liberal internationalism (Iraqis are better off without Saddam and an Iraqi democracy will make the United States, and the world, safer). Bush defended US unilateralism using the values of liberal internationalism even as that defense alienated other liberal democracies.

As Bush foreign policy came into question because of unforeseen events following the invasion (e.g., the Iraqi insurgency, an incursion of foreign terrorists, and the absence of meaningful democratic reform), elite support dwindled and public opinion turned against the war. The incoherent formulation, supported by media elites, continued to influence Obama's Iraq policy as he first withdrew US forces because Iraq would not consent to judicial immunity but later inserted more US troops despite their susceptibility to Iraqi prosecution.

On the eve of the invasion of Iraq, two realist IR theorists presciently warned of the risks ahead:

> If the United States is, or soon will be, at war with Iraq, Americans should understand that a compelling strategic rationale is absent. This war would be one the Bush administration chose to fight but did not have to fight. Even if such a war goes well and has positive long-range consequences, it will still have been unnecessary. And if it goes badly—whether in the form of high U.S. casualties, significant civilian deaths, a heightened risk of terrorism, or increased hatred of the United States in the Arab and Islamic world—then its architects will have even more to answer for. (Mearsheimer & Walt, 2003, p. 59)

Mearsheimer and Walt (2003) offered the equivalent of expert opinion that was overridden by fear and wishful thinking that followed 9/11, the latter endorsed by the elite liberal press. That this was a polarized and belief-driven phenomenon could be seen in the media's reaction to Abu Ghraib and in a more nuanced way in popular culture. Bennett et al. (2006) claimed that the deference of the mainstream press to political elites led to mischaracterization of the Abu Ghraib scandal. By a wide margin, coverage was framed as abuse rather than torture.* The authors attribute this framing to an absence of elite dissent on the matter and downplay the possibility of a cultural explanation because the torture frame only briefly appeared in coverage before being overwhelmingly overtaken by the abuse frame. Although this is plausible within the narrow empirical bounds of the indexing hypothesis, an alternative cultural account cannot be ruled out.

The authors' strongest case for elite influence is that the sources they analyze are generally regarded as liberal and presumably less likely to be sympathetic to a Republican administration, but this fails to take into account the general fear and disquiet after 9/11, the mass of culturally inflected media opinion prior to the invasions of Afghanistan and Iraq, and the predictable uncertainty-based wave of patriotic sentiment that followed. In addition, nearly one-quarter of the electorate cited the war in Iraq and fear of another attack in the United States as the most important issue in the 2004 reelection and said that preventing another attack was their primary consideration in their vote. Isolating this one incident from the context of history that preceded it runs the risk of attributing a single cause to an overdetermined phenomenon that took place in a climate of fear and dread. A later example indicates its lasting impact on the broader political culture.

In 2013 a controversy arose on the merits of *Zero Dark Thirty*, a film that depicted the sequence of events that ended with the killing of Osama bin Laden. Critics on the right and left agreed that the film's depiction of torture was objectionable, but for opposite reasons. Those on the left said the film justified the use of torture because it was instrumental in leading the CIA to bin Laden's hideout. Those on the right complained that the film put torture in an unfair negative light when it had in fact led to unspecified intelligence breakthroughs. The first argument rested on the assumption that the United States held itself to a higher

---

* It is unclear whether the distinction is legal (as the *New York Times* editor claimed in his rationale for explaining the paper's decision to use the term *abuse*) or simply a logically fallacious differentiation of essentially equivalent acts.

moral standard, the second on the assumption that the nation did not need permission to safeguard its interests. The positions were, in fact, different sides of the same rhetorical coin most recently minted by George W. Bush and used by Barack Obama in his speech at West Point. The high risk exposure of 9/11 had led to a flawed foreign policy supported by an emotionally aroused electorate and a culturally resonant appeal of American exceptionalism that was at odds with the new political realities of stateless terror networks operating freely in a globalized world.

By the time Katrina hit the Gulf Coast, the United States had spent an esti-mated $400 billion on the War on Terror. The expenditure added to a growing federal debt (partly the result of two Bush tax cuts intended to stimulate the economy), $8.5 trillion as of September 30, 2005. The growth of the debt and the cost of the war would influence public debate on the government's response to Katrina and on the issue of climate change.

Appendix to Chapter Four

Together with the names of the publications and the sources and affiliations (professional and national) of the quoted sources, the coding protocol also included directions for identifying the themes that signaled the presence of the four frames that structured the text. Coding instructions were as follows:

Code assertions by the author (not merely reports of claims by others, unless these are strongly supported) that reflect on the role of the United States in the world post-9/11. The assertions fall into three main categories: (1) the United States as an exemplar to the world as a model for others to emulate to gain the prosperity and freedom that are the keys to solving the problems that led to terrorism. The United States as a moral exemplar to the world, its system and political philosophy having exceptional status that distinguishes it from other nation-states. This outlook obliges the United States to act in a selfless way. It also facilitates moral judgments made upon others and casts them into the role of evil actors who deserve condemnation rather than a hearing. (2) The United States as part of an interdependent system of nations. It should cooperate with other nations to advance a solution for a problem that affects others. It should work through the UN to gain its sanction or to rely on its help for solving a problem. (3) The United States is one of many unexceptional actors on the international stage who are susceptible to the same forces and self-interests as others. (4) The United States bears responsibility for terrorism and other world problems because of its sheer power. The category also includes other unrelated themes.

Exceptionalist Themes

1. United States as a model for others
   a. Solution to political and economic injustice is to emulate the United States. US self-interest seen as coextensive with the interests of a global greater good (e.g., assumption that because it is the most successful, the US model is good for others to emulate).
   b. Progress (e.g., in human rights, prosperity) inevitable with democracy and free-market capitalism (may also be equated with the United States as its symbolic representation)
2. United States as virtuous
   a. United States as endowed with special moral qualities that distinguish it from other states
   b. Moral language used to judge enemies of the United States (use of terms such as evil, corruption, perversion, darkness, backwardness)
   c. Others may not be capable of acting in this way (e.g., corrupt Europeans) or to receive the exceptional benefits of such treatment (e.g., the states of the Middle East are retarded by tradition, history, and resentment)
   d. With us or against us in the War on Terror

Internationalist/Globalist Themes

    3. United States must engage with the world in a multilateral way

    4. United States should work through the UN either for its sanction or for its help

Realist Themes

    5. United States must punish states that harbor terrorists and retaliate

    6. United States seeks alliances of convenience, necessary in these times (though alliance of other may be two-faced)

Other

    7. United States seeks world hegemony

    8. United States responsible for conditions that led to terror

    9. Bias of United States against Arabs, Palestinians (pro-Israel bias)

    10. United States is a self-serving state (e.g., profits by war)

CHAPTER FIVE

Climate Change and the Flood

This river used to meander all over its floodplain. People would move their tepees, and that was that. You can't move Vicksburg.—*Quoted in J. McPhee*, The Control of Nature, *p. 32*

Responding to arguably the most serious problem facing the globe, in late 2014 President Obama and Xi Jingping, president of the People's Republic of China, struck a bargain on carbon emission reductions. The United States pledged to reduce its carbon emissions by 25 percent by 2025, and China agreed to substitute 20 percent of its fossil fuel consumption with alternative energy sources by 2030. Climate scientists were divided on whether the reductions would be sufficient to avert a tipping point that would trigger irreversible environmental damage, while skeptics doubted the binding force of pledges. Republicans opposed the agreement and promised to pass laws that would permit states to override the EPA regulations that would enforce it.

Using his executive authority, Obama made the most important policy change to date but could not avert domestic politics. Those politics had made climate change a position issue that for nearly two decades had impeded progress on solutions to the problem widely acknowledged by scientists as a clear and present danger.

In this chapter, we review evidence brought to light by the uncertainty model that explains why threats posed by global climate change have failed to ignite the political passions needed to support an effective policy response to a gridlocked position issue. We find that data and information alone are not sufficient for effecting policy change. Statistics that index gradual increases in average global temperature do not have the same capacity to instill the uncertainty that follows hurricanes, flooding rains, and high-intensity tornadoes. These occur in what may be described as punctuated fashion, suddenly and unpredictably after long periods of otherwise unexceptional weather. Climate scientists say that such events are more likely as the atmosphere and the oceans heat up and provide more energy for storms and counterintuitive second-order events such as anomalous cold outbreaks. The weather anomalies provide the "hooks" that stimulate discussion and debate among political and media elites on the need for a policy response. Absent such attention or the emergence of a national movement to force response, the scope of the population that perceives itself to be at future risk is usually confined to the region or locales immediately affected. Outside those areas, perceived risk exposure to climate change is conditioned by cues of political elites as well as the political culture but oddly little by scientific authority. The polarization of opinion on climate change has frustrated attempts by the left to pass laws regulating carbon consumption. In the politics of insecurity, an energetic, passionate response is essential to overcome elite gridlock and the outsized influence of skeptics who doubt the role of human agency in global climate change. As we discover in the historical case study comparison that follows, a hidden, conditioning element is the political culture now tilted against decisive policy change.

Failure of the United States to respond decisively to climate change is significant for two reasons. First, although American political leaders frame climate change as if it were a tragedy of the commons where all nations share in the responsibility, the United States consumes nearly one-quarter of the world's energy supply. Because the United States claims global leadership based on its economic and military primacy as well as claims by political and media elites as to its exceptionalist moral status (as in its foreign policy), the nation's policies provide models for other states. The claims also establish the grounds for inaction on the part of states who criticize the United States for not living up to its standards.

Second, there are recent precedents for mobilizing domestic public opinion to support policy for addressing environmental hazards that cross national borders. These include the damaging effects of acid rain and the chemicals used in household products that erode the protective layer of ozone that shields the globe from ultraviolet radiation. In this context, the absence of the political will to respond to climate change is all the more striking because of the periodic catastrophic weather events that sound loud signals of increasing risk. One such example was Hurricane Katrina. Mediated reactions to the hurricane and its aftermath help explain the current dynamics of the political debate and the paralysis around global climate change, now commonly linked to weather disasters.

As we will see in the following discussion, instead of cueing a national debate on climate change and the risk exposure of the nation's population, Katrina came to symbolize fumbling at all levels of government, an indication of the lack of trust in government in general, as well as a fuel for zero-sum symbolic politics. This will become apparent when we compare national reaction to an earlier catastrophic flood that was used by political and media elites to fuel an energetic response to what was perceived as an intolerable risk to the nation's well-being and collective self-interest. In making the historical comparison, I argue that an overlooked dimension of this issue was a set of assumptions about self, and nature had transparently influenced the course of the mediated debate. The assumptions were the product of painstaking work by political actors on the right and the left that rendered certain mediated appeals culturally resonant and others flat. To explore the influence of these assumptions in the context of the uncertainty model, I compare the mediated discourse on the Katrina flood to the flood of an earlier era when what seemed possible and desirable drew on a radically different set of assumptions that made up the political culture. Before analyzing those assumptions, I provide some background on recent research on the reasons why the debate on climate change remains polarized and largely symbolic.

Climate Change and National Borders

There are three principal obstacles to national policy on climate change. The first is the conundrum of the "action at a distance" quality that characterizes globalization: a remote event has an unforeseen or unperceived impact on the local level. In Anthony Giddens's (1990) example, prosperity in Singapore leads to a factory shutdown in Pittsburgh. One climate example is the 2013–2014 "polar vortex" that propelled record cold and snowfall into the East and Midwest. In Chicago and elsewhere, climate change skeptics sarcastically pointed out that global warming would soon have polar bears frolicking on the frozen waters of the Great Lakes. What they may not have known or avoided mentioning was that anomalously warm air in the arctic had pushed the steering winds of the jet stream farther south and drawn down cold air from the Yukon into the Midwest.

A second is cost-benefit distributions within countries that make some policy changes easier to make (Bernauer, 2013). The most recent example is the case of the ozone hole. In 1976 the National Academy of Sciences concluded that the ozone layer was being depleted by the release of chemicals then commonly present in aerosol spray cans and refrigerants. The erosion of the ozone layer exposed the world's population to dangerous levels of ultraviolet radiation that would lead to increased cases of skin cancer. By 1987, the UN Environment Program had developed the Montreal Protocol, an international treaty intended to phase out the ozone-depleting chemicals. It only took two years for 197 nations to sign the treaty, which led to the gradual restoration of the ozone layer.

One explanation for the success of this international effort is that the few large firms that produced the chemicals could find substitutes and distribute their higher costs over a very large population of consumers, keeping per capita increases relatively small. Such is not the case for carbon consumption, because energy substitutes are more expensive compared to fossil fuels and the infrastructure for their distribution (e.g., charging stations) is in its infancy. Potential consumers and producers are thus faced with a chicken-and-egg problem that requires a government subsidy solution, one that introduces the uncertainties of time horizons for payoffs and pressure from competing interests, now pushed further into the future because of increases in oil and gas supplies due to new extraction processes such as fracking and oil shale processing. A more daunting problem is posed by the free rider problem inherent in setting national targets for the reduction of carbon consumption. President George W. Bush, for example, refused to sign the Kyoto Protocol on the grounds that reduced US consumption would hurt the US economy and because big polluters such as China and India were not required to sign the treaty.

The third obstacle is a less studied area of research: the risk and uncertainty profiles of Americans relative to climate change and the relationship of those profiles to their beliefs. In their analysis of national survey data of perceptions of climate change risk, Brody et al. (2008) found that only those who live near coastlines and low elevations consider themselves at greatest risk to rising sea levels, the most salient indicator of climate change to most Americans. Other more extreme weather events are not widely recognized by the general public as being connected to the phenomenon. In terms of the uncertainty model, the scope of the population at future risk has been confined to specific regions and locales, limiting the force of an effective political response.

The more relevant finding in the study is that personal efficacy is the best predictor of risk perception—the greater the degree to which citizens believe they have the responsibility and ability to reduce the potential adverse impacts of climate change, the greater their concern with potential risks. The logical following question is what influences public perceptions of climate change, information or political allegiance?

Using Stimson's concept of policy mood (introduced in chapter 1), Brulle et al. (2012) found that extreme weather events and information have zero influence on public opinion. Analyzing nine years of data aggregated from 74 surveys led the authors to echo the conclusions of the Brody et al. (2008) study that public perceptions of risk depend on groupcentric political allegiance. The researchers found that media coverage of climate change does influence perceptions of risk but only insofar as it relates to debate among elites. When political leaders make climate change a position issue, citizens rely on party identification or source credibility to decide which side to take. The authors concluded that "given the vested economic interests reflected in this polarization, it seems doubtful that any communication process focused on persuading individuals will have much impact" (p. 185). As the uncertainty model predicts, in the politics of insecurity, beliefs trump information and the strength of beliefs determines political outcomes. Those beliefs arise from a matrix of values and assumptions that make up the political culture, at present tilted against effective collection action on climate change.

Political Culture

As discussed in chapter 2, the concept of political culture is heuristically appealing but notoriously difficult to pin down with conventional measures of the social sciences (Geertz, 1973). This begs a larger issue, though: the absence of a widely accepted, noncontroversial definition of culture itself, described by Raymond Williams (1983) as "one of the two or three most complicated words in the English language."

Scholars differ on the usefulness of the concept (e.g., Laitin, 1995; Semetko, 1996), in part because they fail to adhere to a single definition and the different purposes to which they put those definitions to use. The concept has been used to define the norms that guide the work of journalists (Blumler & Gurevitch, 1995; Semetko, 1996; Pfetsch, 2004) or to probe the implicit assumptions that support commonsense thinking, usually at the national level (Schlesinger, 1997; Altheide, 2004).

In both cases, culture refers to a network of widely understood semiotic relations that allows those who live in that culture to recognize the same set of oppositions and thereby engage in "mutually meaningful symbolic action" (Sewell, 1999, p. 49). Note that this definition of culture as *system* highlights mutual comprehension rather than acquiescence to all of its values and precepts. Sewell's use of the term *oppositions* touches on the *practice* of culture, a potential mechanism for its change. In politics, the practice of culture takes the form of an attempt at persuasion and thereby an opportunity for a change in the cultural system itself, the dialectical view we described in chapter 2.

The success of an attempt at persuasion depends on making a culturally resonant appeal, one that in its weak version affirms the commonsense assumptions of its intended audience (Schudson, 1989) or that in its strong version creates them, a process that may take years of painstaking work. Benford and Snow

(2000) distinguished three dimensions of cultural resonance: real-world evidence, lived experience, and the repeated narratives that derive from the latter two (see Ettema, 2005).

A culturally resonant appeal is the product of interests, selected empirical evidence, mediated messages, and individual reception. A conscious strategy by self-interested political actors may explain why a policy idea can seem outré at one time and orthodox at another. Over the past three decades, for example, conservative think tanks such as the Heritage Foundation have successfully promoted supply-side economics and welfare reform (less so, however, for privatization of social security). A string of GOP political victories and the drift of the Democratic Party to the right influenced by these ideas attest to the success of a sustained campaign at changing the harmonics of American political culture. Resonance thus attaches to interests, but it may become difficult to distinguish interests after the passage of time because tradition establishes an authority that obscures their origins. The received wisdom of a given era is the product of the interaction between historical processes and events, politically motivated agents, and institutions such as the mass media disseminating narratives that reinforce specific values and beliefs.

Dimensions of Political Culture

Analysis of US political culture often begins with the values articulated in the nation's founding documents. That these values often offer incompatible policy guidelines—for example, equality and liberty—did not prevent their inclusion because each was perceived as desirable in its own right (Berlin, 1969). A deeper source of tension originates in the amalgam of Enlightenment reason and religious faith that composes the philosophical matrices from which these values originate. The instability of the amalgam and its influences on perceptions of self and nature support the dynamics that have driven a part of the nation's cultural and political history.

Self

In early colonial US history, religious faith was primarily associated with spiritual introspection and common fate. Historian Karen Halttunen (1998) interpreted late-18th-century sermons spoken prior to the execution of a convicted murderer as partaking of a culture of inner-directed piety: "Not only were all women and men equally burdened by that original sin which was the root cause of murder; all were guilty as well of committing those besetting sins which could lead ineluctably to that worst of crimes" (p. 15)

By the turn of the 19th century, the secular influence of prosperity and science had redirected piety to an outward focus on individual moral conduct, first as individual choice for a good, earthly life and then self-discipline as a prescription for economic prosperity (Lears, 2003). Outward-directed morality combined with the Enlightenment belief in the perfectibility of human nature to inspire political movements to rid the environment of the causes of social ills. The evangelical roots of the abolitionist and temperance movements represent examples of the fusion between morality and reason (Morone, 2003), occasionally yielding unintended and even perverse consequences in that it eased demonization of those who fell short of the mark. It could not otherwise be, for if one believes the environment to be just, only the individual remains blameworthy.

Lears (2003) proposed a binary framework of fate and control for explaining the conversion of the murderer from fallen sinner (one of us) to monster (one of them). The execution sermon represented the culture of fate, a reverence of grace in the religious domain but also luck and fortune in the secular. A message of common fate made all witnesses aware of their own vulnerability: There but for the grace of God go I, its secular counterpart, there but for fortune go I.

By contrast, the culture of control derives from a narrative that links the notion of the self-made citizen to providence. To use a modern example, the perceived success of the civil rights movement in correcting the excesses of racism made it easier for whites to blame those blacks who remained impoverished (Kinder & Sanders, 1996; Bobo, Kluegel, & Smith, 1997). The Reagan administration repeatedly drew on the moralistic tenets of the culture of control to advance its war on drugs ("just say no") and to promote its more general goal of reducing domestic spending. The shift in cultural harmonics was achieved by a disciplined political effort to associate liberalism with ostensibly failed social policies, often using racially charged symbols such as Willie Horton (Mendelberg, 2001) and the welfare queen (Hancock, 2004) to create division within Democrats' traditional constituencies.

Nature

Control of nature has until recently proven as resilient a narrative as that of the modern self. Together with time, money, and God, received conceptions of nature represent a universal trump card in argument (Douglas, 1975). Equated with faith in science and technology, faith in Promethean control of nature has been fueled by industrialization, technical innovation, and scientific advance whose apotheosis was Einstein's insight into the heart of matter. No less than how we think about self, what we assume to be true of nature is susceptible to suprarational appeal, naked political interest, or some alloy of the two. The farms, towns, and cities that dot the floodplain of the Mississippi River—described by Barry (1997) as a writhing, imprisoned snake—are physical manifestations of commitment to a belief in the control of nature.

Like the dikes that protect Zeeland from the North Atlantic, a complex network of levees, dams, reservoirs, floodways, and spillways contain the lower Mississippi—a war on nature (McPhee, 1989). Hardly the passive opponent, nature sometimes launches counteroffensives in what insurance companies call natural disasters or acts of God. Whatever their provenance, they were disasters because humans built cities on floodplains only temporarily secured by great engineering projects. The issue therefore is not whether a disaster can be fairly described as natural or an act of God but what belief needs to be sustained to stiffen the political will required to recapture that which nature periodically reclaims. That political will began to weaken after publication of Rachel Carson's *Silent Spring* (1962), a hugely popular book that questioned faith in technological progress, and in the 1970s when the environmental movement highlighted increasingly apocalyptic visions of the imminent destruction of earth's natural systems (Dunlap, 2004). The influence of Carson's book could be judged by the energetic public relations response of the American chemical industry. One spokesperson remarked, "If man were to follow the teachings of Miss Carson, we would return to the Dark Ages, and the insects and diseases and vermin would once again inherit the earth" (quoted in McLaughlin, 1998).

At the turn of the 21st century, global warming had become an important trump card against arguments for control of nature, an extension of challenges to the idea of progress advanced by the environmental movement of the 1970s. That movement drew on the religious component of American political culture, decoupled from its link to the sacred by the earthly appeals of romanticism (Dunlap, 2004). Increasingly common narratives of human overreach and nature's responding vengeful fury suggested a more fatalistic attitude that could weaken the political will to formulate a comprehensive response to natural disasters. In addition, a mode of reasoning termed by Hulme (2011) as *climate reductionism* wrote human agency—values, cultures, and practices—out of climate change models. The bleak future predicted by the models assumed a rigid set of conditions defined by the necessity of mathematics and computer code, thus discounting contingencies based on human agency. In these models, "humans are depicted as 'dumb farmers,' passively awaiting their climate fate" (p. 256). Narratives of disaster that have shrunk human agency and discounted the power of transformative norms traded on the spectacle of terror that relegated human beings to helpless victims of overpowering nature.

Four possible configurations arise from outlooks on self and nature: for self, solidarity and identification with victims linked to a collective sense of fate, responsibility, and unity; or finding fault with victims or the political actors and institutions that represent their interests, thereby ceding shared responsibility; on nature, a coherent, confident plan for responding comprehensively to a natural disaster and a moral obligation to find resources to do the job; or the absence of such a plan based on claims of scarce resources or a fateful view of nature as untamable and its future course as outside the control of human agency.

To illustrate the changes in the political culture, I contrast the assumptions embedded in mediated discourses on the federal response to two weather-related flood disasters that took place 80 years apart in the Mississippi River valley. The contrast helps explain a hidden cause of the impasse on climate change policy and how application of the uncertainty model points to likely outcomes.

The Great Flood of 1927

By present lights, the 1920s seem a paradoxical decade. On one hand, the period was characterized by prohibition, disillusion, isolationism, and reaction, but also by faith in science and progress on the other. Christian fundamentalism offered a prescription of simple faith as a remedy for the disillusionment and political corruption that followed World War I (Higham, 1965). The Scopes trial erupted from tensions that had developed between science and religion and revealed the diminished standing of the latter, especially its less flexible sects. During the 1920s, church membership continued to grow but churches themselves were being consolidated and religious belief was outshone by the "colossal" prestige of science (Allen, 1931). As Allen put it, "The word science had become a shibboleth. To preface a statement with 'Science teaches us' was enough to silence argument" (p. 199). In 1927 the nation's response to an unusually severe flood would reveal how the nation's political culture had tipped in the direction of the control of nature.

The Great Flood of 1927 resulted from an unusually heavy pattern of rainfall that began in the late summer of the previous year. Heavy rain fell on the entire Mississippi basin, an area encompassing hundreds of thousands of square miles from Pennsylvania to Montana. That winter, the plains states were inundated with snow. The following spring, the snowmelt and unrelenting waves of rainstorms in the basin raised the Mississippi to record heights. Levee breaks ("crevasses") along the lower half of the Mississippi River valley, from Cairo to New Orleans, inundated 28,000 square miles of land, displaced 700,000 people, and killed 246. In his account of the flood, Barry (1997) wrote that affected residents were reminded of their impotence against the forces of nature and God: "In many a church preachers spoke of the rain as a sign from God of man's wickedness. Even without a preacher's sermon, the good, decent folk of the prairie had to be thinking of the story of Noah, of the end of the world, of the coming of judgment" (p. 174).

Despite the moralistic impulses that had led to Prohibition and fundamentalist reaction against science, then commerce secretary Herbert Hoover promoted scientific management and engineering solutions for social problems. Hoover sponsored massive federalization of flood control for the lower Mississippi River valley, seeing in the plan a potential springboard to the White House. Thus began a campaign to build support for an unprecedented expenditure of federal funds for what were regional and local problems.

Katrina

During the 1980s, religion gained increased influence on American politics and culture, in part because its most conservative Protestant denominations had undergone a structural transformation (Wuthnow, 1988) that influenced the rhetoric and political agendas of Republican administrations (Green, 2007). George W. Bush inherited the culture of self-help bestowed by the Reagan and Clinton administrations, to which he added the luster of "compassionate conservatism," partly based on a strategy to attract the support of the Christian Coalition (Domke, 2004).

The Bush administration capitalized on a growing divide between nonbelievers and adherents of conservative religion and on the diminished prestige of science. In 2006, for example, the American Association for the Advancement of Science reported that although Americans continued to embrace science and technology, their belief in evolution had waned and they were torn about the balance of faith between science and religion: 50 percent agreed that "we depend too much on science and not enough on faith."

Americans had also become more wary of the limits of technological progress that threatened the natural environment. A near meltdown of the nuclear reactor at Three Mile Island in 1979 and a catastrophic explosion at Chernobyl in 1986 became symbols of technology run amuck (Gamson & Modigliani, 1989), while global warming became a symbol of the harmful effects of unrestrained consumption. The left merged control of self with nature by coining the concept of the carbon footprint to raise consciousness of individual energy consumption.

On the right, similar to the campaign to build support for supply-side economics, a number of interest groups and individuals had been building a case against evidence of environmental degradation. Termed by Dunlap and McCright (2011) as the *climate denial machine*, the actors included the coal and oil industries, corporate interests groups such as the US Chamber of Commerce and the National Mining Association, conservative foundations that had supported the turn against Keynesian economics in the 1970s, conservative think tanks (e.g., American Enterprise Institute, Cato, Heritage), and the "front groups" and grassroots campaigns that provided a stream of messages to conservative politicians and media.

In the politics of insecurity, the campaign for climate change skepticism had an easier hill to climb than commitment. All that skeptics needed to do was create sufficient conflict and doubt to blunt the force of the environmental movement.* One example is Al Gore's academy documentary "Inconvenient Truth." Though it won an academy award, it failed to reinvigorate the environmental movement. Until the Reagan administration, environmentalism had been a nonpartisan (valence) issue. Because Reagan regarded environmentalism as a pillar supporting government regulation, his administration and proponents began a campaign to undermine it. By the midterm elections of 1994 ("Contract with America"), and especially after the Kyoto Accords of 1997, climate change had become a highly partisan, position issue. In 2001 George W. Bush said he would not sign the treaty. His refusal met with the approval of his constituents. A number of studies demonstrate the success of the right in converting climate change into a position issue, finding that the best predictors of climate change skepticism are identification with the GOP and religious service attendance (Pew Research Center, 2006; Hamilton & Keim, 2009; McCright & Dunlap, 2011; Hamilton, Cutler, & Schaefer, 2012).

By the early 2000s, the economic pressures of the war in Iraq and federal tax cuts had reduced the flow of federal funding for infrastructure projects such as reinforcing the deteriorating levees in New Orleans. The storm surge of Hurricane Katrina that struck the Gulf Coast on August 29, 2005, undermined the levees at three points in the city's elaborate flood control system. The floodwaters overwhelmed the lowest-lying parts of the city, those largely occupied by its

---

* From a psychological standpoint, experimental research shows that "perceived or real uncertainty reduces the frequency of pro-environmental behavior" (Gifford, 2011).

poorest African American residents. Many had stayed in their homes, either because they did not have the means to evacuate, had to care for relatives who were too old to travel, or because they thought they could ride out the storm. Within hours, parts of the Ninth Ward were under 20 feet of water.

Media and the Floods

We now turn to a study of the changes in political culture that hamper the left's ability to convert local weather disasters into culturally resonant symbols for national policy, key conditioning variables for perceived risk exposure, and an effective political response. I use content analysis to detect background assumptions of a given era on the control of nature and identification with the victims of disaster. Self-interest may lie at the foundation of these assumptions, but that interest must be argued within the confines of historically contingent and often uncritical assumptions on what is possible and desirable. Indeed, even social scientists are not immune to making what are tantamount to value judgments in their choice of concepts and theories that appear objective and transhistorical. As Gergen (1973) pointed out, "People may prefer bright shades of clothing today and grim shades tomorrow; they may value autonomy during this era and dependency during the next" (p. 315).

The data for the 1927 flood come from the ProQuest Historical Newspaper database of national and regional newspapers. These include (*N*s in parentheses) *New York Times* (43), *Washington Post* (37), and *Christian Science Monitor* (30), as well as the *Hartford Courant* (10), the *Chicago Tribune* (17), *Atlanta Journal-Constitution* (27), and *Los Angeles Times* (10). The sources were searched for all front-page stories and opinion pieces (*N*=174) on the aftermath of the flood, from June 1927 through the passage of federal flood legislation in May of the following year. For the aftermath of Katrina, I analyzed coverage in the Nexis transcripts of evening news broadcasts of NBC, the most highly rated during the period—August 31, 2005, until the issue faded from attention in early 2006—147 broadcasts in total. Although ratings are down for network broadcasts in general, I selected television coverage because it remains the most relied on news source for more than half of Americans (Pew Research Center for the People and Press, 2012).

To rule out the possibility that differences in coverage of Katrina were due to media differences, I also tracked editorial and op-ed coverage of the 2005 flood in several regional and local newspapers. I selected editorials and commentaries because they represent the most economical distillation of discourse on this event. To test whether an individual source's perspective might be influenced by prevailing partisan sentiments, I sampled several papers in areas that voted heavily for either the Democratic or Republican candidates for president—John Kerry and George W. Bush—in the 2004 election. The papers include: Kerry: *Atlanta Journal* (41), *Los Angeles Times* (41), *New York Times* (65), *Pittsburgh Post* (51); and Bush: *Dayton Daily News* (20), *Greensboro News* (10), *Houston Chronicle* (41), and *Knoxville News* (12).

The analysis began with a coding protocol that identified themes relevant to nature and self. Coders undertook an extensive training process that simultaneously refined the final coding protocol. After completion of the task, each coder sampled 10 percent of the texts for a test of reliability. Intercoder agreement averaged 82 percent for newspaper coverage and 91 percent for broadcast coverage.

Overall Differences

A general comparison of the results reveals a sea change in the political culture of the two eras: in 1927 a culture of common fate regarding self, albeit rooted in collective economic self-interest, and a swaggering confidence in control of nature; and in 2005 what amounted to a defaulted culture of control regarding self and a greatly reduced confidence in human command over the natural environment. To provide some rough sense of the change, I calculated the sum of optimistic and pessimistic themes in each news report or commentary. I define an optimistic theme as one that supports a comprehensive solution for flood control or one that links the fate of the victims with the nation as a whole; a pessimistic theme is skeptical of a comprehensive solution, portrays the victims as unsympathetic, or declares government as incompetent. Thus two optimistic themes yield a score of two, a balance yields a score of zero, and so on. Tables 5.1 and 5.2 show the distribution of the themes, optimistic and pessimistic, respectively.

Using this metric, two-thirds of press coverage on the aftermath of the 1927 flood was optimistic, a near reversal of that in the 2005 coverage. Comparison of television and print content in 2005 reveals some differences: television coverage, perhaps driven by sensational imagery, was more negative than print discourse (76 percent vs. 62 percent), but there were only minor differences across the specific themes. Newspaper editorials in those papers published in counties where Bush received majority support were slightly more negative than Kerry (66 percent vs. 57 percent), largely due to greater skepticism of government-sponsored solutions or concern that budget deficits would make it difficult to find sufficient money to rebuild and protect New Orleans in the event of another catastrophic storm.

Table 5.1. Distribution of optimistic themes
(percentage of total)

	1927	2005 Press	TV
Sufficient resources	37	8	2
Unity of purpose	31	2	1
Control of nature	26	5	4
Optimism in future	14	0	0
Can-do attitude	5	12	14

Table 5.2. Distribution of pessimistic themes
(percentage of total)

	1927	2005 Press	TV
Government ineffective	22	33	32
Insufficient resources	13	13	21
Unsolvable problems	0	16	14
Blaming victims	0	14	11
Fatalism regarding nature	3	5	13

In both eras, media discourse was suspicious of government, the most common negative theme. Also in both time periods, insufficient resources was the second most common, but the specifics differ: a tax cut was on the minds of politicians in the 1920s and a large government deficit in 2005.

By far the greatest difference was on perceptions of unity and, indirectly, on unacceptable future risk exposure to the nation as a whole. As the analysis of the specific events show, in the 1920s the discourse championed national unity to support an engineering solution for containing the Mississippi. In the aftermath of Katrina, the partisan blame-shifting and accusations of incompetence called to mind the image of a circular firing squad. Unique to the later period was a loss of confidence in government's ability to respond effectively to a natural disaster. By 2005, nature had become an unpredictable and untamable force, a reversal of its portrayal in the 1920s, and although skepticism of federal competence was not exclusive to either period, in the mid-1920s skeptics questioned the idea of federal control rather than government competence.

I now turn to a closer analysis of the two cases, beginning with the Great Flood of 1927. Political and media elites drew on a new enthusiasm for science to contain and harness nature and to link the fate, or perceived risk exposure, of those who had built on the floodplain with the greater majority who lived out of harm's way.

1927

On June 1, 1927, the *Los Angeles Times* and the North American Newspaper Alliance asked Hoover whether the massive floods of the lower Mississippi were the result of faulty engineering or the unstoppable force of nature. In a 2,500-word response replete with technical detail, Hoover formulated an argument that fused collective interest with collective obligation. He conceded that floods were inescapable but that an engineering solution was nevertheless essential to protect the investments of individual farmers who had built levees to cultivate the bottom land, of those who built levees downstream to protect their own farmland from the increased volume of water that resulted from the building of the levees upstream, of those who built the towns that sprang up at intervals along the river to service those farmers, and of those innumerable Americans whose economic livelihood was indirectly affected (Hoover, 1927).

Hoover yoked self-interest to collective fate by framing the issue in terms of fairness and justice. After all, the area drained by the Mississippi encompassed most of the United States. Was it right, then, for a lower section to bear the cost for maintaining levees that protected against the waters that originated in an upper section (Evans, 1927)? Hoover also noted the onerous burden borne by those who lived at the end of the line of levees: "It is not the waters of the immediate states which are responsible for the flood; it is the waters that come from 31 states, most of them at a distance from the lower valley. The greatest sufferer of all the states is Louisiana" (*The New York Times*, 1928b, p. E7).

Located at the base of the Mississippi drainage area, New Orleans would bear the greatest weight of the waters contained and channeled by the flood control project. The increase in downstream water velocity and volume would eventually erode the silt deposits and wetlands that acted as a barrier against storm surges from the Gulf, an unforeseen negative consequence of flood control that would contribute to the Katrina disaster. Figure 5.1 shows a striking visual icon that illustrated shared fate, a map that depicts the drainage basin of the Mississippi, an intricate arterial network of streams and rivers that infuse and drain an enormous area of the nation (*Christian Science Monitor*, 1928a).

That the surface of the Mississippi behind the levees would sometimes rise as high as the rooftops of adjacent houses did not strike Hoover as an absurdity of engineering hubris. The river was not a force of nature that mocked human ambition but merely a "wild animal" to be bridled (Hoover, 1927, p. 1). Hoover thus articulated the major themes of a discourse that would dominate press coverage until passage of landmark legislation: control of nature, the commercial

Figure 5.1. Drainage basin of the Mississippi River. *Source: Christian Science Monitor,* March 29, 1928, p. 1. PDF of the newspaper available on ProQuest Historical Newspaper database.

benefits of a coordinated solution, a moral call to action, and the assumption of unified public opinion behind the plan.

Two examples illustrate the link made in the late 1920s between faith in scientific mastery of nature and a moral call to decisive action:

> At a time when radios talk and men fly, when machines set type and buildings scrape the sky, the solution for the problem of controlling a river cannot be longer delayed. (*Christian Science Monitor*, 1927b, p. 16)

> The United States has before it a task of the first magnitude, calling for the patriotism and teamwork of all citizens until it is accomplished. It is an urgent task, with staggering loss of life and property as the price of delay. The greatest river system in the world, running through the heart of this country, must be changed from an agency of death into a helpful and reliable servant. (*The Washington Post*, 1927a, p. S1)

Metaphors for the river ranged from the anthropomorphic—a wild beast, the "father of the waters"—to a metaphysical force that nonetheless could be managed and controlled. Humanity was at war with nature, the outcome in little doubt: "It is no merely defensive purpose that Mr. Hoover outlines, but such an active thoroughgoing dominion as will harness the unruly stream to serve the nation's welfare" (*Christian Science Monitor*, 1927a, p. 20A). More than one-quarter of the coverage made explicit references to the possibility and desirability of the control of nature.

Coverage was not uniformly optimistic: about one in five of the pieces were skeptical of federal control, especially *The New York Times*, whose editorial board echoed Coolidge's opposition to federal relief. Pressured by bipartisan editorial opinion and Congress (Barry, 1997), Coolidge relented and made virtue of necessity: he declared the nation united "in the bonds of sympathy," the "heart of an empire nation . . . quickened by the task at hand" and the river a "fount of untapped energy" (*The New York Times*, 1927b, p. 1). Notwithstanding the focus on financing, nearly four in ten articles mentioned that sufficient resources could be found to fund flood control.

Replete with moral rhetoric, media discourse invoked the patriotism and duty ordinarily associated with a threat to national security. Control of the flood was "a war against an enemy that has invaded the heart of the Republic. Maine and California are duty bound to stand by the States that are invaded" (*The Washington Post*, 1927b, p. S1). The editor of the *New Orleans Item-Tribune* likened it to a battle (Thompson, 1928), and the chief of the Army Engineers declared the problem only less serious "than war itself" (*Chicago Daily Tribune*, 1927a, p. 1). Though *The New York Times* was skeptical of the sources of funding for the project, the editors nevertheless dedicated two entire pages to "Hoover's Plan to Harness Our Waters" (1927a, p. 1). The tone was of unanimous optimism for controlling the Mississippi, provided the engineering plan was "bold and proper."

The often highly technical discourse in the press of the time demonstrated the stature of science and engineering. In the late 1920s, engineers and scientists were held in high regard, as prestigious figures with something to say to common readers. Their opinions were replete with technical details and scientific language that would be opaque to today's audiences (see, e.g., Lane, 1927). And because the problem was defined as a technical task for experts rather than politicians, the discourse carried a sense of inevitability (*The Washington Post*, 1927c), propelled by what was assumed as public unity (*The Washington Post*, 1928). Nearly one-third of the coverage included references to public support, either assumed or illustrated by the travel of lobbyists and delegations from Mississippi

River valley states to Washington to show their support (*Chicago Daily Tribune*, 1927b).

To the extent that public opinion could be read in some impressionistic sense, it was "almost unanimous" in favor of Hoover's plan (*The New York Times*, 1927c). The *Chicago Tribune* used its front page to build support for the national effort: "But not even the engineering research will go forward until we accept the principle that the responsibility—legal, moral, and economic—rests with the federal government" (Evans, 1927, p. 1). When the legislation passed the Senate on an 89-0 vote, even the staid *New York Times* characterized the bipartisan effort behind its success "a love feast" (1928a, p. 1). Except for World War I, the legislation represented the greatest expenditure the government had ever undertaken (Barry, 1997).

While content analysis necessarily highlights what the text contains, what is most striking about media discourse of the 1920s is the comparative absence of portraits of individuals who suffered at the hands of the flood. There were, of course, stories about the hundreds of thousands displaced by the flood and the bleakness of their situation, but the greater part of the coverage was fixed almost entirely on the wild river and the plans designed to subdue it. This is in vivid contrast to coverage of Katrina, almost entirely fixed on human agency and its failings, sometimes cast in religious terms.

Katrina

In contrast to characterization of nature as a scientifically tamable force in 1927, in 2005 Katrina and the ensuing flood were often portrayed in fatalistic terms. Coverage often connected the catastrophe to technical hubris, shortsighted economic rapacity, and corruption. Commentators asked whether the unusually warm waters of the Gulf that fueled the explosive force of the storm were the result of global warming and wondered whether similarly fierce storms would return the following year (NBC Nightly News, September 18, 2005; September 21, 2005; November 30, 2005).*

Others pointed to the disappearance of wetlands south of the city, partly the result of directing an increasing volume of water into the Gulf. The erosion of the barrier islands and the displacement of the sustaining silt into the depths of the Gulf had created an alarming vulnerability for New Orleans. During the storm surges that accompanied hurricanes, the flow of water reversed into the

* All dates cited refer to evening broadcasts of NBC Nightly News.

Mississippi, converting it into a fire hose that shot the water back into the city. The war against nature was now perceived to represent the excesses of unchecked human ambition. Nature had prevailed and no short-term solutions seemed realistic, or wise.

Coverage described New Orleans as a bowl or bathtub, referring to its below-sea-level location and thereby implicitly questioning the wisdom of rebuilding the city: "Three months after the storm, there's no official plan to rebuild and no outline for what it will cost. Instead, there's been debate over who should run the schools, who should get the loans, and lately, whether a city below sea level should be rebuilt at all" (November 22, 2005). Only 5 percent of editorial opinion focused on technical details for flood control, and 4 percent of broadcast coverage. In the absence of a vigorous solutions-oriented discourse, attention turned to the scope of the damage and fault-finding.

Common metaphors for coverage of individual suffering invoked biblical references to the apocalypse: "St. Gabriel, named for the archangel the Bible says will one day trumpet the end of the world, now some in this small town wonder if the end of the world is coming to them. In truck after truck, Katrina's dead are arriving at St. Gabriel, Louisiana" (September 6, 2005).

NBC's science correspondent spoke of "threats from the water, infections that cause vomiting and diarrhea; in crowded shelters, viral illnesses that could spread like wildfire" (September 8, 2005). Reporters used religious language and metaphors to describe the miniatures of human kindness within the disaster. One report commented on the fate of a father who had found a shelter for his family: "what he calls a God send. But the room he shares with his wife and five kids is far from home. Providence and purgatory" (September 11, 2005). Another described a Texas family who had taken in 44 displaced New Orleans residents as "saints" and closed with a common theme: "A family that came together, survived the storm, their prayers answered" (October 7, 2005).

Commercial interests were also at risk, but rather than using the economy to rally public opinion, national news referred to the 2005 Katrina flood as a seemingly insoluble hydra-headed problem: threats to the Gulf shrimp industry (September 10, 2005), to insurance companies (October 11, 2005), and to the economy in general. At no point in coverage would these threats be regarded as a motive for a plan for recovery or prevention of future disaster. Things would only get worse, as, for example, the nation could expect high gasoline prices for the foreseeable future as the refineries knocked out by the flood might bear the brunt of future superstorms. Expectations of such storms drove up oil price futures through the 2006 hurricane season. The underlying attitude was of resigned acceptance rather than an urgent call to action. The absence of a unified strategy for dealing with the issues raised by Katrina partly explains the near absence of a theme of national unity in coverage: 1 percent in broadcast news, 2 percent in print.

Unlike the discourse of national unity and centralized federal control that permeated coverage of the 1927 flood, in 2005 media discourse applauded the voluntary efforts of individuals. It could not be otherwise because of negligence and incompetence on the part of government, its lack of preparation, delay, blame shifting, and bureaucratic obtuseness. Iconic images of dying victims, abandoned school buses, and unused trailers were juxtaposed against repeated images of George Bush praising the head of FEMA. About one-third of broadcast and print coverage referenced the ineffectiveness of the government's response. Victims relied necessarily on the kindness of strangers who randomly dropped out of the sky in helicopters, drove into town in pickup trucks, or floated in on boats. Reporters abandoned canons of objectivity and were openly critical of the federal government—"a White House more interested in damage control than disaster relief: On all fronts today, it was administration damage control (September 8, 2005); and of the state: "a governor working damage control, actively trying to manage her image after these images of chaos at the convention center were first broadcast" (December 4, 2005). Even the president's mother was criticized as being insensitive for implying that displaced flood victims were better off on the floor of the Houston Astrodome than in their New Orleans slums.

The ineffectual response to the disaster became a metaphor for the perilous state of the nation itself. Like the discourse during the Vietnam War that described the United States as a helpless giant, "nations around the world [were] fascinated by the seeming powerlessness of the most powerful, the richest nation on Earth, to handle relief supplies in the immediate aftermath." A London editor declared that "people are watching with absolute horror. . . . Here in Britain and elsewhere, newspaper editorials are asking why the world's only super power appears so helpless. And in today's *Independent*, on the front page, it claims people died because they were poor" (September 6, 2006).

No visual metaphor of national unification appeared in coverage of the Katrina flood; on the contrary, repeated images of local abandoned victims and unused school buses came to symbolize human misery and government incompetence rather than an appeal for common cause. The most visible victims were African Americans whom the media depicted alternately as sympathetic and dangerous. The media passed along rumors of Mad Max lawlessness and gun violence at the Superdome and Convention Center. A flood victim camped at the Convention Center reported that when the National Guard finally arrived five days after the levees were breached, "they acted like we were the Vietcong or something, maybe Indians in a damn concentration camp. They kept shouting for everybody to give up their weapons. Problem was, nobody really had weapons, although a few guys coughed up penknives" (quoted in Brinkley, 2006, pp. 479–80). The Guard had been made wary by media reports that reported rumors of the most grotesque violence in the Superdome—children raped, throats slit, and random gunplay. Media reports focused on looters who were free to pillage stores because much of the New Orleans police force had abandoned their positions either to deal with their own family concerns or because of a lack of discipline (Brinkley, 2006).

In other reports, media coverage was ambivalent about the largely poor African American victims of the disaster (Sommers et al., 2006). The reaction began as disbelief and indignation at government neglect and sympathy for the victims and then followed by concern for the danger they posed to others. A little more than one in ten reports in broadcast news—14 percent in print—highlighted looters or other criminal behavior perpetrated by evacuees. A more subtle form of distancing pitted victims against taxpayers who were being charged "millions of dollars every day" to pay for the evacuees' hotel accommodations. A graphic detailed the scope of the expenses: 596,514 evacuees; 192,424 rooms; 9,606 hotels (October 13, 2005).

The most evident signs that the disaster would not warrant a national mobilization of resources were repeated reports of onerous cost and waste. Just before President Bush's speech in Jackson Square, estimates of $200 billion necessary for disaster relief were accompanied by reports of overextension, budget trade-offs, and waste (September 15, 2005). Some conservatives who objected to "runaway spending" proposed $23 billion offsets in local projects from the highway bill and a $40 billion cut in the seniors' drug program (September 18, 2005). One in five broadcasts pointed to the insufficiency of federal funds for responding to the flood. More ominously, Congress had authorized $3.2 billion to repair the levees, enough to restore them to Category 3 hurricane resistance but only one-tenth of what it would cost to make them immune to a Category 5 storm, repeatedly and fatalistically forecast as a near certainty the following hurricane season (December 15, 2005).

Highly critical coverage of local and state governments began only weeks after the story broke. The New Orleans' public school system was a "disaster area with schools literally falling apart and plagued by violence." The accounts were in such a state of disarray that the district had been pressured into hiring a New York restructuring firm to clean up the books (September 17, 2005). The political leadership then came under attack for its reckless invitation to evacuees to return despite dangers of cholera from the high levels of E. coli and fecal coliforms bacteria in the water (September 18, 2005). Later reports found systemic corruption that may have led to the failure of the levees. Members of the city levee board carried out cursory inspections and rewarded themselves with expensive lunches: "Take this itinerary for the annual low water inspection, October 17, 2003. Start time 9 AM, then drive and drive and drive along miles and miles of levees, canals, and floodwalls, ending about four and a half hours later at the popular Red Maple restaurant, where the tab for 39 people came to $833, including $592 for 32 10-ounce prime ribs" (December 15, 2006).

In this context of corruption and systemic neglect, coverage turned to evacuees who had resettled as far away as Idaho to escape New Orleans (September 21, 2005). By the end of the year, a reporter speculated that even the middle class of the city was not expected to return (December 26, 2005). The flood of pessimism culminated in a report that revealed what Katrina had revealed about "us":

> Katrina didn't just change New Orleans, it also changed us, shattering assumptions. We thought, for example, that 9/11 prepared us to handle catastrophe. Katrina showed we were wrong. It also shook our faith in what's possible and how much we can control fate. Remember World War II when we naively and optimistically decided we could put all of Europe back on its feet and did so with the Marshall Plan? Today, how much along the Gulf Coast believe that's possible? Four months then of sadness, relief, failure, and opportunity to see not just whether we can fix what is broken in New Orleans, but also what is broken in us. (December 19, 2005)

For this report, the culture of control regarding self had turned into a culture of fate, but it was not accompanied by a feeling of kinship with the residents of New Orleans. A number of public opinion polls suggested that Americans were pessimistic about the viability of New Orleans and were as likely to blame the residents as they were all levels of government. In a poll taken at the end of February 2006, only 11 percent thought New Orleans would be rebuilt in a year or two; 60 percent thought it would take longer; and nearly 30 percent thought it would never be rebuilt (CBS, 2006). Only one-quarter of the same sample thought evacuees would be better off returning and nearly three in five believed that evacuees would be better off if they stayed in a new place. If the moment of self-doubt and piety confessed by the reporter were akin to an execution sermon, it had been addressed to an abandoned city.

Conclusion

By the guidelines of the uncertainty model, climate change poses the greatest challenge to an effective policy response. As we have learned, readily available information supported by consensual scientific opinion has little bearing on perceptions of threat. National attention is roused only by punctuated catastrophes that currently send varying signals of future risk exposure to regional or local populations who, like the Native Americans in the path of floods, move their abodes to higher ground to avoid future risk exposure. Partisan elite gridlock provides a structural opportunity for a movement to force the issue, but group identification along party lines diminishes the base for such a movement as does the current political culture. The result is a raised threshold for perceived risk exposure. To illustrate, by the time Hurricane Sandy struck New York City and flooded lower Manhattan in 2012, media reports had begun to use the phrase "the new normal" to refer to extreme weather events, a fatalistic raising of the bar for tolerance (DeMause, 2013).

Cultural resonance underlies valence issues—those that elicit a nearly uniform emotional response on a desired end (Nelson, 1984). New Orleans offers a conspicuous case of failure for building consensus despite the lengthy period during which the issue held the attention of politicians and the mass media. In plotting a middle course between materially determined and interpretive "toolkit" theories of culture, Schudson (1989) proposed a fivefold model that explains which cultural phenomena are more likely to gain influence.

Resonance plays a key role in the model but eludes precise specification because of the circularity between interests and culture. As Schudson (1989) put it: "What is resonant is not a matter of how culture connects to individual interests but a matter of how culture connects to interests that are themselves constituted in a cultural frame" (p. 169). The interests promoted by the right raised the threshold of concern for the fate of New Orleans and its residents. Meanwhile, the fatalistic signal sent by the failure of the left to invest Katrina (and Sandy) with a symbolic connection to climate change did little to disturb the status quo. To be sure, the left had the more daunting task of overcoming the inherent advantage held by climate skeptics. The skeptics merely needed to create some doubt about the reality of global climate change to rationalize doing nothing at the level of national policy. That such was possible despite the evident achievements of science and technology in every dimension of American life spoke to the diminished prestige of scientific authority in the nation's political culture.

From the standpoint of the uncertainty model, the punctuated timing of weather catastrophes like Katrina raised the threshold for effective political action, as did the perceived scope of future risk. Elite consensus of the kind seen in the response to the 1927 flood would have to overcome the limited geographic impact of the disaster. Absent such a consensus or a citizen-led reaction for policy change, Katrina's potential symbolic link to climate change could not be sustained. The symbolic politics that attend climate change reflect the polarization of the nation in general and partisan identification that devalues expert scientific opinion. As this book goes to press, Pope Francis has bolstered the opinion of climate scientists. In his encyclical "Laudato Si," Francis affirms the role of human action in climate change and its heavy costs borne by the world's poor. Should the moral impulse strengthen, particularly among the nation's evangelical population, climate change may become a valence issue that stimulates a debate on the best means of achieving a common goal. Absent a resonant moral appeal, global climate change will remain a symbolic issue that provides an opportunity to invidiously define one's membership in a group. Group identification also plays a large role in the debate on illegal immigration, the topic of chapter 6.

CHAPTER SIX

Porosity and Paradox

Global Cities and the Illegal Immigration Debate

"I'm running for office, for Pete's sake, we can't have illegals."—*Mitt Romney*

Whether 2012 presidential candidate Mitt Romney was addressing the fears of the voter base he sought or his own in a replay of the Bain controversy when he was CEO,* in running for office he was caught up in the dynamics of a controversial, gridlocked position issue. Largely focused on undocumented workers from Mexico and Central America, the controversy on illegal immigration arose in the 1980s, crested in 2006, and surfaced during the healthcare debate of 2009, the rise of the Tea Party movement, and Barack Obama's executive order of 2014. The use of an exploited class of Mexican laborers by a wealthy politician encapsulated some of the underlying issues in the illegal immigration debate.

Mexican immigrants have contributed a steadily increasing share of all immigration to the United States, beginning at 7 percent in 1980 and rising to 32 percent in 2005[†] (Hanson, 2006). Unlike other immigrants, the most recent Mexican immigrants have arrived illegally (Passel, 2005).[†] Current estimates are of nearly 12 million undocumented workers residing in the United States. Notable during this period is the implementation, in 1994, of the North American Free Trade Agreement (NAFTA), a policy that had little effect on the trend it was intended to reverse. NAFTA failed, in part, because it could not overcome increased demand for the kind of labor offered by these workers in the changed economies of some of the nation's largest cities. The shifts in the labor market

---

* When he was CEO of Bain Capital, Romney discovered his company was paying a subsidiary in Pawtucket, Rhode Island, that hired illegal workers for cleaning services. Romney established plausible deniability because Bain did not own the subsidiary, even though its CEO had been fined over $130,000 in the years before he accepted a contract with the Bain-owned firm (see McPhillips, 1998).

　† Nearly three in five Mexican immigrants are estimated to have arrived illegally, compared to less than one in five of immigrant arrivals from other nations

reflected larger changes that can be traced to the uneven effects of globalization on the US economy.

In this chapter, we look at the politics of insecurity underlying the illegal immigration debate, taking special note of the role economic self-interest plays in it and how that has undercut the passion needed to drive a movement aimed at reform. We do this by comparing the way the press covers the issue in cities that have greater and lesser connection to the global economy. In particular, some cities have attracted global multinational companies (MNCs) and organizations that have increased demand for skilled, highly paid professionals. These, in turn, have increased demand for low-wage workers in construction, low-end manufacturing, cleaning services, and food preparation (Passel, 2005), skill profiles readily met by the most recent wave of Mexican and Central American immigrants.

To the degree that economic rationality has played a role in the controversy on immigration, it may have complicated it. Mitt Romney's comment during a GOP primary debate reveals the tangle of economic and political issues underlying the debate: At an individual level, low-cost service labor benefits those whose economic self-interest is at odds with policy that might increase the bargaining power of their employees. At a macro level, a decades-long policy of border enforcement that varies in harmony with price changes in specific labor markets casts doubt on the earnestness of official pleas for reform. Economic self-interest undermines the passion that might otherwise be channeled to support an effective policy response or, minimally, to compete in the symbolic politics long dominated by opponents of immigration reform. In addition, the chronic nature of the issue and its varying risk exposure—often inversely related to its actual local impact—renders the issue the polar opposite of climate change.

To preview the findings, press coverage of illegal immigration differs depending on the global connectedness of a city. For example, though more sympathetic to the human tragedy represented by illegal immigration, the debate in global cities includes a dimension of economic self-interest that tempers its moral passion. The cities create a market for the service skills provided by undocumented workers. By contrast, a potent moral appeal to the rule of law dominates a more singular, policy-coherent, and passionate discourse in nonglobal cities. There perceived future risk exposure to illegal immigration is high and has resulted in a paradox: the absolute numbers of immigrants does not predict opposition to granting legal status to undocumented workers. Economic rationality at individual and sector levels has dampened the prospects for a political movement that would influence political elites to reconsider their positions on an issue that continues to energize a conservative base that blocks reform. The status quo, meanwhile, benefits those who rely on a ready supply of cheap labor.

Global Flows in Theory and Practice

A common metaphor used to conceptualize and theorize globalization is flow. Whether it is information, capital, people, or goods, globalization as a cause or an effect implies the permeability of national borders. The long-term goal is increased efficiency and prosperity, and in the case of the Eurozone, the ability of workers to move readily across national borders. Economists regard national boundaries as a major cause of distortion in labor markets: "all else equal, immigration raises national income by allowing countries to use fixed factors more productively, making free immigration welfare maximizing" (Hanson, 2006, p. 915). While the removal of tariffs and deregulation of capital flows have been relatively uncontroversial, removal of obstacles to the free flows of people have proven more difficult. Globalization may have liberated the movement of goods and capital from the constraints of space, but people remain bound by national boundaries. A textbook example is NAFTA.

Unlike the consolidation of markets in the European Union, NAFTA did not provide for the mobility of workers. It was hoped that NAFTA would accelerate Mexico's economic development and raise wages, which would help restrain migration into the United States. Instead, the withdrawal of subsidies to Mexican farmers, opening the nation's agricultural markets to competition from Canada and the United States, and imposition by the United States of obscure nontariff agricultural trade barriers combined to *decrease* Mexican wages by 10 percent. In effect, NAFTA increased the flow of Mexican workers into the United States (Stiglitz, 2007).

9/11 aggravated the situation as border security tightened and campaign rhetoric became entwined with fear of terrorist incursions at US borders. As a result, immigrants who might have otherwise returned to Mexico weighed the costs of exit and reentry and elected to stay in the United States, greatly increasing their numbers (Fernàndez-Kelly & Massey, 2007). What had been a semiporous border (its porosity influenced by the price of certain US goods and housing starts) became an osmotic border: continued flow into the United States but limited reverse flow into Mexico.

George W. Bush (2010) proposed a compromise that he hoped would satisfy opponents on the right as well as reformers on the left, "a rational middle ground between granting an automatic path to citizenship for every illegal immigrant and a program of mass deportation" (p. 303). Bush failed, not only because opposition, stiffened by fear and resentment, had crystallized (Branton et al., 2011) but also because interests that advanced from the status quo weakened the passion needed for reform. The uneven effects of globalization on the nation's local economies, particularly in the largest cities, contributed to the intractability of the debate. This paradoxical feature of globalization helps us understand the politics of insecurity that underlie the controversy.

Global Cities

Advanced communication technologies and transportation have reduced the primacy of place (Giddens, 1990; Castells, 1996; Tomlinson, 1999), but as functions and supply chains become increasingly dispersed, central coordination and administration become increasingly necessary Scholars have identified a number of processes that accompany this unique and paradoxical development. It is unique because of its unprecedented complexity (Keohane & Nye, 2000) and paradoxical because dispersion and complexity increase the need for centralization. MNCs such as Apple may contract to have components for their devices made in the Philippines, assembled in China, and distributed in Europe, Asia, and North America. What is dispersed must be synchronized and coordinated. Thus the tendency for MNCs to centralize their operations within a single corporate site whose location depends on ready access to service providers with a global footprint (Sassen, 1991). Taken collectively, economies of scale, highly specialized knowledge, and global reach favor centralization of producer services in the same locations, hence the concept of global cities as "command centers" in the organization of the world economy (Friedman & Wolff, 1982).

Although definitions vary in emphasis and detail among scholars (e.g., Meyer, 1986; Abbott, 1999; Abu-Lughod, 1999; Short & Kim, 1999; Sassen, 2006), a global city may be defined as a node through which flow a disproportionate fraction of national and international transactions. Complex, interacting systems of communication channel the resources of international banking, consulting, accounting, advertising, and other economic services applied to "non-routine decision-making employed in coordinating and controlling fiscal, material and people flows at the world scale" (Boschken, 2008, p. 9).

The concept of a global city does not mean all such cities are alike or that they compete with one another for the same business. Like puzzle pieces in a globally dispersed system, they contribute on the basis of whatever unique advantages are offered by their locations and their specialized services. Because of its connection to global economic flows, the global city is also distinguished by its independence from the regional and national economy: the greater the number of MNCs and global producer service providers located there, the greater the city's independence (Sassen, 2006). A global city differs not only in its independence from the regional economy but also in its unique demographic profile, a function of its demand for service workers with contrasting skill profiles. These contribute to the income inequality that is also a distinctive marker of a global city.

Economic and Social Consequences

Immigration has traditionally been a driver of urban development, no less today than during the multiple waves that occurred during the 19th and 20th centuries, but contemporary patterns influence and are influenced by a new transnational political economy that greatly increases inequality. The economy of global cities is marked by a wide income gap between highly educated professionals who work in global firms and a mobile labor force, largely made up of immigrants who work at low-paying jobs. To wit, a UN report (UN-Habitat, 2008) found that US cities such as Atlanta, Miami, New York, and Washington, D.C., have the highest levels of income inequality in the United States (Gini coefficients exceeding .50), comparable to cities in the Ivory Coast, Nigeria, Chile, and Argentina.

The high income inequality found in a global city is the combined product of a post-Fordist economy and rehabilitation of inner-city housing. Deindustrialization lowers wages in nonunionized manufacturing and service jobs, a process accelerated by the reduced bargaining power of undocumented workers and firms incentivized by evasion of regulation and taxes. The two sides of the transaction drive a thriving gray service economy that creates what demographic scholar Douglas Massey calls an "exploitable category" of workers (2007, p. 310). The growth of the gray economy is augmented by gentrification, the inflow of investment by highly educated professionals into dilapidated housing. Gentrification increases income inequality because of its dependence on low-skilled workers who meet demands for labor-intensive renovation and domestic jobs such as landscapers, nannies, and house cleaners. City politicians are surely aware of the presence of undocumented immigrants, but the rising rents and real estate prices that accompany gentrification more than offset their concerns. The added revenues compensate for tax shortfalls caused by white suburban flight (Sassen, 2006).

For undocumented workers, large cities provide an island of support from similar others who seek to improve their economic fortunes. There they are less conspicuous than in places where token internal immigration enforcement efforts typically occur. Crackdowns on undocumented workers often take place in small towns where immigrants are more visible and local officials feel more pressure from residents to take action: "They didn't become part of the community. They didn't speak the language" (Cave, 2008, p. A1). Hopkins (2010), for example, found that local opposition rises when a sudden influx of immigrants is paired with increased media attention.

An inflow of undocumented workers is merely the final step in a largely invisible causal chain that begins with macroeconomic disturbances that affect border enforcement policy. The economists Hanson and Spilimbergo (2001), for example, pointed out that border authorities work under conflicting directives from groups who demand strict enforcement and labor-intensive industries who argue that such enforcement threatens their viability. Typically, these forces are in an equilibrium that sustains a consistent policy of border enforcement. The authors found, however, that border enforcement slackens when housing starts increase and when prices rise for apparel, agricultural products, and meat.* The importance of this finding is magnified by the fact that greater than 90 percent of the INS immigration enforcement budget is spent on border rather than internal enforcement, such as raids on employers. Figure 6.1 illustrates the long-term nature of this imbalance.

Because internal raids are rare, a foreign worker contemplating a move to the United States focuses almost entirely on the costs and risks of border crossing rather than deportation. Once in the States, the risks of being deported are relatively small, especially if the worker decides to settle in a city where changes in labor demand are reflected in new patterns of settlement.

Research shows that while the latest waves of immigrants—those arriving in the 1990s and after—are similar in English language and educational skills to those who preceded them, their favored destinations have changed significantly: "[They are] less likely to move to Los Angeles (the traditional destination of about one-third of all Mexican immigrants) and more likely to move to cities in the Southeast, Northwest, and Mountain states. The geographic shift [is] associated with some change in industry concentration, with fewer of the recent arrivals working in agriculture and more in construction (for men) and retail trade (for women)" (Card & Lewis, 2007, p. 193). In their analysis of employment patterns of recent immigrants, Borjas and Katz (2005) found that immigrants were three times more likely than US natives to be employed in low-skill service jobs

---

* The logic is that higher prices raise the value of hiring additional workers, which raises the incentive for lobbying against border enforcement (Hanson & Spilimbergo, 2001).

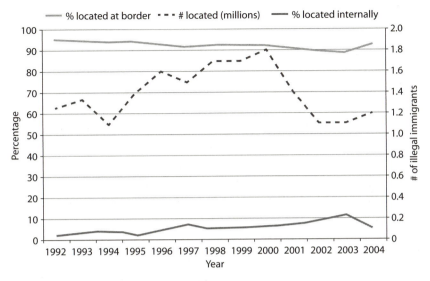

Figure 6.1. Illegal immigrants located by US immigration authorities, 1992–2004. *Source: Department of Homeland Security Yearbook of Immigration Statistics, 2005.*

such as private household occupations, food preparation occupations, and gardening, emblematic of the job growth in nontradable jobs in the United States. Accordingly, "American consumers who spend more on low-skill intensive nontraded goods and services will tend to disproportionately benefit from the recent wave of Mexican immigration" (p. 40).

To draw attention to the self-interested issue at the core of the debate, in 2011 a Texas House legislator from Houston proposed a bill that would punish those who hired illegal workers with two years in jail and up to $10,000 in fines. Reflecting the sardonic motives of the legislator, the bill would exempt those workers whose labor was "performed exclusively or primarily at a single-family residence" (Radcliffe & Fikac, 2011, p. B1). Houston reporters noted that local residents understood the mocking tone of a proposed bill intended to spotlight the mutual self-interest of buyers and sellers in an open gray labor market.

Self-interest and cosmopolitan tolerance combine to explain the cultural allure of the global city for immigrants and professionals: "As a centre of intercultural exchange, the global city brings together many more of these in proximity to each other than cities focused more on regional or national interests, making multicultural awareness an everyday experience" (Boschken, 2008, p. 10). The increased presence of a foreign population in global cities forms an essential component of a cosmopolitan lifestyle based on a symbols-driven consumption, or, as Sassen (1991) put it, "demonstrating taste" (p. 267; see also Clark, 2004). Because cosmopolitan tolerance is largely a function of self-interest and consumption, it is an unlikely support of a passionate campaign for immigration reform.

On the contrary, expansion of the undocumented labor market from its traditional base in agriculture into a US low-wage service sector depends on a tacit policy of don't ask, don't tell that redounds to the benefit of the buyer rather than the seller. What has come to be known as the "Zoe Baird problem"* illustrates the occasional political hazards of a widely known but unacknowledged practice that contributes to the intractability of the illegal immigration issue. It also reflects the capture of an emotionally laden, mobilizing issue by the right in the politics of insecurity. Illegal immigrants have come to represent group threats to the actuarial balance of social security (Winter, 2008) and have been targeted by supporters of the Tea Party movement as undeserving beneficiaries of federal largesse (Skocpol & Williamson, 2012). Evidence for the symbolic nature of opposition to immigration reform comes from a review of the past two decades of research on immigration attitudes (Hainmueller & Hopkins, 2014). The authors found that threats are unrelated to individual self-interest but rather to groupcentric threats to culture and to a lesser degree perceptions of the impact of immigration on the economy as a whole. Additional evidence showed that opposition to Mexican immigrants grew after 9/11 (Hitlan et al., 2007; Branton et al., 2011) and the Great Recession of 2008 had no influence on attitudes toward immigration (Creighton, Jamal, & Malancu, 2015). Like opposition to affirmative action, resistance to immigration reform draws upon group, culturally based sentiments.

Critiques

A growing body of research on the concept of the global city and the theories that explain its rise and manifold effects has stimulated a lively debate. Scholars have taken issue with (1) the economic determinism (Marxist or classical) of global city theorists, (2) the assumption that the state has lost its power to transnational economic forces, (3) the use of an ethnocentric Anglo-American model

---

* Bill Clinton nominated Zoe Baird for United States Attorney General but withdrew her nomination when it was learned her nanny and chauffeur were illegal immigrants and that she had failed to pay their social security taxes. Hence "Nannygate."

on the part of some theorists, and (4) the myopic historic "presentism" of glo-balization theory.

White (1998), for example, argued that globalization does not follow from economic internationalization, and that income inequality found in some global cities is not inevitable. The growth and economic structures of Paris and Tokyo, for example, both widely recognized as global cities, differ in important ways from the US model. France, the most Fordist of mature economies, has not ex-perienced the income inequalities characteristic of the United States largely because the French state has adopted policies that prize social solidarity and equity over unregulated, polarizing economic growth. One indicator of the pol-icy is the strength and ubiquity of unions in France over that in the United States, further evidence that cultural differences temper the effects of a global-ized economy.

In Tokyo, contrary to the assertions of globalist theorists, the state has enacted policies that have prevented the "unbundling" of the city from its hinterlands. Tokyo city officials have de facto presidential power and have used that power to override the wishes of MNCs. Income polarization present in some US global cities is evident in Tokyo as well, but White (1998) pointed out that such inequality is a century old, the product of the nation's dual economy made up of small tra-ditional firms and large modern ones. Moreover, the extreme levels of urban decay found in US cities such as New York and Chicago are nowhere as extreme or as widespread in either Tokyo or Paris. White suggested that a more accurate model of the modern economic change would include indirect causal relation-ships mediated by policy and take into account varying political structures, forms of capitalism, and historical processes.

Other critics of the global city hypothesis argue that globalization changes ethnic identities through cultural processes that are irreducible to economic forces (e.g., Canclini, 1995), while some economists (e.g., Cowen, 2002) champion the growth of cultural diversity that liberates difference from place. Historians, meanwhile, take issue with the "presentism" of global city theorists who place cities outside the flows of history (Sites, 2003). The latter critique pointed out that the current global status of Washington, D.C., can be directly linked to state power (Abbott, 1999), which is also true of Paris (White, 1998).

These are compelling counterarguments, yet the role of economic self-interest in an increasingly competitive global economy and the growth of un-documented immigrant communities in US cities offer a forceful reason to test the influence of the unique social and economic conditions on local political cultures. Based on the uncertainty model, one would expect to see more sympathetic and lenient treatment of the immigration issue in those cities more globally connected, and less sympathetic and punitive treatment in cities less connected to the global economy. There one would expect a more impassioned opposition compared to global cities where economic self-interest tempers passion for reform. Put another way, illegal immigration is a position issue for only one side of the debate.

Ranking Global Cities

Until recently, much of the research on globalization has used the nation-state as the unit of analysis. Scholars have yet to develop definitive measurements of the global connectedness of individual cities. In this analysis, I use a method developed by the Globalization and World Cities (GWC) research program. The GWC index is based on a synergistic rather than a hierarchical view of global cities and assumes that global reach derives from the extent of a city's participation in a communication network of service firms. The firms create and maintain global networks to communicate among themselves and affiliates in branches located in a matrix of global cities (Taylor & Lang, 2005).

The method counts the global service firms in key service sectors—accounting, advertising, banking, insurance, law, and management consulting—and measures the size of the office offering the service and the degree to which the office coordinates the activities of other locations. The resulting index orders US cities into ten strata with a stratum one being the most globally connected (for the United States, only New York falls into stratum one) and a stratum ten the least. The index ranks New York, Chicago, Los Angeles, San Francisco, Miami, and Atlanta in the top strata of global connectivity, and Omaha, Sacramento, Buffalo, and Birmingham, among others, in the lowest.

For media discourse, I analyze front-page coverage in US cities that lie on opposite ends of the global city continuum. I vary coverage by region—East, Midwest, South, Southwest, and West—and, as much as possible, by states that include high and low numbers of illegal immigrants. According to a Pew study (Passel, 2005), over two-thirds of the undocumented population—mainly from Mexico and Central America—live in eight states: California (24 percent), Texas (14 percent), Florida (9 percent), New York (7 percent), Arizona (5 percent), Illinois (4 percent), New Jersey (4 percent), and North Carolina (3 percent).

The purposive sample, described in table 6.1, provides variation on key variables in the analysis. All of the global cities in the sample—New York, Chicago,

Table 6.1. Coverage by source, region, global connectivity, and increase in Mexican population

Source	Region	Global connectivity	% increase in Mexican immigrant pop. 1990–2000	Story count
New York Times	East	1	270	121
Buffalo News	East	8	*	35
Chicago Tribune	Midwest	2	120	77
Omaha World Herald	Midwest	9	*	94
Atlanta Journal-Constitution	South	3	1076	73
Birmingham News	South	10	*	23
Houston Chronicle	Southwest	3	131	160
San Antonio Express News	Southwest	10	53	120
San Francisco Chronicle	West	3	91	66
Sacramento Bee	West	9	112	64
Total				833

Source: Card & Lewis, 2007, pp. 204–205.

*Did not contribute significantly to the increase in Mexican immigrants in the United States.

Atlanta, Houston, and San Francisco—experienced an increase in the growth of their Mexican immigrant population (figures cited are changes from 1990 to 2000), especially so in Atlanta, where the numbers of Mexican immigrants increased tenfold. Note, however, that numbers also increased in some nonglobal cities: San Antonio by 53 percent and Sacramento by 112 percent (a little higher than its global partner San Francisco). The study excludes Los Angeles because its proximity to the Mexican border has always made it a convenient destination for immigrants and because of its relative decline as a desirable location by Mexican workers. The more interesting question was how changes in more distant labor markets would increase incentives for these workers to travel longer distances, thus the rationale for selecting San Francisco.

Targeted coverage includes all front-page stories making any reference to illegal immigrants or the issue of illegal immigration between 2006 and 2007, peak coverage years for the issue during which the George W. Bush administration floated a number of policy proposals for immigration reform. (Figure 6.2 illustrates the coverage trend in the *New York Times* and the peak of interest in the mid-2000s.) Some critics regarded comprehensive reform and its inclusion of a path to citizenship for illegal immigrants as a reward for criminal behavior. More sympathetic views raised a number of arguments in favor of such a path. The controversy split the Republican Party and fueled an ongoing debate that continued well beyond the 2006 midterm elections into the Tea Party movement of 2008 and beyond (Skocpol & Williamson, 2012).

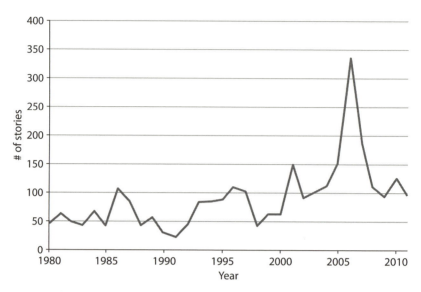

Figure 6.2. Coverage of illegal immigration, *The New York Times*, 1980–2011.

The analysis seeks to determine how each local press framed the issue, as well as its slant. I analyzed front-page coverage because it reflects the imprint of senior editorial judgment as to the relative importance of the issue and coded assertions of fact or opinion, made either by the reporter or quoted source, as an indicator of the range of acceptable, objectively defensible news discourse. I thus adopt Tuchman's view (1972) of the practice of journalism as relying on techniques that offer a procedural standard of objectivity rather than a guarantor of its achievement. Patterns of coverage may reveal an underlying preference otherwise obscured by the procedures of journalistic practice—quotations, limiting space to a restricted range of the issues, and the use of authority figures for expressing opinion. Whether the cause is availability of motivated sources, reporter sympathy, subtle cues offered by senior editors, or some combination of these, the resulting framing reflects the imprint of power on an important venue for the expression of issue priority and slant. As I point out in chapter 2, in the case of news slant, market considerations weigh heavily in favor of catering to existing opinion rather than leading it (Bovitz et al., 2002; Gentzkow & Shapiro, 2010).

Coders were instructed to code assertions of fact or opinion either by quoted sources or by the reporter herself regarding illegal immigrants and the broader issue of illegal immigration. An example from the *New York Times* illustrates one such coded assertion: "Border Patrol commanders say they see no explanation for the drop-off across the entire 2,000-mile border other than stiffer enforcement deterring migrants. The slackening flow, they argue, belies the conventional wisdom that it is impossible to stem illegal migration. Many veteran officers in the force are now beginning to believe it can be controlled with enough resources" (McKinley, 2007, p. 1). This assertion was coded as an endorsement of the effectiveness of border security fences for stemming the flow of illegal immigration, a subcategory of the rule-of-law frame. The finer categories of analysis emerged from successive reading of the texts. The content analysis software (QDA Miner) used by the coders enabled flexible and rapid recoding as new categories emerged that provided subtle distinctions within the broad dimensions of the analysis. The software enabled a low-cost use of grounded theory (Glaser & Strauss, 1967) to refine the categories used to code the large quantities of text for the project.

We began with four broad issue frames to code the discourse: (1) the economy, including consumption of public goods such as health, welfare, and education; (2) national identity, citizenship, and human rights; (3) national security and the rule of law; and (4) power and politics. Collectively, these issue frames make up the issue culture of illegal immigration, the set of media frames available for making sense of the issue (Gamson & Modigliani, 1989; Entman & Rojecki, 2000). A coding protocol that includes the complete set of coding categories and reliability measures appears in the appendix.

Findings

The principle findings include the following: (1) aside from the politics underlying the issue, a roughly even distribution of the remaining framing categories across all five regions; (2) support for the global cities hypothesis in all five regions by one key indicator, but regional variation based on other factors; (3) the importance of local history and national policy in overriding national or global city imperatives; (4) an omnipresent appeal to the rule of law, attached to endorsement of restrictive policy in nonglobal cities, ritually invoked in global cities; (5) a more coherent, policy-relevant, and impassioned discourse in nonglobal cities than in global cities.

The coded discourse on illegal immigration across all regions divided nearly evenly across three of the four dimensions of the controversy: national identity, citizenship, and human rights (33 percent); economy (31 percent); and national security and the rule of law (27 percent). The category of politics (including issues of horse race politics, public demonstrations, allegations of voter fraud, and public opinion) comprised an average of 8 percent of all coded discourse (at

Table 6.2. Frame rank

City	National Identity / Human Rights		Economy		Law / Security	
	Rank	%	Rank	%	Rank	%
NYC	1	39	2	28	3	23
Buffalo	2	28	3	16	1	48
Chicago	1	35	2	31	3	29
Omaha	2	31	3	20	1	36
Atlanta	2	28	1	42	3	26
Birmingham	2	27	1	46	3	19
Houston	1	35	2	33	3	27
San Antonio	3	28	2	31	1	38
San Francisco	1	41	2	29	3	25
Sacramento	2	33	1	43	3	14
Total	1	33	2	32	3	29

13 percent, highest in Omaha where former Nebraska GOP senator Chuck Hagel was dogged by opponents for his liberal stand; at 3 percent, lowest in San Antonio). For illegal immigration, horse race coverage—how the issue was used by candidates for office to improve their chances for election—was comparatively low and notable for that reason. The press found the issue novel enough to warrant majority attention to its substance rather than its use as a wedge issue by contenders in campaign races. Therefore, the category of power and politics is largely discounted from the detailed analysis.

Table 6.2 summarizes the general patterns for each city and for the discourse as a whole: aggregate discourse on illegal immigration is more sympathetic in more globally connected cities (54 percent) than in those less globally connected (48 percent) but not dramatically so. Also notable is that the rank order of issue frames is identical in all but one of the global cities: human rights and citizenship first, the economy second, and law and order third. By contrast, law and order ranks first in nonglobal cities. This broad comparison conceals interesting regional differences in the South and the West, where history and local economic needs resist and reinforce the findings, respectively.

Control over the dimension of the debate is decisive in its slant. For illegal immigration, the two most influential frames are (1) national identity and human rights and (2) law and security. If one wishes to make a winning argument on liberalizing policy toward illegal immigrants, the national identity/human rights frame proves the most successful. In this discourse, 80 percent of the overall coverage is in favor of liberalizing immigration policy, much of it dominated by the specific frames of human rights and the admirable qualities of the immigrants themselves. It also includes the more controversial issue of amnesty, temporary ID cards, and other policies that provide a path to citizenship.

For stiffening resistance, the law and security frame is the most negative, where more than 80 percent of the assertions are opposed to liberal reform. Within this domain, an appeal to the rule of law is by far the most common frame, even in the most globally connected cities: "If you don't get the right papers, you need to go back. . . . You can't just run in and not follow the rules" (Davey, 2007, p. 1). The exceptions are Buffalo and San Antonio, where the cities' proximity to the border attaches pragmatically to calls for increased border security and fences—the most common used subframes in these two locales—with the rule of law running a close second.

Economic concerns represent the swing issue for the debate. Here the range of sympathetic coverage runs from a low of 47 percent (San Antonio) to a high of 78 percent positive (Buffalo). The salience of the issues depends on the region: predictably higher in global cities in the East, Midwest, and Southwest. In the South, economic issues dominate the discourse in both cities, at a little over 40 percent of the coverage. There is no discernible pattern in the mix of economy-related issues across the nation, with reducing of costs and filling an otherwise unmet labor need slightly outweighing the negative slant that illegals take jobs and exploit public goods (health care, public education, welfare, etc.). Notable in this case is the pattern in Atlanta, where the illegal immigrant population increased over 1,000 percent in the 1990s. Perhaps this pattern plays a role in the economic-related concerns being the most common in both Atlanta (and Birmingham), slightly outweighing even the more symbolic issue of the rule of law.

While New York is a prototypical case for global cities, Buffalo is a model for US cities disconnected from the global economy. Here and in Omaha and San Antonio, the dominant frame is on matters of law and security: 48 percent, 35 percent, and 38 percent, respectively. Insofar as the conceptual category itself is derived from a judgment regarding law breaking, the majority of the discourse is thereby unsympathetic to immigrants in general.

The overall tone of the coverage depends on the combination of issue frames prominent in any given area: in global cities, national identity/human rights and the economy, and in nonglobal cities, security and law, with exceptions explained by historical circumstances.

History and State Policy as Mediating Factors

While the issue of illegal immigration is of less concern in the southern sample generally, Birmingham, the region's less globally connected city, is somewhat more sympathetic in the aggregate than Atlanta. (Note, however, that the issue gets less coverage in Birmingham than in any other analyzed source.) The general issue priority is similar in both cities: economics first, national identity and human rights second, and law and security third. However, while Atlanta's discourse includes an important human rights component that outweighs Birmingham's by seven to one, Birmingham's front-page coverage was slightly more sympathetic and less punitive than Atlanta's. It was also twice as likely to carry statements portraying illegal immigrants as victims of nativism or those warning that increased or aggressive enforcement would bring unintended harm to the local economy. A large contemporaneous increase in Atlanta's immigrant population may have made this issue more salient than in other global cities, replicating a finding in a study by Hopkins (2010).

A similar divergence is found in the West, where the agricultural needs of California's Central Valley dominated the news discourse on the issue—nearly one-fifth of the coverage in Sacramento referred to the otherwise unmet demand for labor. As in the South, however, there is a greater emphasis on human rights concerns in the more globally connected city, San Francisco. While Sacramento's front-page news discourse is slightly more sympathetic overall, and slightly less punitive, the contrast in the general issue priority reveals the explanation of the divergence from the overall pattern: in San Francisco (as in all of the global cities except Atlanta), the emphasis is on national identity and human rights concerns; in Sacramento, the emphasis is heavily economic and more positive on economic concerns by a ratio of nearly two to one. Coverage in Sacramento was nearly twice as likely to mention the positive effects of undocumented workers on reducing costs to consumers or filling an unmet need for harvest labor.

In Birmingham and Sacramento, history is inextricably woven into the coverage on illegal immigration. In the South, the more recent arrival of immigrants, despite their relatively smaller numbers compared with other regions, constitutes a disruption that is affected by the region's, and in this case specifically Birmingham's long and still-contentious civil rights history. In the West, the immigration issue has a longer historical arc with coverage often referring to the Bracero program of the 1940s, instituted by a series of agreements between the United States and Mexico to meet the demand for harvest labor during World War II and after (the program continued through 1964).

The long tradition of immigrant labor (often reliant on undocumented workers) in the West makes agricultural interests more sympathetic, as does the salience of civil rights in Birmingham. In both regions, the overall divergence from the expected pattern affirms, upon closer examination, the guiding hypothesis in the relationship between economic self-interest and tolerance. Despite Atlanta's more conservative coverage, its front page includes a human rights component reflective of the importance of undocumented workers to the city's diverse culture and local economy, concerns of less importance in less diverse Birmingham. Similarly, in Sacramento, where reliance on agricultural labor is an important concern, coverage includes less positive national identity and human rights discourse compared with its more globally connected partner, San Francisco.

Issue Domains

Table 6.3 summarizes the order of issue frame priority and the percentage of positive slant in that domain. The numbers here recap the broader patterns discussed previously but reveal the sources of greater sympathy in global cities. The difference between the global city and its regional partner in overall coverage is evident (with the noted exceptions in Birmingham and Sacramento), as is the overwhelmingly positive coverage of national identity and human rights issues across the board. Most striking, however, is the difference on issues of law and

Table 6.3. Frame slant

City	National Identity / Human Rights		Economy		Law/ Security	
	Total	Pro	Total	Pro	Total	Pro
New York	39	79	28	61	23	16
Buffalo	28	81	16	78	48	6
Chicago	35	89	31	49	29	40
Omaha	31	86	20	56	36	6
Atlanta	28	72	42	49	26	22
Birmingham	27	73	46	59	19	11
Houston	35	76	33	55	27	25
San Antonio	28	69	31	47	38	4
San Francisco	41	86	29	61	25	28
Sacramento	33	89	43	69	14	12
Total	33	80	32	59	29	17

security. Though negative wherever they occur, they appear much less in global cities.

National Identity and Human Rights

In all but one of the regions—the South—the modal discourse of the more globally connected city is the overwhelmingly sympathetic set of issues under national identity and human rights. Looking into the specific issues, the global city is much more likely than its regional partner to have a vigorous human rights discourse. Figure 6.3 illustrates the striking ratios: New York 10:1 over Buffalo, Atlanta 7:1 over Birmingham, Chicago 2:1 over Omaha, and San Francisco 2:1 over Sacramento. The exceptions are Houston and San Antonio, where the percentages are nearly identical. Notably, Omaha and Sacramento share agricultural interests, meatpacking for the former and crops for the latter.

Two features of the human rights discourse make it important for understanding the nature of the controversy and the posture of the media on the issue. First, it draws the reader's attention to the dire conditions that drive desperate people to flee to the United States. The tales are often moving first-person accounts of the appalling conditions emigrants wish to escape, peril-filled desert crossings, and of the heart-rending consequences of separation of parents from children born in the United States to undocumented workers. Second, this kind of reporting requires an investment of effort on the part of the reporter (itself a telling indicator of story slant), which often leads to sympathetic

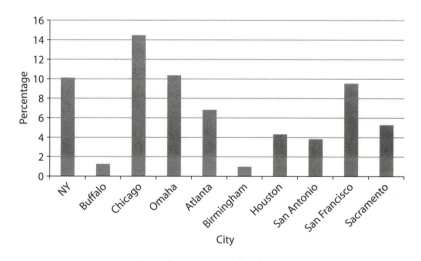

Figure 6.3. Human rights frame.

coverage. One example from the *New York Times* illustrates both the effort invested in getting the substance and personal details of the story and the evident sympathy of the reporter:

> "I can't breathe," Felicitas Martinez Barradas gasped to her cousin as they stumbled across the border in 100-degree heat. "The sun is killing me." They had been walking for a day and a half through the Sonoran Desert in southern Arizona, the purgatory that countless illegal immigrants pass through on their way from Mexico to the United States. Ms. Martinez was 29 and not fit. A smuggler handed her a can of carbonated energy drink and caffeine pills. But she only got sicker and passed out, said her cousin, Julio Diaz. There, near a mesquite tree a little over 10 miles from the border, Ms. Martinez died, her eyes open to the starry sky, her arms across her chest and Mr. Diaz, 17, at her side. Gone was her dream of making enough money in the United States for a house for her four young children in Mexico. (Archibold, 2007, p. 1)

Another telling category within this issue domain highlights the virtuous qualities of the immigrants themselves—their discipline, patriotism, or exemplary adherence to the law. Here the sympathetic coverage ratios favor the globally connected city in every region: New York 5:1 over Buffalo, Chicago 3:1 over Omaha, Atlanta 3:2 over Birmingham, Houston 3:1 over San Antonio, and San Francisco 2:1 over Sacramento. Thus, despite the overall favorable coverage in Sacramento, sensitivity to the human rights of undocumented workers or their estimable qualities is not a significant contributor. More self-interested economic interests (detailed in the following section) are responsible.

As in assertions of human rights, the discourse of "virtuous illegals" uses either detailed reporting that requires substantive remarks from sympathetic third parties—"Most immigrant patients have jobs and pay taxes, through paycheck deductions or property taxes included in their rent, administrators at the Dallas and Fort Worth hospitals said. At both institutions, they have a better record of paying their bills than low-income Americans do, the administrators said" (Preston, 2006)—or statements from illegal immigrants themselves: " 'I want to learn English. I know it would help me get ahead. But I have to work 65 hours a week to raise my children and pay my bills. That has to come first before anything,' says Espino" (Rodriguez, 2006).

Economic Issues

The economic dimension of illegal immigration is more salient in global cities, with the exception of areas in which migrant labor meets the needs of large-scale agriculture, especially the Central Valley of Sacramento, and in that part of the South where the issue of illegal immigration is a relatively new phenomenon. Contrary to the general pattern found in the discourse on citizenship and human rights, when it comes to economic issues, less globally connected cities are slightly more likely to have a positively inflected tilt than their more globally connected partners. Whatever positive difference accrues to the smaller, less globally connected cities, however, is diminished by the decreased prominence of this issue.

In the South, there is a vigorous debate on the economic consequences of illegal immigrant labor. In both Atlanta and Birmingham, slightly more than 10 percent of the assertions focus on the loss of jobs to and the exploitation of public services by illegal immigrants. In Birmingham, the issue of illegal immigration is much less prominent than in Atlanta (table 6.1), but it is more positive on the dimension regarding the nonexploitation of public services by illegal immigrants (greater than 2:1 over Atlanta). A local controversy sparked by a KKK-led demonstration against illegal immigrants may have distorted the overall pattern; an unusually high number of references to undocumented workers as victims of nativism—9 percent, compared to an average of 4 percent nationally—support this hypothesis. Nonetheless, in Atlanta, assertions regarding the otherwise unmet needs of labor supplied by undocumented workers outnumber those in Birmingham by better than 2:1. In these parts of the South, the novelty of the debate may have contributed to the prominence of its economic effects (42 percent, compared to a national average of 31 percent). Here the trade-offs are on the loss of jobs and the unmet needs of the labor market.

In the other anomaly, Sacramento, the increased presence is due almost entirely to the needs of the agricultural labor market. In Sacramento, one in five assertions on the debate referred to the reduced labor costs provided by immigrant labor, and the consequences for farmers and consumers were the flow of immigrant labor to be slowed. The statements are plentiful, substantive, and often impassioned:

> Americans' general ignorance of how their food and drink are produced, farmers say, has allowed immigration hard-liners to attack policies that make perfect sense to the agriculture industry. "Anybody who says they'll pay $10 for a head of lettuce so workers don't have to be here is just talking big," Cunha said. "How will they buy those DVDs they want, eat in those nice restaurants and go to hotels?" He fumed about claims on talk shows that do not match his reality, including one assertion that labor costs are only 10 percent of farm production. To produce fruits

and vegetables in California, labor is more than 30 percent of cost, according to federal agricultural officials. (Ferriss, 2006)

Law and Security

Where the discourse on citizenship and human rights is dominated by sympathetic assertions, and opinion on the economic effects is often divided, the discourse on issues of law and security is overwhelmingly negative. The rule of law, combining the essential illegal nature of the act of entering the country without proper documentation and the alleged criminal tendency of illegal immigrants, is a prominent issue everywhere, though in most cases it is less so in global cities (the sole exception being Atlanta). Despite the predominantly negative tone, coverage in global cities is less negative, even in the South, largely due to skepticism on the *effectiveness* of increased border security or the *impracticality* of deportation.

Border issues are most salient in cities close to national boundaries, but they are also the most negative in cities with the least globally connected economies. Buffalo and San Antonio have an identical high issue priority for border security, 16 percent in both cases. When national security is added to the figure, the numbers jump to 29 and 23 percent, respectively. Despite its own proximity to the Mexican border, the border issue is less prominent in Houston, 11 percent, half that in San Antonio. In no other region is this issue as prominent. In their analysis of illegal immigration coverage in California newspapers, Branton and Dunaway (2009) found that proximity to the Mexican border was positively correlated with negative coverage. Economic incentives for ownership of US newspapers near the border may induce sensational negative coverage, as the authors argued, but there may be cross-pressures induced by other economic factors, as the San Antonio–Houston contrast reveals. In a follow-up agenda-setting study (Dunaway, Branton, & Abrajano, 2010), the authors found that the media paid greater attention in border states than in nonborder states, leading residents of border states to identify immigration as a more important problem than residents of nonborder states.

Assertions on security ranged from simple declarations of majority support for greater border security in public opinion surveys (Preston & Connelley, 2007) to expert opinion that links border security with terrorism: "Even as debate rages in the United States about the influx of illegal immigrants across the Mexican border, some analysts see the arrests in Canada as a reminder of the threat posed by dozens of terrorist cells thought to be active just north of an easily crossed, thinly guarded border. 'It's an enormous worry,' said John Keeley, a

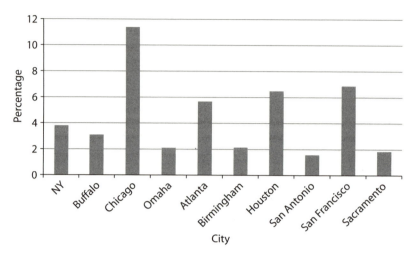

Figure 6.4. Ineffectiveness of enhanced borders and deportation.

spokesman for the Center for Immigration Studies, a Washington think tank that favors tighter immigration controls. 'It's an enormous country with an enormous international population, and the border is basically unguarded'" (Deans, 2006).

The chief reason for the less negative law and security discourse in global cities is skepticism of its effectiveness, as illustrated in figure 6.4. In all regions, the more globally connected cities have a higher proportion of assertions doubting the effectiveness of increased border security measures or the practicality of deporting illegal aliens. The comparatively small differential for *The New York Times* reflects the national character of the debate and of the paper's increased coverage of conservative Washington politicians who often called for more security at the border. The heated debate on border security and the rule of law in nonglobal cities is contrasted with the human rights coverage in global cities. A closer look at these and other dimensions reveals potential areas for compromise as well as incommensurable and irresolvable differences due to the symbolic politics underlying the issue.

Frame Co-Occurrences and Policy Coherence

In the following investigation, I use factor analysis to code assertions derived from frames that either support or oppose liberalization of immigration policy. Factor analysis permits us to track the co-occurrence of these assertions (frames and their slant) to reveal the patterns of opinion and whether they cohere around

Table 6.4. Factor analysis of frames, global cities

Frames	Component 1	Component 2	Component 3
Rule of law (con)	.522	.425	.285
Human rights (pro)	.567	.074	.250
Reduce costs, fill unmet need (pro)	.648	.434	.223
Support amnesty, path to citizen (pro)	.258	.807	.032
Take jobs, exploit services (con)	.734	.204	.384
Border security, fences (con)	−.057	.670	.095
Illegals law-abiding, hard-working (pro)	.705	−.034	.272
Oppose amnesty, temp measures (con)	.255	.841	.052
Employers responsible (con)	.697	.317	.160
Deportation, enforcement impractical (pro)	−.053	.566	−.145
Enforcement brings unintended harm (pro)	.321	.039	.077
Nation of immigrants (pro)	.121	.219	.779
Victims of nativism (pro)	.273	−.023	.649
Pay taxes, do not exploit services (pro)	.788	−.173	−.058
Threaten national identity (con)	−.141	.707	.211
National security threat (con)	.183	.005	.809
Deport illegals (con)	.245	.144	.155

Note: Frames arranged in order of frequency. Extraction method: principal component analysis. Rotation method: Varimax with Kaiser normalization. Rotation converged in eight iterations.

a policy recommendation. I begin with an analysis of the aggregated opinion of global cities, as depicted in table 6.4.

In global cities, three factors explain 61 percent of the variance. The correlations in the first column (the first factor) show the sources of the largely sympathetic opinion. The first factor is the most sympathetic—four pro frames, two con—and highlights mainly economic issues. It also includes the exemplary character of undocumented workers as well as a concern for their human rights. The economic dimension of the coverage features a balanced presentation of opposing views on the pluses and minuses of immigrant labor: the reduction of costs for goods balanced against the taking of jobs and exploitation of services. Though immigrants pay taxes, their illegal status prevents them from receiving the benefits otherwise made available to citizens. The single policy-relevant element of the discourse blames employers for exploiting undocumented workers who are depicted as hardworking and rule abiding. The most common set of frames in global city coverage portray illegal immigrants as virtuous and exploited but do not include liberal reform as policy relevant. On the contrary, exploiting employers are held to account and, by policy extension, would deny undocumented workers the economic opportunities they seek and the lowered costs afforded by their cheap labor. Moreover, as we learned previously, internal enforcement of illegal immigration is comparatively rare and conducted mainly in response to sudden influxes of migrants to small towns.

The second factor is more negative than the first and includes a balance between assertions favoring amnesty and paths to liberal reform against those opposed. The factor also includes a similarly balanced discourse on security and border concerns with skepticism about the efficacy of such measures (deportation is altogether rejected).

The third factor, the least common, coheres around assertions that undocumented immigrants threaten national identity with the view that they are victims of nativism in a country that is historically a nation built on immigrants and immigration. Though mainly positive, this stream of discourse is also disconnected from policy. Significantly, although the potentially powerful and highly symbolic appeal to the rule of law is the most common frame in global city discourse, it is only weakly associated with the three factors.

In summary, mediated discourse on illegal immigration in global cities is complex and diffuse. It highlights an implied policy of punishing unscrupulous and exploitative employers, a thus far rarely enforced policy. This is associated with a balanced discussion of economic issues and anticipated losses given a stricter enforcement regime. Undocumented workers themselves are humanized and depicted as victims of employers. A path to citizenship is argued within a balanced discussion on the questionable merits of border security rather than the economic benefits derived from a captive and undemanding (and albeit virtuous) workforce. In a nutshell, the coverage reflects the complexity of the issue and nods in the direction of liberal reform rather than emphatically affirming it.

In nonglobal cities, three factors explain 60 percent of the variance (see table 6.5). What stands out in the overall coverage is its policy relevance—largely against liberal reform—and its simplicity compared to global city discourse. Unlike the largely positive first factor in global cities, the first in nonglobal locales is mainly negative (five unsympathetic frames, three sympathetic) and charged with an emotional appeal to the rule of law. Also present is a sympathetic frame that acknowledges the cost reductions of immigrant labor; these assertions come largely from Sacramento and Omaha, areas that depend on labor in agriculture and meatpacking.

Significant and in contrast to coverage in global cities are policy-relevant recommendations in nonglobal cities for increased enforcement measures at the border and in the workplace. The factor also includes a balanced discussion between those in favor of amnesty and those opposed.

Table 6.5. Factor analysis of frames, nonglobal cities

Frames	Component		
	1	2	3
Rule of law (con)	.872	.036	.031
Border security, fences (con)	.797	.248	.283
Support amnesty, path to citizen (pro)	.862	−.206	−.080
Reduce costs, fill need (pro)	.571	.201	−.132
Human rights (pro)	.441	.634	−.166
Employers responsible (con)	.658	−.103	.076
Take jobs, exploit services (con)	.326	.439	.611
National security threat (con)	.443	−.387	.353
Enforcement brings unintended harm (pro)	.431	.238	−.028
Illegals law-abiding, hard-working, patriotic (pro	.459	.700	−.221
Pay taxes, do not exploit services (pro)	.237	.648	.240
Victims of nativism (pro)	.541	−.010	.601
Oppose amnesty, temp measures (con)	.729	−.260	−.163
US a nation of immigrants (pro)	.507	.376	−.178
Deportation, enforcement impractical (pro)	.650	−.436	−.344
Threaten national identity (con)	.528	−.455	.310
Deport illegals (con)	.695	.074	−.184

Note: Frames arranged in order of frequency. Extraction method: Principal component analysis. Rotation method: Varimax with Kaiser normalization. Rotation converged in seven iterations.

The second factor is entirely positive. It includes three sympathetic frames that speak to the exemplary character of immigrants, their nonexploitation of public goods, and concern with their human rights. The third balances assertions of immigrants taking jobs and collective goods against those who describe illegals as victims of nativism.

In sum, the policy discourse in nonglobal cities is more coherent on the side of restriction, reinforced by the morally inflected related issues of the rule of law. The discourse is mindful of the human rights issues of the immigrants themselves, but their rights do not accompany policy discussion for liberal reform. This is also true for global cities where the undocumented workforce is regarded as an economic boon justified with recourse to human and civil rights rhetoric that connects to a discourse of employer exploitation. This is an unlikely recipe for a movement in favor of immigration reform.

Conclusion

The uncertainty model predicts that elite gridlock on an issue that creates risk exposure for one or more segments of the population enhances the likelihood of a citizen reaction. As the patterns in the mediated discourse show, the passion

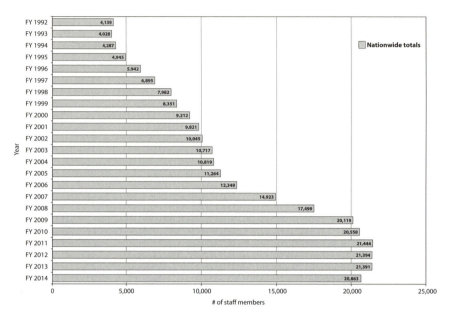

Figure 6.5. US border security staffing, 1992–2014. *Source:* US Customs and Border Patrol, 2014. Report available at http://www.cbp.gov/sites/default/files/documents/BP%20 Staffing%20FY1992-FY2014_0.pdf.

is largely on the side of those opposed to immigration reform, largely expressed in symbolic terms. The obvious dilemma facing policymakers is a conflict between groups who demand enforcement on emotionally laden grounds and those who depend on or take advantage of cheap labor. The former sustain an issue that arouses the ire of a constituency on the right. The latter dampen the prospects for a reform movement on the left. On this score, the right has benefited the most by mobilizing voters on the emotional issue of illegal immigrants as undeserved recipients of and threats to the solvency of Social Security and Medicare. Resentment among Tea Party supporters of illegal immigrants (and other undeserving recipients of government aid) mobilized large numbers of conservatives to vote in the 2010 midterm elections (Skocpol & Williamson, 2012), which led to a House majority that thwarted the Obama administration at every turn. The often-emotional appeals to the rule of law that dominated news discourse in those locations not benefited by globalization of the US economy animated a debate that gave the GOP an important advantage.

Additional support for the continuing dominance of the security frame is the continuing emphasis on border patrols and a failed 2013 bipartisan framework for immigration reform. Figure 6.5 shows the increase in border agents between

1992 and 2011. Since the 2006 flare-up of the debate, the number of border agents has increased by nearly 74 percent. The Obama administration has also stepped up deportations at a monthly rate that exceeds that in the Bush administration by 1.5 to 1. The bipartisan framework for immigration reform had four pillars, the most prominent of which highlighted border security: "Create a tough but fair path to citizenship for unauthorized immigrants currently living in the United States that is contingent upon securing our borders and tracking whether legal immigrants have left the country when required" ("Bipartisan framework for immigration reform," 2013, p. 1).

Immigration reform is once again on the public agenda, and some changes seem inevitable given the importance of the Hispanic vote for both parties. It remains to be seen, however, whether the resistance of immigration reform foes will delay and weaken the aims of proponents. Barack Obama's executive order in late 2014 led to lowered support for immigration reform. A poll showed support for immigrants was at its lowest level ever measured (Quinnipiac University, 2014). "[When] offered three choices on what to do about illegal immigrants: 48 percent of American voters said they should be allowed to stay, with a path to citizenship, down from 57 percent . . . 35 percent said illegal immigrants should be required to leave the U.S., up from 26 percent 12 months ago and higher than this number ever has been" (p. 1). Still to be addressed by reformers is economic self-interest that blunts the passion for effective policy change.

Globalization has changed the US economy from one based on heavy industry and manufacturing to one driven by services and other nontradable jobs. The supply chains that decouple function from place afford transnational corporations incentives to offshore their manufacturing facilities, at one time a principle source of high-paying jobs for the lower and middle classes, now greatly diminished. The result is growing income inequality and uncertainty about the prospects for a growing economy.

A standard measure of income inequality is the Gini coefficient. Ranging from 0 (perfect equality) to 1 (one person has all the wealth), most industrialized states have lower values than nonindustrialized states. For example, the Gini coefficient for Denmark is .25 and .33 for France. By contrast, it is .46 for Mexico and .47 for China. The United States at .41 is closer to the nonindustrialized states than to its modernized partners. The reasons for the disparities are due to differences in income tax levels, rates of capital gains taxation, and much higher rates of unionization in Europe than in the United States.

When examined from the perspective of a global economy, the United States is somewhat of an anomaly, the effects of which are exaggerated in the extremes of income inequality of its most globally connected cities, where undocumented and nonunionized workers fill low-paying service positions. There residents, local politicians, and low-wage employers have few incentives for reform. A survey experiment of attitudes on immigration found that high-income respondents who lived in states with high welfare benefits (e.g., California, New York, and Massachusetts) were more welcoming of low-skilled immigrants than low-income respondents (Hainmueller & Hiscox, 2010). The researchers explained that opposition to immigration was founded less in concern about wages than in "differences in cultural values and beliefs about immigration's sociotropic impacts" (p. 228).

Meanwhile, in those areas where undocumented workers are relatively low in number, they represent a symbolic target for the economic insecurities of Americans who have seen their wages stagnate and have benefitted least by the growth of high-paying service jobs in globally connected cities. The appeals to the rule of law and, indirectly, to American identity echo the rhetoric of the nativist movements of the mid and late 19th century, when industrialization and urbanization drew waves of immigrants to the United States. At the end of the 20th century, the economy had changed again, this time responding to a place-indifferent global network. Globalization of the economy may have reduced the importance of place for the transmission and flow of capital, but these efficiencies do not apply to the flow of people. Appeals to fear create a friction that has resulted in diminished wage bargaining power for undocumented workers, disincentives for immigration reform among companies and individuals who benefit from cheap labor, and a powerful symbolic issue for conservatives that has yet to inspire a countermovement from the left. We explore the reasons for the grassroots imbalance in the politics of insecurity in the next two chapters.

Appendix to Chapter Six: Coding Protocol

Code each assertion of fact or opinion on illegal immigrants and policies relevant to illegal immigration. Quotes are obvious targets of interest for opinion, but also pay close attention to assertions of fact by quoted sources and those assumed by the reporter. For example, the following hypothetical quote is an expression of opinion about the negative impact of illegal immigration on the domestic economy: "Illegals drive down the wages of American workers." One expressing a positive sentiment: "Illegals do work that no one else is willing to do." Assertions of fact or assumptions driven by such assertions are also fair game: "The California peach crop will rot unless migrant workers, even illegals, are given temporary permits so that they can work the fields." Note here that the assertion can be coded as an economic issue—illegals do undesirable work—and a citizenship issue: favor temporary measures.

Ten percent of the text was coded to assess reliability. Agreement percentages followed by Scott's pi coefficients appear in parentheses.

A. Economy
1. Illegals do undesirable work or take jobs that reduce costs to the American consumer. Include all opinion and assertions that illegal immigrants do dirty, backbreaking, or unpleasant work that would otherwise not get done (83%, .61).
2. Illegal workers are exploited by American employers; include any references to holding employers responsible for hiring illegal immigrant labor or for gaining an unfair advantage of employers who adhere to the law (81%, .50).
3. Enforcing the law against illegal immigrant labor will have negative consequences for the economy (e.g., reducing demand for goods and services created by immigrants themselves) (90%, .61).
4. Illegal immigrants take jobs from Americans or reduce their wages; exploit public resources (get welfare benefits, send their children to publicly funded schools, etc.) (85%, .63).
5. Illegals do not take public funds or use public resources; in fact, they are taxed but are prevented by their illegal status from claiming benefits to which they would otherwise have a right (88%, .60).

B. National identity, citizenship, and human rights
1. Illegals are victims of nativism, xenophobia (85%, .48).
2. Illegals threaten national identity and/or integrity by virtue of their numbers, use of language other than English, and so forth. Code as relevant assertions or opinions on desirability of making English the official language in the context of the illegal immigration issue (85%, .51).
3. Support amnesty, temporary measures (issuing a temporary worker or ID card or driver's license), or any mention of a path to citizenship (90%, .72).
4. Oppose any of the measures mentioned in item three (88%, .68).
5. Human rights: mention of dire economic, political, or social conditions that drive people to emigrate illegally to the United States and the risks they take (e.g., hiking through deserts with little or no water or food; any mention of

casualties of such treks); code as relevant also the potential harm to children born in the United States of illegal immigrants who would be separated from their families if deportation would take place (90%, .61).

6. Illegal immigrants are hardworking, law abiding, and/or patriotic. Note first-person accounts that mention working long hours, backbreaking work, and so forth to support family here or in home country (83%, .52).

7. The United States is a nation that has prospered because it has welcomed immigrants; it is a nation with a welcoming tradition to people all over the world: for example, "the US is a nation of immigrants" (93%, .68).

C. National security and rule of law

1. Illegals pose a national security threat, especially in light of 9/11 (85%, .48).

2. Build better fences, increase border security (88%, .68).

3. Border or deportation is unenforceable or impractical (93%, .63).

4. Deport illegal immigrants (93%, .63).

5. The United States is a nation of laws, and illegal immigration represents an affront to the rule of law (80%, .46).

CHAPTER SEVEN

Reaction from the Right

Tea Party Politics

Two organized reactions from citizens followed the first economic panic of the modern age of globalization, the worst since World War II. On the right, predominantly white older Americans mobilized to form what they called the Tea Party, a movement that championed small government, reduced taxes, and other goals that reinforced an economic regime that sustained globalization of the US economy. On the left, a movement made up of younger cohorts of Americans—mainly college students and recent graduates—mobilized to protest the inequalities of globalized capitalism. The contrasting outcomes of the Tea Party and Occupy Wall Street movements help explain the current advantage of the right in the politics of insecurity.

We begin with the Tea Party and analyze the movement's reception in a new information environment that provided an infrastructure for a system of mutually reinforcing interests shared by anxious citizens, partisan media, and political elites. The proximate cause of the movement was the Great Recession of 2008, an economic downturn driven, in part, by a major increase in the flow of capital across national borders. The broader context included the origins of the crash in a housing bubble inflated by Chinese monetary policy and the maturation of a balkanized and politicized information environment. While the former led to magical thinking, the latter led to selective perception and the rise of a lively debate on the dangers of a soaring national debt and the size of government.

The absence of such a reaction among conservatives during the George W. Bush administrations whose tax cuts paired with increased defense spending to fund two ground wars and a new pharmaceutical Medicare benefit pointed to the politicized nature of the debate. The net effect was a doubling of the national debt from about $5.8T in fiscal 2001 to $12T in fiscal 2009. The Obama administration inherited the debt as well as several structural economic problems that would make the recovery difficult. In chapter 1, we saw how the drop of tradable jobs contributed to the precariousness of the American middle class. Their increased reliance on housing values to compensate for stagnant wages was enabled by a rapid increase in the global flows of capital, a major contributor to the depth and length of the recession.

The Economic and Political Discontinuities of Globalization

The distinct markers of this era of globalization are the speed and density of transnational flows, making it qualitatively different from any that has preceded it (Keohane & Nye, 2000b). One might call this the era of hyperglobalization, marked by the institutionalization of a global economy that has produced manifold changes in multiple domains of life. Offshoring of manufacturing from advanced economies, for example, has created a nascent middle class in developing economies, but it has also created stubborn new problems in mature economies.

In the United States, liberalization of the economy has aggravated the results of 30 years of tax legislation that have led to the "hyperconcentration" of income gains by the top tier of the US population (Hacker & Pierson, 2010). Because globalization has increased the mobility of capital, it has also reduced the tax base. In the absence of the political will to raise taxes to strengthen the social safety net, the "race to the bottom" increases those most vulnerable to the risks of the new economy—those without the skills to join or compete in a trans- formed labor market or who lack the diversified investment portfolios necessary to prosper in a globally dispersed economy (Rodrik, 2005; cf., Gilpin, 2000). The interaction of the business cycle with structural changes in the economy has led to an unfamiliar sense of instability and insecurity for Americans steeped in a culture of increasingly high expectations for a more prosperous future.

Notwithstanding arguments about the shrinking role of the state (e.g., Strange, 1996), it remains an essential political actor in managing and stabilizing global- ization. First, there are no comparable institutions at the transnational level for democratically influenced policymaking, regulation, and providing a social safety net to manage globalization-related dislocations. And second, Americans continue to derive identity from nation or state rather than a cosmopolitan sense of global citizenship. At times of crisis, citizens do not turn to global institu- tions for relief or security; they reflexively look to their resident political elites for answers. While economists may rationalize the economic instability of glo- balization as a short-term concern, politicians do not have the luxury of the long view. As Keynes (1924) put it, "Economists set themselves too easy, too useless a task if in tempestuous seasons they can only tell us that when the storm is past the ocean is flat again" (p. 80).

The Great Recession of 2008

The US economy entered a tempestuous season when the global financial system inflated a housing bubble that led to the first economic crisis of the most recent era of globalization. In the late 1990s capital began to accumulate in developing economies and oil-producing nations in what Federal Reserve Chair Ben Bernanke described as a global savings glut.* Seeking investment opportunities that offered greater returns than US treasuries, nations with trading surpluses such as China and Korea began to buy US securities based on complex derivatives of housing mortgages.†

Liberalization of capital flows across borders is a recent phenomenon, dating to the early 1990s. To illustrate, in 1973 average daily trading in foreign currency markets was $15 billion. By 2010, that figure had risen to $4 trillion (Triennial Central Bank Survey, 2010). Foreign exchange permitted the Chinese government to buy US dollars to slow the rise of export prices and thereby sustain the growth of jobs for a large and potentially restive peasant population. The cheap credit that resulted paired with the Clinton administration's deregulation of the US banking industry led to increasingly risky financial instruments and risk profiles. The most perilous turned out to be mortgage-backed securities that exceeded $7 trillion worldwide.

A hierarchy of self-interested participants—investment bankers, mortgage institutions, and local mortgage brokers—steadily reduced the collateral needed to meet increasing demand from overseas investors and Americans who began to buy and sell houses for profit. Increased demand gradually reduced risk thresholds as brokers eventually began to offer what came to be known as NINA loans—no income, no asset—to people who under normal circumstances would have been denied them. The high-risk mortgages were sold in pools called collateralized debt obligations (CDOs) that were underrated on their risk of default. Just as in the dot .com bubble of the late 1990s, expectations of future profits induced citizens to speculate in the real estate market. Cable channels aired programs on how to join the boom in "flipping" houses, further accelerating the growth of the housing market. As the bubble expanded, Wall Street firms converted from private firms to publicly traded corporations and thereby shifted risk to stockholders and eventually to taxpayers. Thus the catchphrase "privatized profits and socialized risks."

---

* Bernanke's hypothesis did not go unchallenged (see, e.g., Borio & Disyatat, 2011), but nearly all economists acknowledged the role of a globalized economy in contributing to the downturn.

† Treasury interest rates had been dropped to one percent by Bernanke's predecessor Alan Greenspan to stimulate the economy following 9/11.

Constraints on the Left

The financial crisis played a large part in Barack Obama's victory in 2008. Shortly after his election, Obama proposed and Congress passed an economic stimulus to provide cash to a frozen credit market and to save the banks and underwriting firms (e.g., AIG) that were responsible for the crash. Despite his attempts to rescue the principal institutions of capitalism, Obama became the target of a sustained attack from the right on his policies and the legitimacy of his presidency. And despite the intellectual incoherence of the attacks leveled at policies that rescued banks and the auto industry as well as the conspiracy theories floated about his true identity, Obama's poll numbers began to fall. Tellingly, increasing numbers of Americans began to doubt he was a Christian. That this was an issue in the first place revealed the influence of religion on what would become the Tea Party movement and the long historical tradition from which it drew familiar antigovernment themes and rhetoric (Noll, 2008; Parker & Baretto, 2013).

The Tea Party's alignment with the Christian Right tapped a potent source of cultural resonance for disciplining group identity and solidarity. The movement would also be assisted by the continued absence of a credible intellectual challenge from the left to economic policies that had been in place since the late 1970s. Bill Clinton's "third-way" doctrine of the Democratic Leadership Council was difficult to distinguish from the economic regime that had been in place since the early 1980s. Often called neoliberalism by its critics, its familiar principles included preferences for low inflation over full employment, deregulation of industry, free trade, and privatization of publicly financed institutions. Rhetorically, these translated to an emphasis on the value of business profits, individual responsibility (e.g., "workfare" instead of welfare), education and retraining, and the demonization of unions that pressured them to make contract concessions. Clinton's pragmatic third way effectively put the left into a position where it would fight a losing battle on terms defined by the right (Mudge, 2011). In terms of the uncertainty model, the movement would be assisted by ideas made resonant by the absence of a credible alternative.

Clinton's concessions to the doctrine were not unusual. Parties on the left in Europe had similarly assumed that voters would not consent to increased taxes to strengthen the social safety net needed to weather economic downturns. Governments reversed course from full employment to a preference for anti-inflationary policy that would constrain public spending. This pressured states to look beyond their borders for economic growth necessary to derive tax revenues (Sassoon, 1996).

The intellectual shrinkage of the public sphere on alternatives for economic policy came at a time when an expansion of the infrastructure for communication had led to its segmentation and polarization.

Segregated Media

In a seminal article, Bennett and Iyengar (2008) analyzed the state of political communication scholarship at a time when an increased number of specialized media outlets—broadcast, cable, and online—made information "hitherto unimaginable" freely and widely available. As we reviewed in chapter 2, the abundance of information arrived in tandem with an order of magnitude increase of channels whose richer entertainment content decreased the size of the audience for news (Prior, 2007).

Summarizing trends in research, Bennett and Iyengar (2008) hypothesized that the new media environment was leading to a wider knowledge gap between motivated and unmotivated citizens. More importantly, the authors noted research that showed that motivated audiences for news were gravitating to sources that reinforced what they already believed while ignoring those from the opposing side. Research following the publication of their article supports their hypothesis in a wide range of contexts (e.g., Iyengar & Hahn, 2009; Pew Research Center for the People and Press, 2010; Stroud, 2011; cf. Gentzkow & Shapiro, 2011).

Partisan media have not benefited equally despite the relatively equal proportions of self-identified liberals and conservatives in the United States. Between 2000 and 2004, Fox increased its audience by 50 percent, while CNN and MSNBC's ratings remained flat (Pew Research Center for the People and Press, 2004). In 2014 Fox averaged 1.7M daily viewers, while MSNBC and CNN had about 600,000 and 500,000, respectively (Pew Research Center, 2015). Illustrating a new symbiosis between partisan media and political movements on the right, members of the Tea Party and their supporters often made a point of avoiding news outlets other than Fox, where coverage of their campaign was heavy and sympathetic (Skocpol & Williamson, 2012).

Notwithstanding its claim of fair and balanced news, Fox permitted a vice president for policy at Americans for Prosperity (AFP)—an arm of oil conglomerate Koch Industries and a prominent financier of the Tea Party movement—to contribute to its website, and a director for the organization often guest-hosted for Rush Limbaugh. Shortly after Obama's election, AFP began a series of training sessions for Tea Party activists. At one such session in Texas, the event was advertised (without apparent irony) as an opportunity to thwart corporate influence on the government: "Today, the voices of average Americans are being drowned out by lobbyists and special interests. But you can do something about it" (quoted in Mayer, 2010, p. 46).

From a media standpoint, the information environment has reduced the threshold for the emergence of ideologically committed publics as news audiences have become more homogenous. A fragmented, partisan information system increases the incentives for offering more extreme points of view. The logic of targeted audiences has led to the creation of an array of ideological distilleries for the consumption of purified points of view. Economic incentives for media increase the value of uniform audiences that can be packaged for advertisers interested in reaching precisely targeted sociodemographic groups (Turow, 1997). With conflict as a staple of audience appeal, partisan media have strong incentives to promote position issues that elicit strident attacks on political rivals. In terms of the uncertainty model, the segmented information environment has raised the perceived risk exposure for disquieting events. New internet-based media have thus far reproduced the same pattern.

At first thought to be a source of increased information and a stimulus for greater political participation (e.g., Benkler, 2006), new media sources such as blogs are read almost exclusively by small partisan audiences (Lawrence et al., 2010). The emphasis here is on *small* as visits to political sites represent less than one-tenth of one percent of all web traffic; the largest traffic goes to shopping and pornography sites. The number of sites visited is also small, the result of a winner-takes-all phenomenon (power law distribution) explained by the logic of search engines (Hindman, 2009). Research also shows that blogs have been "hijacked" by traditional elite media (e.g., *The New York Times*), a result of the circulation of ideas and opinion among trusted sources in partisan networks (Meraz, 2009). The networks tend to homogeneity as, for example, A-list bloggers (especially conservatives) are more likely link to others who reflect their own political views than rivals (Adamic & Glance, 2005). As we reviewed in chapter 2, comparisons of partisan ideological purity (e.g., Lawrence et al., 2010) consistently show increased homogeneity on the right, a resource for maintaining message consistency, identity, and solidarity for the attentive conservative public.

In sum, the present media environment has contributed to selective exposure and increased polarization (Bennett & Iyengar, 2008; cf. Holbert et al., 2010). The structural changes have also lowered the threshold for the emergence of position issue movements that draw upon culturally resonant themes. The rise of the Tea Party illustrates the new symbiosis.

The Tea Party

Supporters of the Tea Party aimed to reduce the size of the federal deficit and of the government, an endorsement of key elements of economic regime promoted during and since the Reagan administration. While critics doubted the movement's authenticity and the sincerity of its stated goals, supporters saw it as a spontaneous, forceful rejection of the Obama administration's Keynesian policy of government spending to revive demand. The movement represented a reaction to a domestic issue entrained in the global evolution of the US economy, namely the offshoring of jobs and rising anxiety about economic security. As in the case of opposition to immigration reform—a high risk exposure issue for the Tea Party—resistance had little to do with economic self-interest. Instead, it was projected on what supporters regarded as outsiders who threatened a way of life, a classic theme of symbolic politics.

Contrary to reports that the movement and its supporters were made up of working-class, out-of-work rednecks, supporters of the Tea Party (about one-fifth of Americans) were middle-class whites who were more likely than the general public to say their personal financial situation was fairly good or very good. A *New York Times* poll (Zernike & Thee-Brennan, 2010) found that despite their present job security, however, over half were worried that someone in their household would be out of a job by the following year. Tea Party supporters faced an uncertain future and resented a governing class that they saw as feckless as it was intrusive, both fiscally and morally.

Movement supporters endorsed an assortment of beliefs and values drawn from neoclassical economics and libertarianism that were charged with the cultural resonance of the nation's founding principles. Beliefs in the inherent fairness and justice of an unregulated market, low inflation, and the primacy of individual liberty amounted to an endorsement of neoliberalism. In her review of the extensive literature on the doctrine, Mudge (2011) traced its roots to moral philosophy: "As an intellectual creation, neoliberalism is rooted in a strand of economic thought that views markets as the spontaneous expression of individual desires—that is, as synonymous with freedom itself" (p. 345). The Tea Party was an expression of neoliberal principles in a tightly disciplined, self-managed political movement that aimed for purity of expression, an ironic turn on its avowed principle of individual liberty. That the discipline would be maintained despite the movement's nonhierarchical structure attested to the strength of identity and solidarity of its participants and supporters.

Unlike traditional movements, the Tea Party had no charismatic leaders or a central geographic location. New forms of mediated information enabled the movement supporters and sympathizers to refine their message and mobilize for events and political campaigns in a dispersed network. The network did include top-down nodes such as traditional advocacy groups that included Freedom Works and AFP. The two organizations had split off from Citizens for a Sound Economy (CSE) but advocated identical goals. CSE was a conservative, libertarian advocacy organization founded by brothers Charles and David Koch, principal owners of Koch Industries, the second largest privately owned firm whose holdings include oil pipelines, refineries, agricultural chemicals, and paper mills. Registered as nonprofit organizations, AFP and Freedom Works were in the early decades of the 21st century two of the most influential conservative issue advocacy groups in the United States. They both sought to leverage the movement to advance their goals of deregulating financial derivatives and the discharge of greenhouse gases.

Despite the outsized influence of Freedom Works and AFP, the Tea Party movement retained its autonomy, at least in the opinion of its local organizers (Von Drehle et al., 2010).* One reason for the movement's ostensible independence was its structure, an estimated 800 local groups with memberships that ranged from 1,000 to as few as 20 or 30. In their study of the movement, Skocpol and Williams (2012) estimated 200,000 members nationwide.

The movement expressed its independence as distrust of mainstream GOP politicians and a movement culture that prized liberty. The latter embodied a paradox that explains the solidarity and ideological coherence of the movement. Although members cherished individual liberty, they policed one another on adherence to first principles. In policy terms, this meant reducing taxes and the federal deficit but, especially, repealing the Affordable Care Act (Obamacare).

Supporters were deeply resentful of who they considered undeserving recipients of federal largesse—illegal immigrants, African Americans, and the younger generation, key voting blocs in Obama's winning coalition. As the policy embodiment of threats to the Tea Party's goals, Obama and liberals were regarded as political enemies. The line of demarcation between us and them yielded a potent source of identity and solidarity for the movement. In a sum-

---

* Skocpol and Williamson (2012) reported that "most Tea Party activists we interviewed knew little or nothing about Freedom Works or the other national free-market organizations promoting the Tea Party brand."

mary of their analysis of Tea Party websites, Atkinson and Berg (2012) found a world populated by "villains who do not live up to the standards set in the Bible and established by the Founding Fathers" (p. 530).

The pairing of religion with politics revealed the composition of the coalition that made up the Tea Party's constituencies. The Tea Party shared the Christian Right's distrust of the federal government, so much so that a Venn diagram of Tea Party supporters and white evangelical Protestants would show considerable overlap. A Pew Research Center Forum on Religion and Public Life report (2011) found that Tea Party supporters had conservative opinions about economic matters as well as social issues such as abortion and same-sex marriage. The organizational skills of religious groups that joined the movement improved the ability of the Tea Party to publicize, organize, and mobilize around issues of culture and identity (Guth & Green, 1996), while ties to partisan media such as Fox News formed a recursive system that preserved ideational uniformity and movement solidarity.*

Public figures who failed to adhere to standards of ideological purity were exposed as "frauds" at rallies and in new media. A study of the campaign Facebook sites of Tea Party primary candidates (Morin & Flynn, 2014) found an efficient system of policing Tea Party primary candidate websites by using polarizing language to identify and expose "trolls." Facebook comments revealed an identity perceived to be under siege: "Thus it is imperative that the identity be sustained through attacking opponents and encouraging supporters and candidates" (p. 128). Tea Party primary candidates maintained the ideological purity of their campaigns by creating an impression of victimhood at the hands of their political rivals.

Contrasting left-wing from right-wing movements in the new information environment, Atkinson and Berg (2012) concluded that unlike OWS, the Tea Party was "not nearly as nebulous or vague as the themes from liberal-leaning alternative media, as it outlines quite clearly who is welcome to take part . . . and who is not" (p. 531). As is discussed in chapter 8, OWS denied itself a clearly defined identity by welcoming any and all who made up all but the highest one percent of income groups. Ironically, until the emergence of OWS, the politics of cultural difference had largely replaced the more universal issue of economic inequality, effectively ceding it to conservative populist movements like the Tea Party. The left had been fractured in the late 1970s and early 1980s, crucially

---

* The network sponsored Tea Party events and sent its celebrity hosts to speak at those events.

among left-leaning evangelicals who were divided on issues of identity and separation of church and state (Swartz, 2011).

Disintegration of the evangelical left ceded majority influence to conservative evangelicals, growing in number, wealth, and political organization (Guth & Green, 1996). With the party realignment that followed the civil rights revolution, the GOP inherited the support of a large group of constituents whose tight social networks formed through intensive church activity could facilitate rapid and intense political mobilization (Campbell, 2004). The Tea Party drew on this network for organizational support and its antigovernment rhetoric. The latter represented a common impulse in US political history, the threshold for its most recent manifestation significantly lowered by the uncertainties of the new economy and nearly universal risk exposure of the Great Recession. Suspicion of illegal immigrants and of conventional party politics amplified the solidarity of the Tea Party.

Suspicion of the mainstream GOP did not mean, as in the case of OWS, disengagement from institutionalized politics, however. The Tea Party promoted its candidates for office in primary campaigns, often nominating those who were too extreme for voters in the general election. Interest groups gain by the difference between primary and general election voters, because motivated voters who pay close attention to primary campaigns are also affiliated or are in touch with interest groups and activists. The attending solidarity and message discipline enhances the capacity of policy demanders to influence primary elections (Bawn et al., 2012). Voter ignorance also contributes to more extreme positions as swing voters who might otherwise change their vote instead retain their support. Bawn and colleagues called this the "electoral blind spot."

The public event credited with giving birth to the movement took place on cable television on February 19, 2009. Amid a federal bailout of banks and other large financial institutions, as well as the US auto industry, Rick Santelli, a CNBC business editor, redirected blame to those who would bear the tax burden of federal bailouts and, inadvertently, focus groupcentric ire on irresponsible individuals: "How many of you people want to pay for your neighbor's mortgage that has an extra bathroom and can't pay their bills? Raise your hand!" The question reframed the bailout as rewarding the moral hazard of irresponsible individuals rather than the institutions that had caused it.

A group naming itself the Tea Party Patriots thanked Santelli for the "spark" that started a movement that morphed several times to subsume several themes and political ends. In the framework of the uncertainty model, Santelli's statement resonated with a segment of the population who shared an anxious view of their future status, distrust of the federal government, and of the "takers" who benefited by government support. That the party out of power and partisan media shared in the propagation of these sentiments helped the movement gain considerable influence in the 2010 midterm elections.

Despite its small number of supporters, the movement's passion and mobilizing skills led to a major shift in power just two years after Barack Obama's decisive victory. In 2010 Tea Party candidates won the House, reduced the Democratic majority in the Senate, and increased the number of GOP governors. The success of the movement would depend on its legitimation by supporters beyond its relatively small circle of activists. In a partisan information environment, acceptance by mainstream media would be an indicator of the movement's success.

Media and Contemporary Movements

Prior to the 1990s, political movements calibrated their strategies in part to anticipate the reaction of the mass media, principle carriers of movement messages to a potentially responsive public, a hopeful application of Schattschneider's (1960) proposition that "the outcome of all conflict is determined by the scope of its contagion" (p. 2). Until the collapse of the Soviet bloc and the proliferation of information technologies, the scope of conflict could be contained by the discursive limits imposed by political and media elites (Gitlin, 1980). The disappearance of the signature exemplar of opposition to capitalism deprived elites of an ideological demon for vitiating political dissent, and the rapid growth and development of a digital communication infrastructure offered the promise of reducing the power of corporate media and thereby the hegemony of state control over responses to challenges to its preferred issue frames. To be sure, elite dissensus would remain a key structural resource for political movements (Eisinger, 1973; Bennett, 2003), but those lower in the cascade of power (Entman, 2004) seemed particularly advantaged by the changed environment, especially because of the emergence of partisan media.

Because of these changes, the mainstream media (i.e., "broadcast news") gained a newfound status as nonpartisan referees in the national debate. Owing to a balancing practice in the service of the journalistic norm of objectivity, mainstream media content provides an indicator of legitimation for political movements. Media reaction to the Tea Party movement in national partisan and mainstream outlets provides an opportunity to test this hypothesis and to gauge the group and message cohesiveness that would contribute to its influence on national politics.

Broadcast Coverage

For the analysis, I focus on television news. As I pointed out in chapter 5, it remains the principal source of information for more than half of Americans. I coded Nexis broadcast transcripts of Tea Party coverage between February 19, 2009 (the day of Santelli's rant on CNBC), and November 9, 2010 (election day), on Fox Special Report, the network's daily evening news show (194 stories), and MSNBC's Countdown, then the most highly rated program on the cable channel (229 stories). I also analyze coverage of ABC World News (105 stories) on the hypothesis that mainstream network news provides an indication of movement success. A balanced account that traces a path between partisan sources would indicate a neutral perspective that does little to induce independents to one side or another; one that favors one side or the other indicates either a resource for movement mobilization or one that dampens its efforts. I analyze media framing of the movement's origins, participants, and goals.

For origins, I coded whether the movement represented (1) a spontaneous, authentic impulse from ordinary citizens who felt disempowered by institutional politics or (2) a confected movement organized by corporate interests for advancing narrow interests. For movement participants, I coded media source perceptions of their (1) rationality and (2) their representativeness of mainstream public opinion. For goals, I coded the (1) legitimacy and (2) desirability of movement policy ends.

Origins

Analysis of the overage reveals a recurring pattern, a mainstream ABC fulcrum that tilted toward the positive Fox side of the ledger and presented a largely sympathetic view of the movement. The partisan outlets, meanwhile, presented accounts of contradicting realities. Thus where Fox reported the spontaneous appearance of a grassroots movement, MSNBC defined it as an "astroturf" movement sponsored by Washington lobbyists and the product of "a familiar circle of Republicans, including former House Speaker Newt Gingrich and former House Majority Leader Dick Armey, both of whom have firm support from right-wing financiers" (April 13, 2009). Over the course of its coverage, MSNBC's reporters and guests mentioned *astroturf* or *fake tea party* 39 times and linked the movement to Fox News 40 times, singling out its cable rival as a key supporter and as (accurately) involved in organizing and sponsoring movement events.

Fox used the term *tea partiers* for the first time in mid-March 2009 and framed the movement as a bottom-up, spontaneous, nationwide protest by taxpayers "largely ignored by the mainstream media" (March 16, 2009). Sample frame indicators that highlighted the authenticity and spontaneity of the movement included "sprouting up coast to coast" (April 19, 2009), large numbers of "independently sponsored" events (April 14, 2009), the mundanity of home-made materials—markers and posterboard—used by individuals to articulate individual grievances, and the use of volunteer websites and social networking to link movement sympathizers: "The political right seems as adept, if not more adept, at using social networking, the Internet, Twitter, Facebook, to use the Internet to have these net roots sort of organizations. These people turned out because of organizations that were plied online" (April 15, 2009).

ABC opened its coverage of the movement with a reference to Fox and talk radio "cheering on" the movement (April 15, 2009), but subsequent reports made only one reference to then Fox personality Glenn Beck's role in providing a face for what it described as a leaderless, "loosely organized," and "self-styled" movement (April 15, 2009). Like Fox, and very much unlike MSNBC, ABC credited social networking sites as the organizing locus of what it judged a spontaneous movement. The absence of any further references by ABC reporters to the symbiotic relationship between Fox News and the Tea Party could be explained by the negative reaction to the Obama administration's complaint in fall 2009 of Fox as a communications arm of the Republican Party. The mainstream press rallied to a professional defense of Fox as a legitimate journalistic competitor and, coincidentally, dropped references to its institutional connection to the Tea Party. ABC reporters never used the term *astroturf* in its coverage of the movement.

Participants

Fox's most frequent characterization of Tea Party backers was as a cross-section of the entire nation. Early reports described participants as earnest, ordinary citizens who had sacrificed the comforts of home to make their voices heard: "In Philadelphia, just blocks from Independence Hall, where our democracy was born, several hundred tea party protesters braved the cold, piercing rain and called on the spirit of our founding fathers" (April 15, 2009). Later coverage referred to the broad base of the movement: "It's not just, you know, white, you know, white voters. It's old people, young people, housewives, you know, people from all walks of life and, by the way, many minorities included" (July 24, 2010).

Fox analysts used *energized* as their most frequent descriptor (26 references), and found the source of that energy in the movement's moral duty to future generations and to the redemption of a federal government "hijacked" by overreaching liberalism. When the NAACP denounced the movement as racist, Fox offered a spirited defense: "Any organization that has honored the likes of Louis Farrakhan, Jeremiah Wright, Jesse Jackson, [and] Al Sharpton has no credibility on this issue and has no business casting stones" (July 18, 2010). A lone dissenter, Juan Williams said the charges were understandable given the large number of Tea Party supporters who doubted Obama's US citizenship and the signs at rallies that declared him a socialist and a communist.

MSNBC did not regard Fox reporting of movement participants as credible in the least and offered a yin to Fox's yang. Where Fox saw an energized mainstream electorate, MSNBC saw "tea baggers" as irrational extremists: "They don't know their history at all. This is about hating a black man in the White House. This is racism straight up" (April 16, 2009). MSNBC reporters and guests made 226 references to racists and 199 to racism in the course of their coverage of the Tea Party.

In general, MSNBC depictions of the participants gravitated between two poles: as driven by unreason and hatred or as dupes led by self-serving GOP elites (e.g., Dick Armey) or Fox television commentators (Sean Hannity, Glenn Beck) and right-wing radio hosts: "a bunch of sheep ordered around by professional politicians" (May, 19, 2009). The sheep-like quality of movement sympathizers was explained by ignorance of their own best interests: "Tea party protestors who believe they are against government-run health care either don't know or don't care that they are at this moment receiving government health care" (August 5, 2009). Occasional references to movement leaders (coalition builders) derided their hypocrisy as tax cheats (May 14, 2009) or as employers of illegal immigrants (June 16, 2009). As the movement matured, MSNBC analysts traced disruptions at town hall meetings of health care reforms to "fake tea partiers" (August 4, 2009), a reference to the influence of GOP operatives rather than good-faith protests from informed citizens.

ABC presented a momma bear account of movement supporters, angry (14 references) and occasionally as "fringe" but more frequently as rationally motivated and as representative of a cross-section of Americans: "Meet the tea partiers: A nurse from Pennsylvania with her daughter. An American Airlines pilot from Texas with his son. A property manager from Atlanta" (April 15, 2010).

Over time, ABC commentators noted the uncompromising ideological tenor of the Tea Party's demands but regarded this as symptomatic of American politics in general rather than as extremism of Tea Party supporters or as a calculated attempt by the GOP to restore its political influence: "Once upon a time, there were moderates in the Republican Party, and there were conservatives in the

Democratic Party. No more. That era is gone. The parties used to be coalitions of diverse interests, kind of a hodgepodge of people from around the country. They have shifted to more European style, ideological parties. And that makes governing tough. That makes compromise hard" (February 20, 2010).

By contrast to the dominant theme of racism in MSNBC coverage (nearly two references per show), ABC barely touched on the topic, making only ten references to racism or racists altogether (one-twentieth that of MSNBC), the majority in a single story that balanced NAACP accusations of Tea Party racism against denials by Congresswoman Michelle Bachmann and a cofounder of a NYC Tea Party (July 13, 2009).

Goals

In keeping with the partisan nature of their reporting, Fox and MSNBC framed the goals of the movement as praiseworthy or blameworthy, respectively. The interesting dimension of Fox reporting was its cautionary view of the movement as a potential threat to the mainline GOP. In this respect, Fox coverage saw the movement's goals for small government and reduced taxes as laudable goals but also showed concern for its tendency to nominate unelectable candidates or break up the GOP coalition: "Republican candidates like Sharon Angle in Nevada and Rand Paul in Kentucky have benefited from grassroots tea party support, but whether they can win in November is still an open question and if they do make it to Washington, it's unclear whether they will change the GOP or whether the GOP will change them" (July 24, 2010).

MSNBC dismissed the goals of the movement as, at best, a distraction from its true purpose, an attempt by GOP elites to rebuild the party decimated by the excesses of the Bush administration and the poor leadership of then minority House leaders John Boehner and Eric Cantor: "They don't have a great deal of faith in this strategy and that's why it's been delegated somewhat at arm's length. That's why they're pretending that this is a grassroots movement" (April 13, 2009). Portrayal of movement participants as dupes dovetailed with MSNBC's dismissal of their aims at reducing spending as distractions from their anger at the architects of the financial crisis and expression of their hatred of the president (April 16, 2009).

While not taking a position on the movement's goals, ABC's coverage echoed that of Fox with respect to the implications of the Tea Party for the fortunes of the Republican Party. Especially after Scott Brown's surprise Senate victory in Massachusetts, ABC framed the movement more as an institutional challenge to the GOP and, by implication, of its record of deficit spending during the

George W. Bush administration: "Republicans have benefited from this movement, but they may not be immune from Tea Party activist anger themselves" (January 20, 2010).

As the movement became integrated with the institutional structures of the GOP itself (e.g., CPAC), ABC commentators echoed the Washington establishment concerns of Fox analysts, whether the sometimes undisciplined energy and anger of a populist movement could be contained by the mainline party. Within a month of the 2010 midterm elections, ABC political analysts said that the GOP had in fact contained the movement. The most extreme candidates were fated to lose, while the winners would become conventional Republicans. This may have been a premature conclusion.

Successful Tea Party candidates formed a Congressional caucus that successfully pressured the GOP for the end of earmarks and for fiscal austerity that had important implications for economic recovery and policy that would cushion the effects of a globalized economy. They also forced a hardline on raising the debt ceiling that led to a lowered Standard and Poor's credit rating for the nation. In the negotiations, Barack Obama was prepared to "reform" social security and Medicare in a deal with House Republicans, an indication that the movement had succeeded in putting the social safety net at risk and thereby fueling the politics of insecurity that had given it its impetus.

In summary, the first successful political movement of the post–Cold War era drew on a number of structural advantages and a resonant historical tradition. The movement benefitted by the aid of a partisan, self-interested media ally and corporate interests that provided financial and ideological support that belied the spontaneous, home-grown public image it projected. Fox legitimated the Tea Party in a symbiotic feedback loop that enhanced the power of the movement as well as the network's political influence. The reaction from MSNBC perhaps unwittingly provided the movement with a more muscular identity than it could have achieved through the more measured and tempered coverage it received on mainstream television. By avoiding the extremist characterizations common on MSNBC, ABC lent the movement the legitimacy it needed to reach beyond an ideologically committed minority.

From the standpoint of institutional politics, the movement's ties to the GOP were unencumbered by compromises made by the most recent Democratic presidents that shifted the party away from its base of support. Both Clinton and Obama had moved to the right on issues of fair trade, accepting major elements of the deregulated free-market economic regime put in place by Ronald Reagan. Claiming to be better stewards of the economy, Democrats adopted a pragmatic, opportunistic style of leadership that increased their vulnerability to charges of inauthenticity, nihilism, and manipulation (Skowronek, 2008) but, more importantly, distanced them from their base. Though GOP leadership had some problems containing Tea Party House members, the party had reinforced its position with its base.

Political culture also played a key role in the success of the movement in hampering the Obama administration's plan for economic recovery by denying it the additional tax revenues needed to sustain the social safety net. As we learned in chapter 1, there is greater support for the social safety net in the advanced economies of Western Europe. The groupcentric politics of the Tea Party point to the heterogeneity of the US population as one explanation for resistance. Another is the resonant belief that individual effort rather than luck leads to success, the ironic residue of Calvinist Protestantism that led to greater effort for a heavenly reward despite the doctrine of election. This has been noted by political scholars as one of the reasons for Americans' preference for liberty over equality for economic outcomes (McCloskey & Zaller, 1984; Bartels, 2008). The demographic homogeneity of Tea Party supporters, their strategic and ideological link to conservative Protestant religion, and the zeal they practiced for policing their message and those of their favored candidates provide a textbook example of effective (though perhaps misdirected) movement politics under conditions of high insecurity and partisan gridlock.

Conclusion

The Tea Party responded energetically to the uncertainties of the Great Recession. The absence of an alternative vision led to a doubling down on a set of beliefs that supported policies that had led to the crisis in the first place. An efficient system of message policing maintained group solidarity and concomitant pressure on Tea Party–endorsed candidates to hew to their demands.

A wider perspective on macroscopic changes and the history of US moral reform movements suggests that right-wing movements gain an advantage over left-wing movements in this new environment on four fronts: (1) a disjuncture between the high-speed investment circuits of a global political economy and the diminished life chances of labor, place-rooted and weakened by its diminished bargaining position; (2) labor's continuing reliance on a fiscally weakened state for relief from the disruptions of a globalized economy; (3) the inertial advantage of a political culture that draws on a tradition of evangelical Protestant political activism (and, ironically, to reactions to federal enforcement of institutionalized reforms); the latter strengthened by (4) the failure of the left to develop an effective political critique and a discourse for promoting a less state-centric form of global citizenship.

The latter were reinforced by elite policy consensus on economic and security issues that restricts the discursive space for dissent, the increased organizational prowess of interest groups on the right that draw on elements of political culture made resonant by a succession of religiously founded moral reform movements and their effect on the coherence and consistency of beliefs, and a new information environment that has changed the partisan risk profile for news media. Exposure to one-sided perspectives generates increased emotional, belief-driven energy, the fuel for group solidarity.

Like the Tea Party movement, OWS responded to the universally felt risk exposure of a continuing economic downturn, but its target was income inequality rather than fiscal policy. The evidence suggests that left-leaning movements will experience greater resistance achieving their ends than movements on the right. The chief reasons for their comparative disadvantage are both structural and cultural. The most daunting structural barriers include the lacuna between political and economic institutions and the rightward shift of the Democratic Party on economic policy. On the first point, democratically responsive institutions have yet to be established that align with economic institutions such as the WTO, World Bank, and the IMF. The political remains bound to geography and nation even as the economy is unconfined by either.

On the second point, the mainstream Democratic Party continues to be influenced by the Democratic Leadership Council on fiscal policy. Both Clinton and Obama emerged as standard bearers of its policy platform. In a statement posted on the DLC website, Harold Ford (2010), chairman of the organization, articulated a position that would not meet much resistance from Tea Party supporters:

> American disgust with politics is driven by the fact that, unlike families who have to make tough choices about their own budgets, Washington seems unable to live within its means. The Fiscal Commission has forced Democrats and Republicans to sit down across a table and hash out their differences. In the near term, we need to embrace tax cuts that spur business investment, stimulate job creation, and lift wages for the middle class. But the Commission's recommendations—cutting spending and reforming the tax code—get to the meat of our long-term challenge: lowering our national debt. This is the dose of fiscal sanity we need.

The movement's cultural deficit is a more serious problem, the result of the fragmentation of the left on identity politics (e.g., Gitlin, 1995), most serious among evangelicals who inherit the nation's history of political reform. The appellation Christian Right is less assertion of a singular identity than what remains of what was once a unified religious movement that championed civil rights and other progressive causes.

OWS is the latest eruption of what was once the misnamed "antiglobalization" movement, this time focused on a nascent politics rather than specific policies, a necessity borne of the unique circumstances it faced in the politics of insecurity. We now turn to an analysis of these movements on the left.

CHAPTER EIGHT

Reactions from the Left
Global Justice and Occupy Wall Street

Two years after the Tea Party came into existence, the economic uncertainties created by the Great Recession continued to reverberate, so much so that a second political movement arose in reaction, this time on the left. While political movements can be studied individually, they do not exist in historical isolation. The Tea Party and Occupy Wall Street movements shared a number of common features: both were suspicious of mainstream political and media institutions, both adopted the affordances of the World Wide Web to mobilize participants and share ideas, and both maintained a leaderless, nonhierarchical structure. On the latter point, both replicated the social media savvy and organizational agility of the global justice movement, an indication that the information environment was having an independent influence on the nature of grassroots politics. Where the two movements differed was on the nature and degree of their political influence. While the Tea Party would achieve a lasting impact on conservative politics, OWS only landed a glancing blow on the liberal establishment. OWS did not survive the winter of 2011–2012, less than five months after its birth in New York City. It did, however, leave a meme—the 99 percent and the one percent—a potential cultural anchor for future movements, but no discernible immediate effect on the ways Americans thought about policies that would respond to their economic uncertainties.

There were multiple reasons for OWS's failure to effect immediate change. From the standpoint of the uncertainty model, it failed to sustain the passion of its participants and supporters, in part because of the continuing inability of the intellectual left to articulate a compelling alternative to the existing neoliberal economic regime. As a result, the movement necessarily fell back on a nebulous vision that sought inspiration in wistful possibility rather than hard-edged policy. OWS was also handicapped by the continuing absence of a resonant appeal to equality of outcomes for Americans. For example, poll data show that although large majorities of Americans believe that the wealth gap is a problem, when asked to choose the greater problem between the income gap and economic mobility, more than two-thirds select the issue of economic mobility (Timiraos, 2015). As we reviewed in chapter 2, continuing ambivalence among Americans about equality—in favor of equal opportunity but against redistributive policy—indicates that the belief in individual effort that drove the Tea Party continues to be a potent cultural force multiplier.

In this chapter, we study the declining fortunes of the political movements on the left that responded to the economic uncertainties of globalization. We begin with the global justice movement. Though it had some early success, it could not withstand the cumulative effects of the issues and changes in political culture that followed 9/11.

Global Justice

From a scholarly perspective, leftist movement politics in the age of globalization have sailed into uncharted waters. This is because their target for reform is no longer exclusively the nation-state but corporations and intergovernmental organizations (IGOs) that govern cross-border economic transactions and capital flows. Nation-states have the power to negotiate agreements with institutions such as the World Trade Organization (WTO), but discussions are conducted in secret and insulated from democratic influence. As we reviewed in chapter 1, threats to individual economic security expose citizens to risks that cannot be entirely addressed by state policy. Americans are particularly disadvantaged in this respect because there is diminished public support for reinforcing the social safety net that would help those whose lives are disrupted by structural changes in the economy.

In a contest between advocates and opponents of global economic integration, advocates have the simpler argument to make. Advocates of economic globalization extol the long-term benefits (e.g., Wolf, 2004; Friedman, 2005), while opponents object to multiple unrelated issues that include despoilment of local environments, exploitation of unorganized labor, and increased income inequality (Rapley, 2004). The left has a more challenging task than the right not only because of the multiplicity of its policy aims and constituencies, but also because key political actors such as corporations and IGOs like the IMF are more immune to direct political pressure than elected representatives. The story of the global justice movement illustrates these and other obstacles to its success in the politics of insecurity.

The Battle of Seattle

A mass demonstration in 1999 that successfully disrupted the WTO meetings in Seattle signaled a change in movement politics and in the dynamics of the demonstration itself. Protestors mounted a politically effective coalition with (among other key Democratic constituencies) labor unions that put Bill Clinton in an untenable position. By supporting increased free trade, Clinton would tacitly agree to the acceleration of off-shoring US manufacturing operations to the cheapest labor pools abroad, to those nations with no labor unions or little or nonexistent environmental regulation. As Clinton conceded that the movement had a point on the exploitation of labor, protestors evaded the best efforts of the Seattle Police Department to prevent the shutdown of the meetings by using a variety of web-based functions to mobilize members, coordinate strategy, and provide expertise.

A flat, network-based model of organization enabled protestors to use a flexible strategy of confrontation that eluded containment (Rojecki, 2002). The Seattle protests also marked the birth of what came to be known as Indymedia—Independent Media Center (IMC)—a group of independent journalists who used the web to provide an alternative source of reporting freed from what they regarded as the constraints imposed by mainstream commercial media. Taking their cue from national and local political elites who could not defend WTO immunity from democratic governance, mainstream media treated the protest with much more nuance and deference than one would have expected from earlier studies of political protest during the Cold War (Bennett, 2003b). Compared to media reception of Cold War movements (e.g., Gitlin, 1980; Entman & Rojecki, 1993), the GJM received unusually sympathetic media treatment, a striking indication of material change that had weakened a once resonant component of US political culture. The collapse of the Soviet Union made it more difficult for movement opponents to link dissent with disloyalty to the state. GJM participants could now lay claim to the mantle of loyalty to country and state, its environment, and its workers, while corporations and the regulatory bodies that sought to enlarge world markets struggled to find an ethical high ground other than that based on efficiency, profit, or trickle-down economics. The conditions enlarged the field of acceptable discourse and positioned global justice appeals within a field of resonant political values. The national press accepted the authority and sensibility of movement leaders, portrayed participants as having sufficient grasp of underlying issues, and acknowledged the movement's political effectiveness (Rojecki, 2002).

In the years after the black swan of 9/11, the GJM faced numerous obstacles. Worried that mass demonstrations could be interpreted as threats to state security, GJM leaders pulled back from confrontations. For their part, anticipating disruptions, state organizers of meetings of the WTO, G8, IMF, and other IGOs opted for remote (e.g., Doha) or easily secured venues for their meetings. Meanwhile, the web-based sites for mobilization and training of movement activists also became useful resources for the effective design of countermeasures by political elites who learned not to be surprised as Seattle authorities. The Seattle demonstration led to increased cooperation, cross-training, and border control among states for crowd control, and even to negotiations between local police forces and demonstrators themselves (O'Neill, 2004).

Most important, as we learned in chapter 3, after 9/11, political elites on the right and the left had prescribed a beefed-up security state and economic liberalization to reduce terrorism. A discursive field dominated by elite consensus on free trade reduced opportunities for the GJM to advance provisions for unionization of foreign workers and measures for environmental regulation. These largely unchallenged prescriptions reduced movement leverage on free-trade policy, so much so that by the end of his presidency, George W. Bush had signed 14 free-trade agreements. Weakened by elite consensus on free trade as well as the absence of a persuasive intellectual critique of market capitalism—in part the product of a failure on the academic left to imagine a new kind of society (Rorty, 1998; Jacoby, 1999)—the GJM lacked the resonant ideas (and financial support) to withstand attacks by its foes.[*]

Meanwhile, de facto US policy reflected the preferences of powerful interest groups: for example, its selective enforcement of NAFTA (Stiglitz, 2007), which increased the perceived risk exposure and anger that fueled the Tea Party. By the mid-2000s, the GJM had become a virtual, networked transnational movement with diminished influence (Rojecki, 2011). The GJM had some success in influencing consumption and lifestyle choices, but its larger ambitions had been thwarted.

Explaining Transnational Global Movements

Because its targets included a transnational set of political actors, scholars identified the GJM as the first widely reported example of transnational protest, a "coordinated international campaign on the part of networks of activists against

---

[*] Arrighi (1990) argued that the left has weakened to the extent it has divided along gender and ethnicity lines to obtain privileged treatment from capital.

international actors, other states, or international institutions" (della Porta & Tarrow, 2005, pp. 2–3). The protests represented a signal example of post–Cold War protest in a new media environment that called for a reassessment of the concepts and theory on the media politics of dissent (Cottle, 2008).

Scholars who sought to map the multiple changes in movement strategies and tactics opened new theoretical grounds for explaining such things as the resurgence of once quiescent political structures (e.g., NGOs) and seemingly spontaneous outbursts of collective dissent. McAdam, Tarrow, and Tilly (2001) formulated the concept of scale shift to define the broadening of protest beyond state borders, and della Porta and Tarrow (2005) coined the concepts of diffusion, domestication, and externalization to map the dynamics of protest that hopscotched national borders.

Skeptics, meanwhile, doubted the staying power of these new political actors or the promise of an energized public sphere. Capitalism had retained and even enhanced its ideological power, and states continued to rely on nationalism to shore up their political power, especially in times of crisis. The fall of the World Trade Center may have brought down a symbol of US economic prowess, but it reinvigorated the power of the national security state. Thus far, the reaction against the global economic downturn of the late 2000s has focused less on neoliberalism than the Tea Party's opposition to government application of Keynesian policy. This demonstrates the resilience of an economic regime whose excesses would spark OWS. In sum, the GJM could not articulate a resonant critique of an economic regime that had contributed to the economic uncertainties that faced American workers.

In his analysis of the GJM, Bennett (2003b) noted its ideological thinness, an overdetermined effect that resulted from the numerous interests involved in the GJM coalition. Thus a campaign against Microsoft included competing businesses such as Sun and Oracle, consumer protection organizations, "hacktivists" (individuals who engage in civil cyber disobedience, e.g., flooding a website with numerous requests and thereby effectively shutting it down), and even a Republican senator. From this broad spectrum, conflicting interests inevitably arise, making it difficult to sustain a coherent and powerful "collective action frame" (Snow & Benford, 1992; cf. Van Aelst & Walgrave, 2004; le Grignou & Patou, 2004). Moreover, the low costs of involvement explain corresponding low commitment and weakness of self-identification. It is one thing to sign a petition on a Facebook page, but it is quite another to give time to a campaign committed to a movement goal.

To this analysis I would add that the movement's ideological thinness was largely a product of its inherently reformist nature. The GJM was not opposed to global market capitalism per se but merely its governance (see, e.g., Clark, 2000).* Further, it is unclear whether a hard-edged critique can be launched from the consumption-driven lifestyle and identity politics of postmodern society (e.g., Jameson, 1984; Giddens, 1991, Castells, 1997). Bennett (2003b) argues that individual narratives linked to networks of other such lifestyle narratives have displaced hierarchical institutions as sources of identification and social recognition. Some theorists (Castells, 1996; Arquilla & Ronfeldt, 2001) declare this seeming weakness a strength: robust and adaptable, networks of activists are led more by a reliable common political agenda than a potentially vulnerable centralized leadership. Harcourt and Escobar's (2002) concept of "meshworks" draws on the systems and information theory–driven concept of "emergence" to describe the self-organizing dynamics of a movement embedded (and constituted) in a communication network:

> [M]eshworks tend to be nonhierarchical and self-organizing. They are created out of the interlocking of heterogeneous and diverse elements brought together because of complementarity or common experiences. They grow in unplanned directions. Anti-globalization social movements, in their heterogeneity and self-organizing character, might be seen as incipient meshworks of this kind. Meshworks involve two parallel dynamics: strategies of localization and of interweaving. Localization strategies contribute to the internal consistency of each particular point in the network, as well as making it more distinct from the rest. Interweaving, on the other hand, links sites together, making use of and emphasizing their similarities. (pp. 12–13)

Harcourt and Escobar's concept uses a network metaphor as a heuristic to develop a conceptual and theoretical vocabulary for analyzing transnational movements. Grassroots political actors are conceptualized as nodes in the dispersed communication technology of the World Wide Web. For example, unlike the civil rights and new left movements that preceded it, what is most striking about the GJM is its facelessness, fluidity, and organizational anonymity (also true for Tea Party members). A large number of networked individuals of indeterminate identity (nodes) linked to one another and to organizations that come and go (hubs) have replaced the charisma of readily identifiable leaders. The consequence of this low-cost membership is resilience that avoids the pitfalls of coalition

---

* Scholarship on globalization has also moved from issues regarding its authenticity and desirability (e.g., Jameson, 1991; Gray, 1998; Hardt & Negri, 2000) to its proper management (Stiglitz, 2007; Howse, 2008).

building, compromise on a single issue, and cooptation but also ideological clarity and coherence (Bennett, 2003b).

Recent work by Bennett and Segerberg (2013) has reoriented traditional research on grassroots politics by replacing the concept of collective action with their concept of *connective action*. The innovative concept redefines movements on a spectrum that moves from traditional top-down organizational movements to individual, crowd-based actions, the latter animated by individual rather than collective action frames. As in Harcourt and Escobar's model, the properties of emergence defined by Bennett and Segerberg describe the dynamics of contemporary movement mobilization. Unaddressed in the meshworks and connective action models, however, are characteristics of movements that determine their political effectiveness. As disparate individuals and groups join a movement based on a multiplicity of identities, beliefs, and goals, tolerance necessarily replaces discipline as the glue that holds together a coalition or a multiplicity of individual action frames.

Thus in an analysis of the participants in the European Social Forum (ESF), della Porta (2005) coined the concept of "tolerant identity" to characterize the diversity and overlapping identities of the participants in the Florence counterdemonstration to the G-8 Genoa summit. People from diverse backgrounds could agree on short-term concrete goals, on "immediately gratifying action" rather than "old style militancy." Critics might characterize this as making virtue of necessity as a heterogeneity of interests made it more difficult to create the force majeure to sustain political pressure. Echoing trends in the United States, left-leaning participants in the ESF had also become wary and distrustful of institutionalized politics, thereby further weakening the GJM's political effectiveness.

Emergent and diffuse in structure, the GJM has also become polymorphous in its tactical repertoire. Though mass demonstrations and other confrontational modes of action remain part of the standard playbook of dissent (an estimated seven million people worldwide protested the US invasion of Iraq in 2003), these have higher costs and risks that diminish their effectiveness. For example, the movement sometimes attracts disruptive elements such as the Black Bloc, a group of anarchists who (are logically compelled to) deny they have an organization but who do otherwise agree on a set of tactics intended to provoke confrontation with the police (infoshop.org/Blackbloc-Faq). The ensuing vandalism and disruption guarantees mainstream media coverage and thereby a focus for elite marginalization of the movement's progressive goals.

Whether the increased costs of confrontation have put off movement organizers is uncertain, but it is the case that the movement has turned to more traditional pressure activities, such as lobbying efforts and consumer awareness campaigns. This is where the GJM has had its most conspicuous success. Nestle, Nike, and Monsanto are now tainted as brands because of movement projects focused on raising consumer awareness of unfair labor practices and potential dangers to health and the environment. One could argue that a movement defined by lifestyle and consumption has had its greatest success by adopting the practices and techniques of its lifestyle-creating opponents. Indeed, some movement organizations have marketing strategies that can scarcely be distinguished from their establishment foes. For example, Global Exchange, one of the pioneering organizations at the Seattle WTO protests, offers reality tours, a gift registry, and stores where one can purchase fair trade goods and gift baskets, the latter available for corporate clients who wish to project an image of concern for social justice (globalexchange.org).

From the standpoint of political effectiveness, the evidence is mixed. Bimber (2001) found that despite the increase in information generated by movement activists and other Internet information providers, survey evidence shows little evidence of increased political activity among the general public. Nevertheless, Garrett (2006) pointed out that the Internet permits an astonishing potential for aggregating small monetary contributions and online coordination of canvassing and phone banks, thus lowering coordination costs. The most prominent example is Moveon.org, essentially a web address that since 2004 has raised nearly 60 million dollars from visitors to its website.

The politics of dissent in a networked, economically interdependent world derives from the disturbance of interests driven by comparative advantage and the velocity and scope of "complex interdependence" (Keohane & Nye, 2000b). The primary issue is whether one can speak of a single transnational movement for the GJM. The category itself subsumes a number of issues that hold different priorities depending on the interests of specific groups in specific locations. Members of a transnational movement that remains geographically bound have the capacity to think beyond parochial interests; Tarrow's (2005) concept of "rooted cosmopolitans" squares the circle of the apparent paradox.

Nevertheless, it is very unlikely that the welter of groups and individuals who have an interest at stake in the new political economy make up a unitary movement. Interests may be specific, local, and disconnected from a conscious membership in a broader global movement. The research cited here does not always specify whether the various groups under study subscribe to a single collective action frame. Members of labor unions in the industrial regions of the US Midwest may be opposed to free-trade agreements for entirely different reasons than members of the Sierra Club, with whom they may differ on the order of priority for environmental regulation. Scholars such as Bennett and della Porta have coined concepts that relax standards of membership in networked movements, and Harcourt and Escobar's concept of meshworks posits an intriguing picture of the self-organizing dynamics of a new form of political organization; yet it is still unclear whether this nascent form of organization or the identities of lifestyle politics are sufficient for dislodging entrenched interests, effectively countering the power of professional lobbyists, or for reaching a public of sufficient size to elect representatives that respond to movement goals. OWS offers the most recent test case.

Occupy Wall Street

In September 2012, on the first anniversary of OWS, the editors of *Adbusters* declared that "capitalism, infinite growth based economics, the sacred morality of Western leadership, the invincibility of totalitarian and corporate driven regimes, the cult of individualism—all the sacred touchstones of our civilization—are reeling under attack like never before" ("What is Occupy morphing into?" 2012). The source of the claim was a publication whose call for an occupation of New York City led to the September 2011 encampment at Zuccotti Park. Published in Vancouver, British Columbia, the stated editorial mission of *Adbusters* is to identify and critique the culture of consumerism that supports globalized capitalism.*

Among the publication's repertoire of critical concepts is "culture jamming," a way of subverting the meaning of a commercial message to draw attention to its exploitative influence. The approach draws on a twining of the Marxist concept of false consciousness with the ironic juxtapositions that defined the visual icons of the Dada and surrealist movements to unmask concealed sources of power. The substance of the editors' hopeful claims identified multiple themes of uncertainty that aroused OWS and its ambitious but diffuse agenda.

OWS arose with little advance notice, maintained a large number of public sites for about four months, and then, like the GJM, retreated to a virtual presence on the web. The movement left a resonant meme but little influence on

---

* A number of its regular contributors include intellectuals who took part in and wrote critical analyses of OWS (e.g., David Graeber, Slavoj Žižek).

electoral politics as contrasted with the Tea Party, a movement with which it was often compared.

Participants in OWS regarded the movement as unique, living in a parallel reality that denied the legitimacy of the institutions that surrounded its encampments and steadfastly refused to articulate its vision of an alternative. To quote one of its characteristically enigmatic claims, "We are our demands." As Harcourt (2012) put it, OWS was best understood as a new form of political rather than civil disobedience: "Civil disobedience accepts the legitimacy of the political structure and of our political institutions but resists the moral authority of the resulting laws. Political disobedience resists the very way in which we are governed" (p. 33). OWS sought a new political paradigm to respond to the high risk exposure of the Great Recession. The profoundly unsettling event exposed a large number of young Americans to an unfamiliar and toxic mixture of high levels of debt and sharply increased unemployment.

Although OWS declared itself sui generis, its historical roots could be traced to the transcendentalist movement of the 1820s and 1830s. Ralph Waldo Emerson, the movement's intellectual touchstone, wrote an essay titled "Nature" (1836), in which he asked why his generation continued to look backward to Europe for their spiritual inspiration. Why should not Americans have their own poetry, their own philosophy, and their own religion? A period of spiritual reflection would yield an enlightened and educated will that would advance a forward-looking good: "Build, therefore, your own world. As fast as you conform your life to the pure idea in your mind, that will unfold its great proportions" (p. 48).

Like the transcendentalists, OWS combined elements of idealism and socialism. The impulse of the achievable here-and-now led to such experimental communities as Brook Farm, where $500 bought members a voting share in determining communal policy. A more recent expression, the counterculture of the 1960s, combined elements of transcendental idealism and Marxist-inspired socialism that combined an unstable mixture of tolerance and authoritarianism. OWS inherited a legacy of communal yearning and Marxist and other critical concepts to articulate political and economic alternatives to existing regimes. OWS participants would find, as did Emerson, that the movement's ideals would represent a Platonic ideal rather than an achievable reality.

OWS materialized in New York City in mid-September 2011, and within weeks had spread to 300 different cities and 80 other nations. Despite its remarkable growth and national notice, the movement had by that winter abandoned most of its encampments and protests. In the short period of its public life, OWS gained nearly universal awareness of its existence and its trademark meme-slogan, "We are the 99 percent."

Movement participants developed distinctive modes of self-governance and adapted to the constraints of their local encampments. During its short life span, OWS enjoyed remarkable resilience and tactical success and raised public awareness despite its defiance of convention, its secrecy, and the opacity of its methods. The Guy Fawkes mask became a symbol of a movement less interested in persuasion than in demonstrating its enigmatic presence, mobilizing potential, and cultural significance. These strengths stood in marked contrast to its inherent weaknesses. OWS defied conventional understanding of how a political movement behaved: its goals more suggestive than definitive, its membership scattered yet readily mobilized, and its notable reluctance to gain acceptance by existing political institutions or adherence to conventional norms.

Building without a Blueprint

OWS represented the union of political dissent with the internet-driven phenomenon of emergence, the growth of novel and coherent structures and patterns through rapid nonlinear interactivity. The self-organized, participatory nature of the movement's structure provided tactical mastery, but its absence of ideological rigor and refusal to connect with institutional politics limited its strategic reach. The New York City General Assembly declared: "We wish to clarify that Occupy Wall Street is not and never has been affiliated with any established political party, candidate or organization. Our only affiliation is with the people."

Its paradoxical nature extended to declarations of principles confined to single sites. I focus on the New York encampment because of the attention it garnered nationally, although Oakland was prominent as well. The New York Occupation of 2011 declared, as did Brook Farm in the 1840s, that only those who devoted resources—time and labor—were its caretakers. Yet no single caretaker could speak for the whole; hence its time-consuming, consensus-building general assemblies that over time frustrated some participants. If no one could speak for the whole, no one outside the movement—including politicians and scholars—could appraise its success. As one OWS participant wrote, "Who decides success? Success has to be decided by those people in struggle, those who are fighting or organizing for something. Success of a movement, movement goals and people's desires come from those people, those social actors, not those studying them or politically desiring to lead them" (Sitrin, 2012, p. 3). Yet understanding OWS's significance requires an appraisal based on the stated objectives of its participants and its forms of identification.

Identity is an individual's affective, cognitive, and moral connection with a group. It is the perception of a shared status or relation, the answer to who we are and to its politically significant inverse, who (and what) we oppose. My analysis of OWS entails three dimensions of movement structure and dynamics: identification, goals, and conflict. I look for sources of conflict as obstacles that ideals cannot overcome and limit what the movement can achieve. Conflict is not necessarily a mortal blow to a movement. It may set off a constructive, dialectical reorienting dissent. Absent such a solution, conflict marks the fault lines that undermine political effectiveness. It leaches the movement of the passion needed to sustain the high-cost investment of time and energy needed to sustain it.

Per the uncertainty model, I seek themes that allow movement participants to maintain solidarity and collective identity, as well as the passion to remain committed to the movement's goals. These recurring and interconnected ideas operate as a cultural anchor, which activists use to engage in a meaningful dialogue with one another within what may appear to be a cacophonous, though not unintelligible, public forum (Ghaziani & Baldassarri, 2011).

Movement Discourse

OWS replicated the networked structures of globalization itself (Castells, 1996), distributed across the United States and Europe with hubs that reflected local issues of concern. Participants developed innovative forms of political deliberation and decision-making. Flexible adaptation to common problems and obstacles, a pattern that emerged at the Seattle WTO protests, enabled the movement to avoid potential cooptation by the conventions and institutions that OWS wished to replace. Technologically savvy organizers used cheap and ubiquitous forms of communication to replicate occupation sites and to form rapid responses to events on the ground. In short, the mass media were less important for OWS to mobilize participants and to get its message out.

Rather than studying mass media coverage, I look at the evolution of discourses among participants themselves. I do this because OWS not only declared itself autonomous of existing structures but also because it distrusted the mass media, a quality it shared with the Tea Party.

A movement that announces itself independent of dominant political institutions and the discourses that sustain them needs platforms of its own if it is to develop a robust discourse, a way of thinking. A number of sympathetic leftist and alternative press outlets provided sources of reporting on the movement. While the sly ironies of culture-jamming may have been used by movement participants to engage with the mainstream press, I posit that internal dialogues and reports are more credible and straightforward accounts of what movement participants were thinking.

I selected a gazette published by the editors of $n+1$, a literary journal that was founded in the mid-2000s in New York City by a young generation of writers steeped in leftist theory but also wary of it and open to exploration of hunches, experiments, and new ways of thinking. As they put it, "theory is dead, long live theory." The editors produced five special issues of what they called "an OWS inspired gazette."

Why this particular publication? In the estimate of a *New York Times* critic, the editors of $n+1$ were keen to "organize a generational struggle against laziness and cynicism, to raise once again the banners of creative enthusiasm and intellectual engagement" (Scott, 2005, p. 38). *The New Left Review* lauded the magazine for "establishing itself . . . as a distinctive presence on the intellectual left, in the United States and beyond" (Mulhern, 2015). The mixing, matching, swapping, and rediscovery quality of the magazine also reflected the technological cultural dominant present in the movement itself. The magazine was also noted for representing the critical zeitgeist of its time, as was *The Dial* for the transcendentalists of the 1830s and *Dissent* for the new left of the 1950s.

For the second half of this chapter, I analyze five months of the OWS gazettes—October 2011 through March 2012—issued by $n+1$, 138 stories altogether. OWS participants in New York City and Oakland contributed most of the material, although each issue also included stories from participants in other US encampments (e.g., Atlanta, Minneapolis, and Philadelphia) as well as in Europe. Issues 1 through 3 were the most forward looking as they reported events on the ground in New York City and elsewhere. By issue 4, the content turned inward, when the encampments began to be abandoned as winter and the police set in. Issue 5 was retrospective, a look back at what had been accomplished.

Analyzing the corpus of articles that made up each issue of the gazette proved to be a challenging task. Unlike mainstream publications and broadcasts, there was no discernible structure that organized the content. Front page headlines announced six or more stories on the inside pages with no indication of their relative importance, as contrasted, for example, with the upper right–hand corner of a newspaper (see figure 8.1).

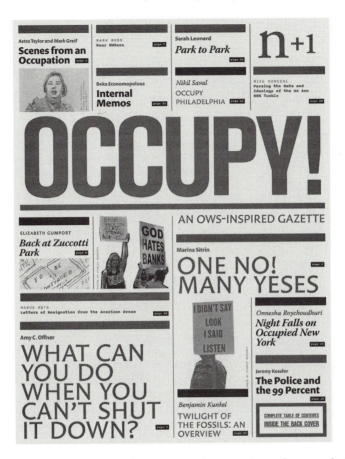

Figure 8.1. Cover of the first issue of *n+1's Occupy!* gazette, September 2011, designed by Dan O. Williams. Reprinted by permission.

The size of a headline also provided no clue as to the importance of an item. For example, in issue 1, the two largest headlines announced stories on pages four ("One No, Many Yeses") and five ("What Can You Do When You Can't Shut It Down?"). In issue 2, the most prominently announced stories appeared on pages sixteen ("Throwing Out the Master's Tools") and twenty-two ("We Are our Demands"). Opinion pieces, philosophical mediations, diaries, chronologies, and panel discussions at local universities appeared in no particular order. The carnivalesque treatment suggested that each item deserved equal treatment, by far the most dominant value that structured both form and content of the publication.

I treat each issue of the gazette as a snapshot of the movement at a given moment in time. The stories that make up the quilt of each issue offer a multifaceted account of a movement improvised by participants and sympathizers. The successes and failures of an experiment in direct democracy enacted at the encampments provide an insight into the potential and limits of the response of the newest generation of Americans on the left to the politics of insecurity.

I coded each of the stories using QDA Miner, a program that permits dynamic coding and analysis of text. The software tool made it possible to organize the large amount of unstructured data that represent the wide range of identities, goals, and conflicts in the database. For example, a first pass at the content revealed nine categories of identity, fourteen goals, and ten sources of internal conflict. Although I provide tables that list these raw frequencies, I also rely on semantic network analysis to simultaneously depict two dimensions of the text: (1) the proximity of the coding categories to one another in the stories and (2) the strength of their relationships, or how often they co-occur in the same story.

The five issues of the gazette describe the arc of the movement's public life and death. They include (1) a discursive period in which participants effusively praised the possibilities inherent in conversing about possible futures (e.g., "prefigurative society"), economic and political equality, and the promise of direct democracy; (2) a self-conscious period of identity dominated by issues of race and gender, specifically why white males were dominating the assemblies and political decision-making; (3) conflict on the slowness of the deliberative process and on the secret deliberations among an elite within the movement that contradicted its principles of direct democracy; (4) coalition-seeking as some movement participants concluded that the rewards of reaching out to potential partners outweighed the risks of cooptation, especially as court orders, police action, and cold weather were bringing the public life of the movement to a close; and (5) introspection, analyses by participants of why the movement foundered: in particular, tensions between the movement's ideals of radical individualism and equality, the conflict between a utopian imaginary and the realities of dealing with the mundane, the rejection of conventional politics (including coalition-building) and engaging with a wider public, frustration with the consensus model in decision-making, and the aforementioned issues of race and gender in weakening collective identity in the movement.

We now turn to a thematic analysis of the text, structured by identities, goals, and conflicts.

Identities and Goals

The wide range of identities used by the contributors reflects the broad coalition of interests in the movement (see table 8.1). The two largest categories were race/gender and people in debt. For convenience, I link race and gender because they were often mentioned together in the text and, more importantly, composed a source of internal conflict. Race and gender were mentioned 41 times in 13 of the stories. In the early stages of the movement, women said they were concerned with issues of power and personal security.

"I went to the anti-patriarchy meeting because even though I was impressed by the General Assembly and its process I also noticed that it was mostly white men who were in charge of the committees and making announcements and that I had only seen one woman of color get up in front of everyone and talk" (issue 1). In this case, a black woman successfully lobbied the while male authors of the New York declaration to change the language of its opening line by excluding the words "one race, the human race." In the eyes of this participant, conflict had led to dialogue and to an improvement:

In that circle, on that street-corner, we did a crash course on white privilege, structural racism, oppression. . . . It was hard. It was real. It hurt. But people listened. . . . It felt worth it to sit down on a street corner in the Financial District at 11:30 p.m. on a Thursday night after working all day long and argue for the changing of the first line of Occupy Wall Street's official Declaration of the Occupation of New York City. It felt worth it not only because we got the line changed but also because while standing in a circle of twenty mostly white men and explaining racism in front of them, carefully and slowly spelling out that I as a women of color

Table 8.1. OWS identities

Identity	Mentions		Stories	
	N	%	*N*	%
Race–gender	41	7.1	18	13.0
Student debtor	21	3.6	13	9.4
Virtual–digital	24	4.2	13	9.4
Marxist	20	3.5	8	5.8
Debtors	11	1.9	7	5.1
Everyone	9	1.6	7	5.1
Generational	6	1.0	5	3.6
Utopian	5	0.9	4	2.9
Students	4	0.7	3	2.2
Jobless	1	0.2	1	0.7

experience the world way differently than the author of the Declaration, a white man, that this was not about him being personally racist but about relations of power, that he urgently needed to listen and believe me about this, this moment felt like a victory for the movement on its own. (Issue 1)

In this instance, the issue was resolved, an example of constructive, guiding dissent. But the race–gender tensions in the movement were never fully resolved. In November a story quoted a female medic in the Oakland encampment who was upset by the violent behavior of Black Bloc anarchists: "The onslaught was disturbing and disgusting in ways I can't even articulate because I am still so angry at the empty bravado and cowardice that I saw. . . . I want those kids to be held accountable [for] the damage that they did, damage made possible by their class and race privilege" (issue 1).

In Zuccotti Park, "a People of Color caucus degenerated into a shouting match, and it made me want to leave for good. Three black men had jumped to their feet, pointing fingers and yelling over everyone else that now was a good time for us to talk about racial and economic oppression in their communities. . . . One of them, clearly an instigator, had been keeping a running commentary on how OWS was some kind of white conspiracy, launching into a tirade about the hand signals—'those goddam hand signals!'" (issue 2).

Another writer observed the gender–race segregation that had replicated the stratification of society outside the boundaries of Zuccotti Park: "Domination loves to split mind and body, and this was being mapped onto assembly and circle: the drums became 'ethnic,' race-coded; the assembly, 'white.' The drums become male; the assembly, female" (issue 2). In Philadelphia, another female participant complained that "the tasks of caring, cleaning, keeping on schedule, mending bruises, resolving disputes, and so on has consistently devolved to women" (issue 2).

Roughly half of the instances in which race or gender were mentioned included such divisive observations. The others depicted OWS as an opportunity to bridge differences: "These new alliances are challenging. They must work across class, gender, and racial divisions, must link up with ongoing struggles, and must be aware of their variegated, rich, and often painful histories. Our distinct histories and divisions can easily become political fissures when we do not take them on as the heart of new alliances" (issue 2). In contrast to the forceful policing of issue identity practiced by the Tea Party, participants in OWS repeatedly negotiated their way through issues of power that derived from race and gender.

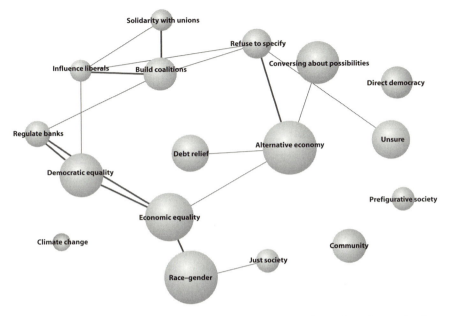

Figure 8.2. Race–gender identity and goals. *Note:* The size of a circle indicates the frequency of a theme. Line thickness indicates the proximity of a theme to another.

The semantic network depicted in figure 8.2 shows that in those articles mentioning race and gender, the goal most often mentioned was economic equality. The category itself included explicit critiques of income inequality, neoliberal policy, and decreased funding of public institutions such as higher education. The multiple goals sought included such redistributive policies as free health care and university tuition, increased budgets for public services, increased taxes on the rich, and livable wages. Because women were doubly penalized by virtue of their gender, the wage inequality issue resonated the most (but not exclusively) with this group: "It is thanks to this concentration on women's participation in the labor market as the measure of improvement in their social condition that women in the US today still lack entitlements (like paid maternity leave) common even in poor countries, leaving them to function as 'plugs' in the gaps opened by the cuts in social services" (issue 3).

The second largest category of explicit mention of identity referenced those crushed by debt, student and otherwise. By far the most common link between status as a student debtor and movement goals was debt relief, one of the principle threads of discourse in the New York encampment. Those who had other sources of debt also sought relief but were more likely to entertain ideas about alternative economic models. An analyst who studied Tumblr OWS microblogs found two clusters of age groups—20 and 27—in the 1,000 entries he studied. Because Tumblr is, as the writer reported, a "technology of the young," it skewed to the concerns of the youngest participants in OWS. For this prominent group, student debt was a "metaconcern" (issue 1).

Interestingly, to the extent that this group had preferences for an alternative economic model (the most frequently cited goal in the database), it was not a Marxist alternative but one that predated industrialization. The youngest OWS microbloggers were not seeking access to the rewards of modernity—large houses, luxury cars, and cheap gas—but freedom from "the bondage of these debts and . . . a bare minimum to survive on in order to lead decent lives (or, in preindustrial terms, give us some land)" (issue 1). The author cited a historian who declared that these were "the demands of a peasantry, not a working class." It's not clear whether the preferences followed the logic of anthropologist David Graeber's* rejection of the concept of debt or the reduced expectations of a generation shocked by the ravages of the first economic crisis they had ever faced.

I created the generic category of alternative economy, the most frequently mentioned goal, to capture all permutations of proposed system-level remedies (see figure 8.3). These included explicitly Marxist models of socialism: "Though I have difficulty imagining a scenario in which workers voluntarily destroy their own means of subsistence, it seems right to insist that any alternative to the capitalist system will have to begin by abolishing private property" (Marcus, 2011, p. 31). But they were outnumbered by more general calls for shared, public goods under the rubric of a "commons," a concept adopted from the GJM: "I'd like to see OWS use some of its grassroots clout . . . to make its own noncommodified institutions and structures. In the alter-globalization movement we called this 'reinventing the commons'" (Gautney, 2011, p. 34). The term *noncommodification* appeared in various contexts to denote rejection of *privatization*, a term equated with the unslaked thirst of capitalism for diverting funds used to produce public goods. The encampments represented spaces where an anti-consumer-capitalist alternative could be enacted: providing security, food, and media without using credit cards.

The variety of alternatives presented—from theoretical Marxist to preindustrial to wishes for other unspecified models—did not approach anything

---

* David Graeber is an influential New School theorist for OWS.

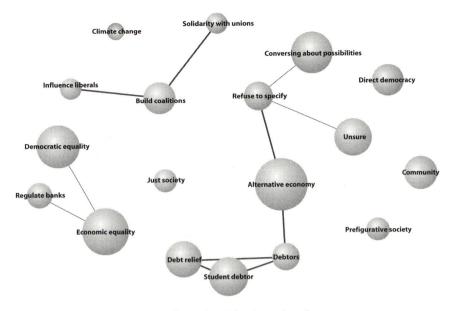

Figure 8.3. Debtor identity and goals.

resembling a consensus on what was to be done. This contrasted with the clarity and specificity with which the current system was universally critiqued: "But above all, against the misery of 'the job' as offered in the capitalist market, we need to revalue the work involved in our reproduction, as the foundation for finding new revolutionary alternatives to the capitalist failure to produce a life worth living, in the homes, the farms, the schools, and the factories of the world" (Federici, 2011, p. 34).

The third largest category of identity was virtual–digital. This referred to mentions by writers of their participation in networked forms of communication, a new and welcome mode of sociality. In one example, the writer referred to the use of social media to link participants with sympathizers and virtual participants: "Ten years ago, we interacted online based on protocols of face-to-face. Today we introduce ourselves to one another based on how we meet online—following interesting-looking strangers on Tumblr or Twitter. Maybe we've seen their faces already as tiny icons, friends of somebody else we know on the screen" (issue 1).

As the network in figure 8.4 shows, virtual identity was most closely linked to a sense of community and thereby to discussions about OWS representing what participants termed a *prefigurative society*. The latter referred to experimental models of a new kind of society (an echo of Emerson's proposition) that

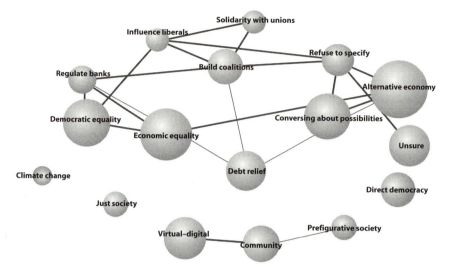

Figure 8.4. Virtual–digital identity and goals.

were being tried out in the encampments: "The most beautiful thing about the Occupy Movement is that we can create, on a small scale, a version of the society in which we would like to live. A society with free education and health care— where democracy is participatory and real and our social relationships are founded on community, mutual aid, equality, respect, and solidarity" (issue 1).

Taking a close look at the numerous goals expressed by participants (table 8.2), one sees broad abstract categories of political and economic equality in various guises—as well as the sphinxlike refusal to state any goals—but few specific policies. Only three—regulation of banks, debt relief, and climate change—were specific enough to be translated into policy and outweighed by refusing to say what goals OWS had on its mind. Notably absent in the list is the issue of immigration, and climate change appears as the least frequently mentioned goal.

Conflict

The most telling indication of the failure to build a disciplined sense of solidarity and identification was the movement's preoccupation with the police. The police that surrounded the encampments represented an authentic threat to the movement, but their menacing presence and use of pepper spray did not produce sufficient passion to overcome internal differences in the movement itself.

Table 8.2. OWS goals

Goal	Mentions		Stories	
	N	%	N	%
Alternative economy	39	6.8	24	17.4
Economic equality	33	5.7	24	17.4
Conversing about possibilities	25	4.3	21	15.2
Democratic equality	28	4.9	20	14.5
Unsure	21	3.6	15	10.9
Refuse to say	13	2.3	12	8.7
Community	15	2.6	11	8.0
Direct democracy	15	2.6	11	8.0
Debt relief	19	3.3	9	6.5
Build coalitions	15	2.6	8	5.8
Bank regulation	10	1.7	8	5.8
Just & fair society	9	1.6	8	5.8
Prefigurative society	8	1.4	6	4.3
Influence liberals	7	1.2	4	2.9
Solidarity with unions	7	1.2	4	2.9
Climate change	5	1.0	2	1.4

Table 8.3. OWS conflicts

Conflict	Mentions		Stories	
	N	%	N	%
Police	86	14.9	29	21.0
Unwieldy consensus model	16	2.8	14	10.1
Ideological conflict	16	2.8	13	9.4
Purposelessness	13	2.3	8	5.8
Unrepresentative	10	1.7	5	3.6
Drummers	9	1.6	6	4.3
Violent protestors	5	1.0	4	2.9
Failed movement	5	1.0	4	2.9
Leaderlessness	4	1.0	3	2.2
Homeless	2	.3	2	1.4

Putting aside the issue of external sources of conflict, table 8.3 shows that the two most frequent sources of internal conflict were the means by which the movement deliberated and ideological differences. An inability to develop a sense of common purpose naturally led to complaints of purposelessness.

A glance at the diagram in figure 8.5 reveals the logic of the relationships that weakened OWS. A quote from one of the participants summarizes the points of ideological division within the movement: "The winter months had taken their toll on the Occupy movement, drawing out divisions to the point of outright conflict between reformists and revolutionaries, socialists and anarchists, all the familiar shades of internecine dispute" (issue 4).

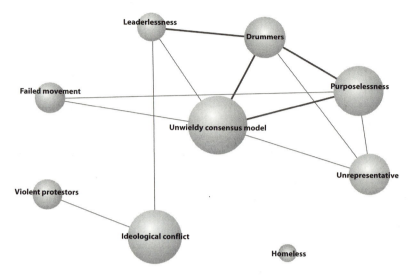

Figure 8.5. Sources of conflict.

The ideological differences that existed between participants could not be resolved either because of their inherent incompatibility or the means selected by the movement to make decisions. The ceaseless drumming at the edge of the encampment exacerbated the tedium of long discussions in the General Assembly on decisions big and small. Participants associated the drumming with the directionless quality of the movement and, in moments of frustration, its futility. Underlying these sentiments were suspicions that the real decisions were being made elsewhere by individuals who may not have represented the views of those at the General Assemblies. This was clear to one writer in the opening weeks of the encampment in Philadelphia: "That there was an issue of transparency was not news to me. The GA was not, as I understood it, where core planning was being formulated, where key decisions were being passed—at least not anymore, not now that the numbers were so unwieldy. Partly this was gleaned from talking to people embedded deep in the organization of OWS—already there were rumors of backroom dealings with various NGOs and unions" (issue 1). In New York, a regular contributor to the gazette complained: "The general assembly model, which already masks underlying divisions, should be a tool and not a fetish" (issue 1). A later report from the Minneapolis site said that the movement was being led by people who were not or very rarely "actually sleeping on the plaza" (issue 3).

In mid-November OWS was evicted from Zuccotti Park by an order from the New York Supreme Court. On December 31 movement participants attempted a reoccupation but were turned away by the police. By then, the movement was in full retreat from its occupation sites.

Later that winter, writers began to reflect on the movement's successes and failures. The consensus model used by organizers not only had failed to bring a focus but had shut out a dialogue with potential sympathizers: "Meetings, and the processes they entailed—the seemingly endless reminders not to jump stack or block just from spite, the presence of constant disruptors, the cyclical, often unsuccessful efforts to reach consensus—were far more difficult to greet zealously without the invigorating balance of a more informal and organic public commons" (issue 4). It was during this period of introspection, in February and March 2012, that participants entertained making overtures to the institutions and groups (unions, liberals) they had spurned at the height of movement ardor. By then, the opportunity had passed.

Coda

The final issue of the gazette was a meditation on the significance of a movement that had gone into retreat. Participants pointed out that although the movement had not achieved tangible policy results, it had succeeded in making participants politically engaged and prepared for future action. Several wrote of the exhilaration of being with others in the same physical space and sharing communal feelings in an otherwise isolated life of alienation. The willingness of individuals to prefer life in tents in the center of cities, to endure hours of slow-moving discussion spoke to the need to connect with others face to face rather than in the ersatz "spaces" afforded by new media. At the very least, participants could make virtue of defeat by denying empathy to their oppressors. Quoting David Halberstam, one participant wrote:

> There is something powerful in being wrong, in losing, in failing and all our failures combined might just be enough, if we practice them well to bring down the winner. Let's leave success and its achievement to the Republicans, to the Matthew Barneys of the world, to the winners of reality TV shows, to married couples, to SUV drivers. The concept of practicing failure, perhaps, prompts us to discover our inner dweeb, to be underachievers, to fall short, to get distracted, to take a detour, to find a limit, to lose our way, to forget, to avoid mastery and to [as Walter Benjamin put it] "withhold empathy from the victors." (Issue 5)

Conclusion

OWS's primary identity discourses alternated between gender and race, those in debt (primarily students and those who could not afford to pay their mortgages), and anyone and everyone disaffected by politics manipulated by corporations and Wall Street. The goals of OWS embraced political and economic equality in general terms, but rejection of extant political structures and inability to put a policy point on the general force animating participants limited the movement's reach. Sympathizers noted the movement's "prefigurative politics," an experimental miniature of politics on the ground, as a model for future political and economic formations.

Other reasons for the movement's collapse included the inherent difficulties of living outdoors and continual pressure by local police forces. On the latter, one item spoke to the ineffectiveness of virtual tactics for mobilizing a mass movement: "Millions of Facebook posts, Tweets, and policy white papers have failed to galvanize a mass movement. Instead, it was the occupation of public spaces, marching without permits, and disruption of daily life in the financial district [that] signaled an open ended defiance lacking in previous efforts" (issue 2).

The movement's lack of immediate success was contrasted by dissemination of its potent rhetorical frame—"we are the 99 percent." This has become a resonant element in political discourse, even among elites. Although mainstream media coverage saw confusing disarray in the movement, network analysis of OWS's internal dialogue reveals a potential organizing hub for future use. Three examples illustrate the cultural anchor of communal affinity that for a time kept the movement together (note here also the underlying themes of alienation and insecurity):

A network of groups—affinity groups, project groups, working groups, general assemblies, neighborhood assemblies, worker-owned cooperatives, and new forms yet to spontaneously develop—was always part of the plan.

It is hard to contrast the joy of community I feel at Occupy Wall Street with the isolation I felt on Wall Street. It's hard because I cannot think of two more disparate cultures.

I believe that this longing for integrated existence and group identity provides much of the conviction behind prefigurative politics—more so than any stated instrumental goals. So many of us feel alienated and isolated in our everyday lives. (Issue 5)

Theorists have emphasized the need for movements to develop collective identities that mobilize participants and sustain their interest in them and to provide collective action frames that mobilize public opinion. A new school of analysis (Ghaziani & Baldassarri, 2011) argues that it is a mistake to conclude that heterogeneity is ipso facto an empirical indicator of cultural incoherence and political disorganization.

In this case study, heterogeneity by itself did not prove fatal. After all, the movement survived for a number of months under harsh conditions, an indication of the passions that drove those who participated in it. However, those passions proved to be insufficient for the movement's long-term survival. Issues of group identity divided the movement at times despite the best efforts to overcome them in a failed model of deliberation. A network analysis of identities and goals showed some divergences in goals: students in debt wanting debt forgiveness, women chafing under economic and political inequality, the latter even present in the "prefigurative politics" of the encampments. The glue that held the movement together for as long as it did was a surge of communal feeling that was not satisfied by exchanges in social media. In the end, the movement derived its greatest energies from individuals who felt a surge of camaraderie as they worked and talked together. But ideas matter, and the movement could not overcome the resonant appeals to individual effort and simple policy goals (reduced taxes, stopping Obamacare) that supported the Tea Party. Despite the claims of the editors of *Adbusters* that the "cult of individualism" was reeling under attack like never before," the GOP nevertheless made major gains in the 2014 midterms at all levels of government, actively supported by the Tea Party. Democrats stayed at home, evidence that passions delinked from ideas could not be sustained.

Although OWS offered a critique of the present economic regime, it did not offer a resonant alternative. This was the result of a division within the movement between traditional Marxists and an emerging model of "everyday communism" that proposed, among other things, substitution of communal sharing and cooperation for the concept of debt (Graeber, 2011). A new utopian vision may yet spring from a model that the movement haltingly tried to adopt, but it remains the task of intellectuals and influential interest groups to convert the ideas into a coherent and persuasive alternative. Absent such an outcome or another destabilizing event, it is likely that diminished expectations will become the "new normal" as they have become for tolerance of events related to climate change.

It remains to be seen whether the communal passions that drove OWS can be rekindled to advance the cause of economic equality threatened by a globalized economy, and if rekindled, whether the left can garner voter support around an issue that has to this point been captured by the populist right in the politics of insecurity.

CHAPTER NINE

The New Normal and the Limits of Insecurity

The crises that confronted Americans in the first decade of the 21st century will not recur in exactly the same way. Policy responses to those crises set in motion a chain of events that interacted with the flows of global processes and media frames to influence later events and subsequent reactions. In this concluding chapter, I review the main findings of the book in historical context, relate them to later events, and draw some implications based on the patterns I see.

Policy Echoes of 9/11

Just as the oil shocks of the 1970s contributed to a loss of confidence in the economic regime, 9/11 crystallized a pervasive sense of uncertainty among American citizens. Of all the crises of globalization the United States faced in the 2000s, the only one that created a nearly universal affective response was terrorism on US soil. Divergence happened at the point of diagnosis and response. This is not unexpected. Where citizens live in the state of dread that accompanies the metaphysical uncertainty and high risk exposure of black swan events like 9/11, elites have the advantage of analytical distance and unparalleled political support to respond however they deem necessary.

Elite diagnosis of the causes of the al-Qaeda attacks elicited two policy responses. One empowered the state's security apparatus for foreign and domestic policy. The other increased the flows of trade and capital. As the research on terror management theory predicts, the first heightened Americans' attachment to their nation, while the second increased the outflow of jobs and stagnation of wages that weakened their economic security. In addition, the increased flows of capital exposed citizens to obscure, ever-riskier cross-border investment innovations. Innovated by a deregulated banking and investment sector and driven by investors overseas, they inflated a real estate bubble. When it burst, the circuits of trade froze and a severe financial crisis ensued.

The economic meltdown sent a loud signal of economic insecurity, but ardent opinion supportive of neoliberal policy—one cause of the economic crisis—limited the president's range of policy options. The Great Recession aroused supporters of monetarism and deregulation to double down on the policies that had contributed to the crisis. They reined in a more forceful use of Keynesian policy, a clear indication of the strength of prevailing sentiment in favor of an economic regime that contributed to the worst economic crisis in 50 years. This counterintuitive outcome resulted from an imbalance in the passion of the two sides in the national debate. Among the causes of that imbalance was the reduced authority of the left. The earliest indication of weakness came from the precipitous decline of the GJM.

Prior to 9/11, the GJM had some leverage on policy by virtue of its support of American workers and unions, whereas after the terrorist attacks, the movement suffered by its association with disruption and confrontation in a climate of dread and nationalistic reaction. The wave of patriotic sentiment that followed 9/11 supercharged that part of the cultural matrix that associated the United States with high moral purpose. The Bush administration took every opportunity to leverage the cultural force multiplier of American exceptionalism to justify the costly military invasions of Afghanistan and Iraq to fight the War on Terror. The reappearance of terrorist groups in weak and failed states elsewhere attests to the ineffectiveness of a conventional state security response (land invasion) to the marriage of an ideology to a tactic unconfined by a national border. The rhetoric did not remain confined to one policy area.

Freedom and individual autonomy, among the bedrock values of American exceptionalism, were used as resonant cultural force multipliers to create a favorable environment for the growth of a movement on the right. Tea Party participants and sympathizers used the symbolic rhetorical appeal of liberty as well as groupcentric resentment of the "takers" to urge fellow citizens and candidates to support limited government and reduced taxation. The most visible takers were undocumented workers from Mexico and Central America, who became lightning rods for the resentment of citizens who sensed the erosion of their future economic security.

The movement's effective use of resentment and position issues hampered Barack Obama's and moderate Republicans' policy options and room to negotiate on fiscal issues. They thus exposed the nation's population to future risk by refusing to expand the social safety net beyond existing programs of Social Security and Medicare. One notable example was the movement's constraint on the design of the Affordable Care Act (Obamacare), taking off the table the possibility of a single-payer system used by nations with advanced economies such as Canada and in Western Europe. The effect was to enhance what *Adbusters'* editors condemned as the "cult of individualism," a keystone in the rhetoric of neoliberal economic policy. The magazine's precipitating role in OWS revealed the influence of a new information system on the dynamics of present-day movement mobilization.

OWS emerged from the transnational network that had supported the GJM. Its themes of equality and crushing debt had the potential to drive public opinion against the predations of the banking and investment establishment, but the movement's refusal to engage with policy elites or politicians—the target of the movement's frustration and anger—limited its influence. By its rejection of alliance with the liberal establishment, traditional allies (civil rights and labor), and institutionalized politics in general, OWS counted largely on its public model of direct democracy to persuade sympathizers to support its nonspecific calls for economic and democratic equality. The practical limitations of the model—criticized by participants and mocked by detractors—undermined the movement, but its failure to present a coherent and persuasive alternative economic vision proved to be its fatal weakness. In this respect, the movement reflected a continuing inability of the intellectual left to do so (see, e.g., Arrighi, 2009).

The outcome of two movements aroused by the same loud signal of economic uncertainty was perverse: exacerbated by the downward forces of globalization, the wealth gap as a source of political energy had not only failed to reduce inequality but created a populist reaction that helped to increase it. The Tea Party's influence on the GOP and the Obama administration's pragmatic willingness to compromise reduced the political pressure to regulate the banking industry and continued to place taxpayers at risk for subsidizing future financial meltdowns. To wit, at the end of 2014, Congress passed a $1.1 trillion budget bill that rescinded a key regulation passed four years earlier in the Dodd–Frank Wall Street Reform and Consumer Protection Act. That regulation required banks to trade their riskiest financial instruments without the bailout protection of the Federal Deposit Insurance Corporation or the Federal Reserve. Privatized profits were once again to be secured with socialized risk.

OWS's disinterest in specific policies such as banking regulation, climate change, and immigration reform deprived liberal reformers of a source of potential energy among sympathizers, especially college students, for the most prominent insecurity-borne issues of the 2000s. The Tea Party's success amounted to a reversal of the 1960s new left and counterculture movements, this time with older cohorts on the ardor-driven winning side of the generation gap.

In the 2016 election cycle, populist passions on the right driven by familiar Tea Party issues such as illegal immigration and nationalism met a growing passion on the left. Faced with the continuing fallout of the Great Recession, largely younger voters were drawn to the themes of Bernie Sanders's presidential campaign. Sanders distilled the ideas that defined the core appeal of the Occupy movement into a simple but sturdy platform—reform of the political system by curbing the influence of Wall Street and corporate money on political campaigns along with universal healthcare and free college tuition as remedies for reducing income inequality. Because Hillary Clinton could not sufficiently distance herself from the economic regime that had been in place since Reagan (and that of Bill Clinton's administration, affirmed by his support of the repeal of Glass-Steagall), her campaign fell back on incrementalism and identity politics to draw support. While Sanders hoped class would trump gender, Clinton relied on the latter to trump the absence of an aspirational policy appeal in her campaign. The outcome of that contest could reveal whether the communal appeal of OWS overcomes the structural weaknesses in its coalition.

Passionate resistance to immigration reform and the failure of the left to rally support led to President Obama's executive order of 2014. Notably, its first element was a crackdown on illegal immigration at the border, a concession to opponents of reform. They vowed to resist implementation of the part of Obama's order that would allow parents of those born in the United States since January 1, 2010, to request a three-year exemption from deportation. The Tea Party shifted its issue priority to illegal immigration shortly after President Obama announced his decision to a small television audience. Polls taken after the order was issued showed conflicted opinions. Although over 70 percent of respondents favored the three-year moratorium on deportations (Public Religion Research Institute, 2014), 53 percent disapproved of Obama's handling of the issue (CNN/ORC, 2014). Predictably, Obama's approval rating rose among Hispanic Americans, but the muted reaction among other citizens indicated the conflicted interests and groupcentric sentiment that underlay the issue. The complexity of the discourse on immigration reform, documented in chapter 6, indicates that it is unlikely to be settled anytime soon.

The incremental effects of climate change distinguish this issue from the others analyzed in the book. Because rising ocean waters are the most salient indicator of future risk, the majority of the population has not been exposed to the signals of high future risk exposure to melting icepacks and the occasional superstorms that only leave a temporary impression on those geographically unaffected. Citizens pay attention only as long as the media do, and research shows that such attention does not last long, even for such influential sources as *The New York Times* (Boydstun, 2013).

More importantly, the cultural matrix that would support national policy for reduction in oil and gas consumption is currently unfavorable. A combination of increased and cheaper supply of oil and fatalism has leached the environmental movement of the passion needed to compete effectively in the politics of insecurity on the issue of climate change. One instructive counterexample that illustrates the change in the harmonics of the political culture is public reaction to the damaging effects of industrial chemicals on the environment brought to the public's attention in the 1960s.

Borne by popular alarm to images of birds falling dead from ingestion of insecticides, an environmental movement quickly arose in response to widespread perceptions of large-scale risk after publication of Rachel Carson's 1962 book *Silent Spring*. Carson's words to Congress (1963), "our heedless and destructive acts enter into the vast cycles of the earth and in time return to bring hazard to ourselves" (p. 1), were indistinguishable from the core message of Al Gore's academy award–winning documentary "Inconvenient Truth," yet the film had little effect on public sentiment to press for a federal program that would address the problem. The fatalistic inaction of the left empowered the right, whose voice was amplified by a lobbying campaign on behalf of the oil industry that in 2013 spent over $144 million and contributed $17 million to political candidates (opensecrets.org).

Implications

For a number of reasons, the politics of insecurity analyzed in this book are likely to continue for some time. First and foremost, income inequality, the principal driver of economic insecurity, is unlikely to decrease any time soon. Given the absence of political will among Americans to support income redistribution or to expand the social safety net, technological advances and the continued off-shoring of manufacturing put a premium on long-term education and retraining as the main drivers of social mobility. Even if this were to be achieved, however, it would be unlikely to expand the economy sufficiently to overcome the wealth advantages of those with investment capital. Thomas Piketty's (2014) analysis of trends in income distribution for the past century showed that unless the US economy grows at a robust rate of 4 to 5 percent a year, capital accumulation provides a greater return on investment than wages. A helpful analogy is imagining a relay race where wage earners join capital-rich runners who started earlier and run faster. In Piketty's words, "the past devours the present" (p. 431).

Paul Krugman's repeated calls for increased government borrowing to stimulate the economy by rebuilding the nation's infrastructure at a time when interest rates were essentially zero could not overcome conservative resistance to government borrowing. This view was also advocated by economist Martin Wolf (2010), whose book championing free markets and globalization (2005) became a fixture on academic syllabi. Resistance to an increased federal deficit became a rallying issue for the Tea Party, whose success at fielding and electing deficit hawks to Congress undermined Obama's capacity to negotiate with the GOP on fiscal issues.

Absent a change in cultural beliefs regarding the value of effort over luck and identification with the fortunes of the rich as a surrogate for the strength of the economy (Bartels, 2008), Americans' attitudes on redistributive policy are unlikely to change. OWS signaled the potential for a populist movement on the left to lobby for such a reversal of opinion, but that remains to be tapped. A more daunting challenge is posed by the scale mismatch between a movement on the left opposed to the inequalities of a global economy and the authority of the nation-state, fortified by the fear of terrorism.

As this book goes to press, the Supreme Court has ruled that the Constitution guarantees a right to gay marriage and refused to strike down the Affordable Care Act (Obamacare). In addition, southern governors were under pressure to remove the confederate flag from state capitals after an avowed racist went on a killing spree during a Charleston black church service. Some media analysts opined that removal of these once resonant symbols was putting the GOP at a disadvantage in electoral politics and, by extension, in the symbolic politics of the culture wars. There is little evidence to support this conclusion. Research in political science and political psychology points to stable moral and value orientations that align with partisan preferences that drive the politics of insecurity. Jacoby (2014), for example, found that morality, patriotism, and social order are highly correlated with conservative identification and that economic security, equality, and, to a lesser extent, freedom align with liberal self-identification.

Meanwhile, Graham, Haidt, and Nosek (2009) found that conservatives and liberals rely on different core values (the authors prefer the term *virtues*) for informing their intuitive moral judgments. More optimistic about human nature, liberals rely on considerations of harm and fairness to individuals when making moral judgments. As the authors put it, "We refer to these two foundations as the individualizing foundations because they are (we suggest) the source of the intuitions that make the liberal philosophical tradition, with its emphasis on the rights and welfare of individuals, so learnable and so compelling to so many people" (p. 1031). By contrast, conservatives rely on the groupcentric values of in-group loyalty, authority, and purity, a potent marker of group boundaries.

Among conservatives, loyalty, patriotism, and sacrifice combine with "extreme vigilance for traitors" to create a groupcentric system of hierarchy and loyalty.

These patterns may not endure for the long run, but they reinforce a recurring finding of this book, that the right holds a structural advantage based on strength of group identification and belief coherence in the politics of insecurity. The issues that attach to symbolic concerns and position issues may change, but the underlying cultural dynamics remain. These issues will continue to divide the nation until its politics return to a more consensual pattern.

In reviewing the policy responses to the globalization-related crises analyzed in this book, one disturbing pattern emerges: as citizens become familiar with the dynamics of globalization, the perceived risk exposure of some disruptions are attenuated by familiarity and adjustment—the "new normal," as in the short-lasting uncertainties raised by weather disasters. Tolerance for the disruptions of global processes translates into a policy paralysis that puts off short-term costs that increase with the scale of the damage of future disruptions.

What is most significant about the issue of climate change is that majority public response is unrelated to information, one of the two dimensions that define the risk exposure of an event, its capacity to arouse concern and effective political action. An important contribution to the political dysfunction of this and other issues is the polarized state of the information environment and its incentives to divide audiences on the basis of their preexisting beliefs. The conversion of universal national concern to narrow partisanship impugns not only the judgment of experts but also of fellow citizens whose opinions differ. A transformation of discourse from reason and tolerance to emotion and prejudice doubles the risk by putting off consensual policy change and embittering citizens along partisan lines.

The politics of uncertainty do have their limits. As we reviewed in chapter 2, rigid belief-driven attempts to minimize uncertainty at all costs and the motivated reasoning that rejects information that contradicts one's worldview inevitably leads to adaptive failure. The functional limits of partisan group solidarity exist at the frontier delineated by new ideas that redefine the terms of public debate. Eventually, globalization will again change cultural signal sensitivities, and the resulting flashpoints will elicit new ideas and sparks to collective action.

Abbott, C. (1999). *Politics of terrain: Washington, DC, from tidewater town to global metropolis*. Chapel Hill: University of North Carolina Press.

Abramowitz, A. I. (2010). *The disappearing center: Engaged citizens, polarization, and American democracy*. New Haven, CT: Yale University Press.

Abramowitz, A. I., & Saunders, K. L. (2008). Is polarization a myth? *Journal of Politics, 70*, 542–55.

Abu-Lughod, J. (1999). *New York, Los Angeles, and Chicago: America's world cities*. Minneapolis: University of Minnesota Press.

Acemoglu, D., Robinson, J. A., & Verdier, T. (2012). *Can't we all be more like Scandinavians? Asymmetric growth and institutions in an interdependent world*. MIT Department of Economics Working Paper No. 12-22.

Adamic L., & Glance, N. (2005). *The political blogosphere and the 2004 U.S. election: Divided they blog*. HP Labs. Available at: http://www.blogpulse.com/papers/2005/AdamicGlanceBlogWWW.pdf

Aday, S. (2010). Chasing the bad news: An analysis of 2005 Iraq and Afghanistan war coverage on NBC and Fox News Channel. *Journal of Communication, 60*, 144–64.

Alderson, A. S., & Nielsen, F. (2002). Globalization and the great U-turn: Income inequality trends in 16 OECD countries. *American Journal of Sociology, 107*(5), 1244–99.

Alesina, A., & Glaeser, E. L. (2004). *Fighting poverty in the US and Europe: A world of difference*. New York: Oxford University Press.

Alesina, A., Glaeser, E. L., & Sacerdote, B. (2001). Why doesn't the US have a European-type welfare state? *Brookings Papers on Economic Activity, 2*, 187–277.

Algan, Y., Cahuc, P., & Sangnier, M. (2011). *Efficient and inefficient welfare states*. Discussion Paper No. 5445. Institute for the Study of Labor, Bonn.

Allen, F. L. (1931). *Only yesterday: An informal history of the nineteen-twenties*. New York: Harper & Brothers.

Allenby, B. R. (2000). Environmental security: Concept and implementation. *International Political Science Review, 21*(1), 5–21.

Altheide, D. (2004). Media logic and political communication. *Political Communication, 21*(3), 293–96.

Anderson, C. W. (2011). Between creative and quantified audiences: Web metrics and changing patterns of newswork in local US newsrooms. *Journalism, 12*, 550–66.

Anonymous. (1999). America's best newspapers. *Columbia Journalism Review, 38*(4), 14–16.

Anonymous. (2014). *An unbalanced recovery.* National Employment Law Project, New York.

Archibold, R. C. (2007, September 15). At U.S. border, desert takes a rising toll. *The New York Times*, p. 1.

Arquilla, J., & Ronfeldt, D. (2001). The advent of netwar (revisited). In J. Arquilla and D. Ronfeldt (Eds.), *Networks and netwars: The future of terror, crime, and militancy* (pp. 1–25). Santa Monica: Rand.

Arrighi, G. (1990). Marxist century, American century: The making and remaking of the world labour movement. *New Left Review, I*(179), 29–63.

Arrighi, G. (2009). The winding paths of capital. Interview by David Harvey. *New Left Review, 56*, 61–94.

Atkinson, J. D., & Berg, S. V. L. (2012). Narrowmobilization and tea party activism: A study of right-leaning alternative media. *Communication Studies, 63*(5), 519–35.

Atkinson, M. L., Baumgartner, F. R., Coggins, E. K., & Stimson, J. A. (2011). *Mood and agendas: Developing policy-specific conceptions of mood.* Paper presented at the annual meetings of the Midwest Political Science Association, Chicago, March 31–April 3, 2011.

Atlas, J. (2001, October 7). Among the lost: Illusions of immortality. *The New York Times*, section 4, p. 5.

Autor, D. H., Dorn, D., & Hanson, G. H. (2013). The China syndrome: Local labor market effects of import competition in the United States. *American Economic Review, 103*(6), 2121–68.

Bafumi, J., & Shapiro, R. Y. (2009). A new partisan voter. *Journal of Politics, 71*, 1–24.

Baldassarri, D., & Gelman, A. (2008). Partisans without constraint: Political polarization and trends in American public opinion. *American Journal of Sociology, 114*, 408–46.

Balzar, J. (2001, September 17). Brothers, fundamentally. *The Los Angeles Times*, part 2, p. 9.

Barber, B. (1996). *Jihad vs. McWorld.* New York: Ballantine.

Barbieri, K., & Reuveny, R. (2005). Economic globalization and civil war. *The Journal of Politics, 67*(4), 1228–47.

Barry, J. M. (1997). *Rising tide: The great Mississippi flood of 1927 and how it changed America.* New York: Touchstone.

Bartels, L. M. (2006). What's the matter with *What's the Matter with Kansas? Quarterly Journal of Political Science, 1*, 201–26.

Bartels, L. M. (2008). *Unequal democracy: The political economy of the new gilded age.* Princeton, NJ: Princeton University Press.

Bawn, K., Cohen, M., Karol, D., Masket, S., Noel, H., & Zaller, J. (2012). A theory of political parties: Groups, policy demands and nominations in American politics. *Perspectives on Politics, 10*(3), 571–97.

Beck, U. (1992). *Risk society: Towards a new modernity.* London: Sage.

Beck, U. (1994). The reinvention of politics: Towards a theory of reflexive modernization. In U. Beck, A. Giddens, & S. Lash (Eds.), *Reflexive modernization: Politics, tradition and aesthetics in the modern social order* (pp. 1–55). Cambridge, UK: Polity.

Bénabou, R. J. M., & Tirole, J. (2006). Belief in a just world and redistributive politics. *Quarterly Journal of Economics, 121*, 699–746.

Benford, R. D., & Snow, R. A. (2000). Framing processes and social movements: An overview and assessment. *Annual Review of Sociology, 26*, 611–39.

Benjamin, D., & Simon, S. (2001, September 14). At war with a wraith. *The Washington Post*, p. A37.

Benkler, Y. (2006). *The wealth of networks*. New Haven, CT: Yale University Press.

Bennett, W. L. (2003a). *News: The politics of illusion*. New York: Longman.

Bennett, W. L. (2003b). Communicating global activism. *Information, Communication & Society, 6*, 143–68.

Bennett, W. L., & Iyengar, S. (2008). A new era of minimal effects? The changing foundations of political communication. *Journal of Communication, 58*, 707–31.

Bennett, W. L., Lawrence, R. G., & Livingston, S. (2006). None dare call it torture: Indexing and the limits of press independence in the Abu Ghraib scandal. *Journal of Communication, 56*, 467–85.

Bennett, W. L., & Segerberg, A. (2013). *The logic of connective action: Digital media and the personalization of contentious politics*. New York: Cambridge University Press.

Berger, P. L., & Luckmann, T. (1966). *The social construction of reality: A treatise in the sociology of knowledge*. Harmondsworth: Penguin.

Berlin, I. (1969). *Four essays on liberty*. New York: Oxford University Press.

Bernauer, T. (2013). Climate change politics. *Annual Review of Political Science, 16*, 421–48.

Bimber, B. (2001). Information and political engagement in America: The search for effects of information technology at the individual level. *Political Research Quarterly, 54*, 53–67.

Bipartisan framework for immigration reform. (2013). US Senate. Available at http://www.flake.senate.gov/documents/immigration_reform.pdf

Black, E. (2001, September 16). Terrorism: Hatred of America has many complex roots. *Minneapolis Star Tribune*, p. 6A.

Blij, Harm de. (2009). *The power of place: Geography, destiny, and globalization's rough landscape*. New York: Oxford University Press.

Blumler, J. E., & M. Gurevitch. (1995). *The crisis of political communication*. London: Routledge.

Blyth, M. (2002). *Great transformations: Economic ideas and institutional change in the twentieth century*. New York: Cambridge University Press.

Bobo, L., Kluegel, J. R., & Smith, R. A. (1997). Laissez-faire racism: The crystallization of a kinder, gentler, antiblack ideology. In S. A. Tuch & J. K. Martin (Eds.), *Racial attitudes in the 1990's: Continuity and change* (pp. 15–41). Westport, CT: Praeger.

Borio, C., & Disyatat, P. (2011). Global imbalances and the financial crisis: Link or no link? BIS Working Papers no. 346. Basel, Switzerland: Bank for International Settlements.

Borjas, G. J., & Katz L. F. (2005). *The evolution of the Mexican-born workforce in the United States*. NBER Working Paper no. 11281. Cambridge, MA: National Bureau of Economic Research.

Boschken, H. L. (2008). A multiple-perspectives construct of the American global city. *Urban Studies, 45*, 3–28.

Bovitz, G. L., Druckman, J. M., & Lupia, A. (2002). When can a news organization lead public opinion? Ideology versus market forces in decisions to make news. *Public Choice, 113*, 127–55.

Boydstun, A. E. (2013). *Making the news: Politics, the media, and agenda setting.* Chicago: University of Chicago Press.

Boykoff, M. T. (2007). Flogging a dead norm? Newspaper coverage of anthropogenic climate change in the United States and United Kingdom from 2003 to 2006. *Area, 39,* 470–81.

Branton, R. P., Cassese, E. C., Jones, B. S., & Westerland, C. (2011). All along the watchtower: Acculturation fear, anti-Latino affect, and immigration. *The Journal of Politics, 73*(3), 664–79.

Branton, R. P., & Dunaway, J. (2009). Spatial proximity to the US-Mexico border and newspaper coverage of immigration issues. *Political Research Quarterly, 62,* 289–302.

Brewer, P. (2001). The many faces of social identity: Implications for political psychology. *Political Psychology, 22,* 115–25.

Bright, J., & Nicholls, T. (2014). The life and death of political news: Measuring the impact of the audience agenda using online data. *Social Science Computer Review, 32*(2), 170–81.

Brinkley, D. (2006). *The great deluge: Hurricane Katrina, New Orleans, and the Mississippi Gulf.* New York: HarperCollins.

Brody, S. D., Zahran, S., Vedlitz, A., & Grover, H. (2008). Examining the relationship between physical vulnerability and public perceptions of global climate change in the United States. *Environment and Behavior, 40*(1), 72–95.

Brooks, D. (2004, May 18). In Iraq, America's shakeout moment. *The New York Times,* p. A23.

Brooks, S. G., & Wohlforth, W. C. (2002, July-August). American primacy in perspective. *Foreign Affairs, 81*(4), 20–33.

Brown, M. E., Lynn-Jones, S. M., & Miller, S. E. (Eds.). (1996). *Debating the democratic peace.* Cambridge, MA: MIT Press.

Brulle, R. J., Carmichael, J., & Jenkins, J. C. (2012). Shifting public opinion on climate change: An empirical assessment of factors influencing concern over climate change in the U.S., 2002–2010. *Climatic Change, 114*(2), 169–88.

Brzezinski, Z. (2003, February 19). Why unity is essential. *The Washington Post,* p. A27.

Bush, G. W. (2010). *Decision points.* New York: Crown.

Buzan, B. (1983). *People, states, and fear: The national security problem in international relations.* Chapel Hill: University of North Carolina Press.

Calibrating the use of force. (2001, September 22). *The New York Times,* section A, p. 24.

Campbell, D. E. (2004). Acts of faith: Churches and civic engagement. *Political Behavior, 26,* 155–80.

Canclini, N. G. (1995). *Hybrid cultures: Strategies for entering modernity.* Minneapolis: University of Minnesota Press.

Card, D., & Lewis, E. G. (2007). The diffusion of Mexican immigrants during the 1990s: Explanations and impacts. In George Borjas (Ed.), *Mexican immigration.* Chicago: University of Chicago Press.

Carmines, E. G., & Stimson, J. A. (1980). The two faces of issue voting. *American Political Science Review, 74,* 78–91.

Carragee, K., & Roefs, W. (2004). The neglect of power in recent framing research. *Journal of Communication, 54,* 214–33.

Carson, R. (1962). *Silent spring*. New York: Houghton Mifflin.

Castells, M. (1996). *The rise of the network society*. Oxford: Wiley-Blackwell.

Castells, M. (1997). *The power of identity*. Oxford: Wiley-Blackwell.

Cave, D. (2008, June 9). Local officials adopt new, harder tactics on illegal immigrants. *The New York Times*, p. A1.

CBS. (2006, February 26). *News Poll*.

CBS News / *The New York Times*. (2007, September). Poll. Retrieved from the iPOLL Databank, The Roper Center for Public Opinion Research, University of Connecticut. http://www.ropercenter.uconn.edu.proxy.cc.uic.edu/data_access/ipoll/ipoll.html

CBS News / *The New York Times*. (2011, June). Poll. Retrieved from the iPOLL Databank, The Roper Center for Public Opinion Research, University of Connecticut.

CBS News / *The New York Times*. (2015, May). Poll. Retrieved from the iPOLL Databank, The Roper Center for Public Opinion Research, University of Connecticut.

Cherry, C. (1971). *God's new Israel: Religious interpretations of American destiny*. Englewood Cliffs, NJ: Prentice-Hall.

Chetty, R., Hendren, N., Kline, P., & Saez, E. (2013). The economic impacts of tax expenditures: Evidence from spatial variation across the US. http://scholar.harvard.edu /hendren/publications/economic-impacts-tax-expenditures-evidence-spatial -variation-across-us

Chicago Council on Foreign Relations. (2002). *Worldviews 2002: American public opinion and foreign policy*. http://www.worldviews.org/detailreports/usreport/index.htm

Chicago Daily Tribune. (1927a, June 4). U.S. will act to curb flood, official pledge.

Chicago Daily Tribune. (1927b, November 8). Big bill helps Congress solve flood control.

Chong, D., Citrin, J., & Conley, P. (2001). When self-interest matters. *Political Psychology*, 22, 541–70.

Christian Science Monitor. (1927a, November 4). Utilizing flood control.

Christian Science Monitor. (1927b, November 16). Power with flood control.

Christian Science Monitor. (1928a, March 29). Flood control bill puts cost on government.

Clark, C. M. (2014). *Sleepwalkers: How Europe went to war in 1914*. New York: Harper Perennial.

Clark, T. N. (Ed.). (2004). *The city as an entertainment machine*. New York: JAI Press/ Elsevier.

Clark, W. C. (2000). Environmental globalization. In Joseph S. Nye & John D. Donahue (Eds.), *Governance in a globalizing world* (pp. 86–108). Washington, DC: Brookings Institution Press.

Clarke, R. A. (2004). *Against all enemies*. New York: Free Press.

Conlin, J. (1999, December 27). Hey, what about us? *Business Week*, p. 52.

Cornia, G. A., Addison, T., & Kiiski, S. (2004). Income distribution changes and their impact in the post second world war period. In G. A. Cornia (Ed.), *Inequality, growth, and poverty in an era of liberalization and globalization* (pp. 26–56). New York: Oxford University Press.

Cottle, S. (2008). Reporting demonstrations: The changing politics of media dissent. *Media, Culture & Society*, 30, 853–72.

Cowen, T. (2002). *Creative destruction: How globalization is changing the world's cultures*. Princeton, NJ: Princeton University Press.

CNN/ORC International. (2014, November). Poll. Retrieved from the iPOLL Databank, The Roper Center for Public Opinion Research, University of Connecticut. http://www.ropercenter.uconn.edu.proxy.cc.uic.edu/data_access/ipoll/ipoll.html

Creighton, M. J., Jamal, A., & Malancu, N. C. (2015). Has opposition to immigration increased in the United States after the economic crisis? An experimental approach. *International Migration Review, 49*(3), 727–56.

D'Angelo, P. (2002). News framing as a multiparadigmatic research program: A response to Entman. *Journal of Communication, 52*, 870–88.

Davey, M. (2007, December 13). Immigration, and its politics, shake rural Iowa. *The New York Times*, p. 1.

Deans, B. (2006, June 6). Raid exposes border risk with Canada. *Atlanta Journal-Constitution*, p. 1.

della Porta, D. (2005). Multiple belongings, tolerant identities, and the construction of "another politics": Between the European Social Forum and the local social fora. In D. della Porta & S. Tarrow (Eds.), *Transnational protest and global activism* (pp. 175–202). Lanham, MD: Rowman & Littlefield.

della Porta, D., & Tarrow, S. (2005). Transnational processes and social activism: An introduction. In D. della Porta & S. Tarrow (Eds.), *Transnational protest and global activism* (pp. 1–20). Lanham, MD: Rowman & Littlefield.

DeMause, N. (2013, January). Sandy and climate. *Extra!* pp. 8–9.

DiFonzo, N., Bourgeois, M. J., Suls, J. M., Homan, C., Stupak, N., Brooks, B., Ross, D. S., & Bordia, P. (2013). Rumor clustering, consensus, and polarization: Dynamic social impact and self-organization of hearsay. *Journal of Experimental Social Psychology, 49*, 378–99.

Dolny, M. (2008). *The incredible shrinking think tank: Fairness in Accuracy and Reporting (FAIR).* http://www.fair.org/index.php?page=3322

Domke, D. (2004). *God willing? Political fundamentalism in the White House, the "War on Terror," and the echoing press.* London: Pluto Press.

Douglas, M. (1975). *Implicit meanings: Essays in anthropology.* London: Routledge.

Dowd, M. (2003, February 16). The Venus trap. *The New York Times*, section 4, p. 11.

Druckman, J. (2001). The implications of framing effects for citizen competence. *Political Behavior, 23*, 225–56.

Drury, S. D. (1997). *Leo Strauss and the American right.* New York: St. Martin's Press.

Dunaway, J., Branton, R. P., & Abrajano, M. A. (2010). Agenda setting, public opinion, and the issue of immigration reform. *Social Science Quarterly, 91*(2), 359–78.

Dunlap, R. E., & McCright, A. M. (2011). Organized climate change denial. In J. S. Dryzek, R. B. Norgaard, & D. Schlosberg (Eds.), *The Oxford handbook of climate change and society* (pp. 144–60). Oxford: Oxford University Press.

Dunlap, T. R. (2004). *Faith in nature: Environmentalism as religious quest.* Seattle: University of Washington Press.

Eisinger, P. K. (1973). The conditions of protest behavior in American cities. *The American Political Science Review, 67*, 11–28.

Ellis, R. J. (1993). *American political cultures.* New York: Oxford University Press.

el-Nawawy, M. (2006). U.S. public diplomacy in the Arab world: The news credibility of radio Sawa and television Alhurra in five countries. *Global Media and Communication, 2*(2), 185–205.

Entman, R. M. (1993). Framing: Toward clarification of a fractured paradigm. *Journal of Communication, 43*, 51–58.

Entman, R. M. (2003). Cascading activation: Contesting the White House's frame after 9/11. *Political Communication, 20*, 415–32.

Entman, R. M. (2004). *Projections of power: Framing news, public opinion, and U.S. foreign policy.* Chicago: University of Chicago Press.

Entman, R. M., & Rojecki, A. (1993). Freezing out the public: Elite and media framing of the U.S. anti-nuclear movement. *Political Communication, 10*, 155–73.

Entman, R. M., & Rojecki, A. (2000). *The black image in the white mind.* Chicago: University of Chicago Press.

Ettema, J. S. (2005). Crafting cultural resonance: Imaginative power in everyday journalism. *Journalism, 6*(2), 131–52.

Evans, W. A. (1927, August 7). Flood control is nation's job, Evans insists. *Chicago Tribune*, p. 1.

Excerpts from Pentagon's plan: 'Prevent the re-emergence of a new rival.' (1992, March 8). *The New York Times*, section 1, p. 14.

Fearon, J. D., & Laitin, D. D. (2003). Ethnicity, insurgency, and civil war. *The American Political Science Review, 97*(1), 75–90.

Federici, S. (2011). Women, austerity, and the unfinished feminist revolution. *Occupy! An OWS-Inspired Gazette*, no. 3, pp. 32–34.

Fernàndez-Kelly, P., & Massey, D. (2007). Borders for whom? The role of NAFTA in Mexico-U.S. migration. *The Annals of the American Academy of Political and Social Science, 610*, 98–118.

Ferriss, S. (2006, July 2). Out in the fields, farmers sweat out immigration issue. *Sacramento Bee*, p. 1.

Fiorina, M. P., Abrams, S. J., & Pope, J. (2011). *Culture war? The myth of a polarized America.* Boston: Longman.

Fischhoff, B., Slovic, P., Lichtenstein, S., Read, S., & Combs, B. (1978). How safe is safe enough? A psychometric study of attitudes towards technological risks and benefits. *Policy Sciences, 9*(2), 127–52.

Ford, H. (2010, November 10). *DLC chair Harold Ford Jr. statement on bipartisan fiscal commission in Democratic Leadership Committee.* http://www.dlc.org/ndol_ci.cfm ?kaid=125&subid=162&contentid=255207

Friedman, T. (2000). *The Lexus and the olive tree.* New York: Anchor.

Friedman, T. (2001, September 13). World War III. *The New York Times*, p. A27.

Friedman, T. (2003, January 22). Thinking about Iraq (I). *The New York Times*, p. A21.

Friedman, T. (2005). *The world is flat.* New York: Farrar, Straus and Giroux.

Friedmann, J., & Wolff, G. (1982). World city formation: An agenda for research and action. *International Journal of Urban and Regional Research, 6*, 309–44.

Fukuyama, F. (1992). *The end of history and the last man.* New York: Avon.

Gabler, N. (2001, October 7). Fundamentalism: An eternal war of mind-sets. *The Los Angeles Times*, part M, p. 6.

Gaddis, J. L. (2002). *The landscape of history: How historians map the past.* New York: Oxford University Press.

Gaddis, J. L. (2004). *Surprise, security, and the American experience.* Cambridge, MA: Harvard University Press.

Gamson, W. A. (2001). Forward. In S. D. Reese, O. H. Gandy, & A. E. Grant (Eds.), *Framing public life: Perspectives on media and our understanding of the social world* (pp. ix-xi). Mahwah, NJ: Lawrence Erlbaum Associates.

Gamson, W. A., & Modigliani, A. (1989). Media discourse and public opinion on nuclear power. *American Journal of Sociology, 95*, 1–37.

Gans, H. J. (1979). *Deciding what's news*. New York: Pantheon Books.

Garrett, R. K. (2006). Protest in an information society: A review of literature on social movements and ICTs. *Information, Communication & Society, 9*, 202–24.

Garrett, R. K., & Danziger, J. N. (2011). Internet electorate. *Communications of the ACM, 54*, 117–23.

Gautney, H. (2011). Occupy the commons. *Occupy! An OWS-Inspired Gazette*, no. 2, p. 34.

Geertz, C. (1973). *The interpretation of cultures: Selected essays*. New York: Basic Books.

Gelpi, C., Feaver, P. D., & Reifler, J. (2009). *Paying the human costs of war: American public opinion and casualties in military conflict*. Princeton, NJ: Princeton University Press.

Gentzkow, M., & Shapiro, J. M. (2010). What drives media slant? Evidence from U.S. daily newspapers. *Econometrica, 78*(1), 35–71.

Gentzkow, M., & Shapiro, J. M. (2011). Ideological segregation online and offline. *The Quarterly Journal of Economics, 126*, 1799–1839.

Gergen, K. J. (1973). Social psychology as history. *Journal of Social Psychology and Personality, 26*(2), 309–20.

Ghaziani, A., & Baldassarri, D. (2011). Cultural anchors and the organization of difference: A muti-method analysis of LGBT marches on Washington. *American Sociological Review, 76*, 179–206.

Giddens, A. (1990). *The consequences of modernity*. Palo Alto, CA: Stanford University Press.

Giddens, A. (1991). *Modernity and self-identity: Self and society in the late modern age*. Palo Alto, CA: Stanford University Press.

Giddens, A. (2000). *Runaway world*. London: Routledge.

Gifford, R. (2011). The dragons of inaction: Psychological barriers that limit climate change mitigation and adaptation. *American Psychologist, 66*(4), 290–302.

Gilens, M., & Page, B. I. (2014). Testing theories of American politics: Elites, interest groups, and average citizens. *Perspectives on Politics, 12*, 564–81.

Gilpin, R. (2000). *The challenge of global capitalism: The world economy in the 21st century*. Princeton, NJ: Princeton University Press.

Gitlin, T. (1980). *The whole world is watching: Mass media in the making and unmaking of the New Left*. Berkeley: University of California Press.

Gitlin, T. (1995). *The twilight of common dreams: Why America is wracked by culture wars*. New York: Metropolitan Books.

Glaser, B. G., & Strauss, A. L. (1967). *The discovery of grounded theory: Strategies for qualitative research*. Chicago: Aldine.

Gosselin, P. G., & Shiver, J. (2001, September 23). After the attack: Financial fallout. *The Los Angeles Times*, part A, part 1, p. 1.

Graeber, D. (2011). *Debt: The first 5,000 years*. Brooklyn, NY: Melville House.

Graham, J., Haidt, J., & Nosek, B. A. (2009). Liberals and conservatives rely on different sets of moral foundations. *Journal of Personality and Social Psychology, 96*, 1029–46.

Green, J. C. (2007). *The faith factor: How religion influences American elections*. Westport, CT: Praeger.

Greenberg, J., Poole, S. L., & Pyszczynski, T. (2004). *Handbook of experimental existential psychology*. New York: Guilford.

Greenberg, J., Porteus, J., Simon, L., Pyszczynski, T., & Solomon, S. (1995). Evidence of a terror management function of cultural icons: The effects of mortality salience on the inappropriate use of cherished cultural symbols. *Personality and Social Psychology Bulletin, 21*, 1221–28.

Greenberg, J., Pyszczynski, T., Solomon, S., Rosenblatt, A., Veeder, M., Kirkland, S., & Lyon, D. (1990). Evidence for terror management theory II: The effects of mortality salience on reactions to those who threaten or bolster the cultural worldview. *Journal of Personality and Social Psychology, 58*, 308–18.

Greenway, H. D. S. (2001, October 8). The deep roots of terrorism. *The Boston Globe*, p. A15.

Greider, W. (1981). The education of David Stockman. *The Atlantic*. http://www.theatlantic.com/magazine/archive/1981/12/the-education-of-david-stockman/305760/

Grueskin, B., Seave, A., & Graves, L. (2014). *The story so far: What we know about the business of digital journalism*. Tow Center for Digital Journalism, Columbia Journalism School. http://towcenter.org/research/the-story-so-far-what-we-know-about-the-business-of-digital-journalism/

Guth, J. L., & Green, J. C. (1996). The moralizing minority: Christian Right support among political contributors. In J. C. Green, J. L. Guth, C. E. Smidt, & L. A. Kellstedt (Eds.), *Religion and the culture wars: Dispatches from the front* (pp. 30–43). Lanham, MD: Rowman and Littlefield.

Hacker, J. S., & Pierson, P. (2010). *Winner-take-all politics: How Washington made the rich richer—and turned its back on the middle class*. New York: Simon and Schuster.

Haidt, J. (2001). The emotional dog and its rational tail: A social intuitionist approach to moral judgment. *Psychological Review, 4*, 814–34.

Hainmueller, J., & Hiscox, M. J. (2010). Attitudes toward highly skilled and low-skilled immigration: Evidence from a survey experiment. *American Political Science Review, 104*, 61–84.

Hainmueller, J., & Hopkins, D. (2014). Public attitudes toward immigration. *Annual Review of Political Science, 17*, 225–49.

Hall, P., & Soskice, D. (2001). *Varieties of capitalism: The institutional foundations of comparative advantage*. New York: Oxford University Press.

Hallin, D. C. (1992). The passing of the "high modernism" of American journalism. *Journal of Communication, 42*, 14–25.

Halttunen, K. (1998). *Murder most foul: The killer and the American gothic imagination*. Cambridge, MA: Harvard University Press.

Hamilton, L. C., Cutler, M. J., & Schaefer, A. (2012). Public knowledge and concern about polar-region warming. *Polar Geography, 35*(2), 155–68.

Hamilton, L. C., & Keim, B. D. (2009). Regional variation in perceptions about climate change. *International Journal of Climatology, 29*(15), 2348–52.

Hancock, A. (2004). *The politics of disgust: The public identity of the welfare queen*. New York: New York University Press.

Hanson, G. H. (2006). Illegal migration from Mexico to the United States. *Journal of Economic Literature, 44*, 869–924.

Hanson, G. H., & Spilimbergo, A. (2001). Political economy, sectoral shocks, and border enforcement. *Canadian Journal of Economics, 34*, 612–38.

Harcourt, B. E. (2012). Political disobedience. *Critical Inquiry, 39*, 33–55.

Harcourt, W., & Escobar, A. (2002). Women and the politics of place. *Development, 45*, 7–14.

Hardt, M., & Negri, A. (2000). *Empire*. Cambridge, MA: Harvard University Press.

Hart and Teeter Research. (1997). Available: Roper Center at University of Connecticut, Public Opinion Online.

Heine, S. J., Proulx, T., & Vohs, K. D. (2006). The meaning maintenance model: On the coherence of social motivations. *Personality and Social Psychology Review, 10*(2), 88–110.

Held, D., & McGrew, A. (2007). *Globalization/anti-globalization: Beyond the great divide.* Cambridge: Polity.

Herman, E. S., & Chomsky, N. (2002). *Manufacturing consent: The political economy of the mass media.* New York: Pantheon.

Hetey, R. C., & Eberhardt, J. L. (2014). Racial disparities in incarceration increase acceptance of punitive policies. *Psychological Science, 25*(10), 1949–54.

Higham, J. (1965). *Strangers in the land: Patterns of American nativism, 1860–1925.* New York: Athaneum.

Hindman, M. (2009). *The myth of digital democracy.* Princeton, NJ: Princeton University Press.

Hirschman, A. O. (1991). *The rhetoric of reaction.* Cambridge, MA: Belknap Press of Harvard University Press.

Hirsh, J. B., Mar, R. A., & Peterson, J. B. (2012). Psychological entropy: A framework for understanding uncertainty-related anxiety. *Psychological Review, 19*(2), 304–20.

Hitlan, R. T., Carrillo, K., Zárate, M. A., & Aikman, S. N. (2007). Attitudes toward immigrant groups and the September 11 terrorist attacks. *Peace and Conflict: Journal of Peace Psychology, 13*(2), 135–52.

Hoagland, J. (2001, September 26). Government's comeback. *The Washington Post*, p. A25.

Hochschild, J. L. (1981). *What's fair? American beliefs about distributive justice.* Cambridge, MA: Harvard University Press.

Hogg, M. A., Adelman, J. R., & Blagg, R. D. (2010). Religion in the face of uncertainty: An uncertainty-identity theory account of religiousness. *Personality and Social Psychology Review, 14*, 72–83.

Holbert, R., Garrett, K., & Gleason, L.S. (2010). A new era of minimal effects? A response to Bennett and Iyengar. *Journal of Communication, 60*, 707–31.

Holstein, W. J. (2001, October 28). Sharing the wealth, for capitalism's sake. *The New York Times*, section 3, p. 7.

Hoover, H. (1927, June 12). Hoover outlines plan to bridle Mississippi. *The Los Angeles Times*, p. 1.

Hopkins, D. J. (2010). Politicized places: Explaining where and when immigrants provoke local opposition. *American Political Science Review, 1044*, 40–60.

Howse, R. (2008). The end of the globalization debate: A review essay. *Harvard Law Review, 121*, 1528–54.

Huebner, J. (2005). A possible declining trend for worldwide innovation. *Technological Forecasting and Social Change, 72*, 980–86.

Hulme, M. (2011). Reducing the future to climate: A story of climate determinism and reductionism. *Osiris, 26*, 245–66.

Huntington, S. P. (1996). *The clash of civilizations and the remaking of the world order.* New York: Simon & Schuster.

Intergovernmental Panel on Climate Change. (2014). *Climate change 2014: Synthesis report.* Geneva, Switzerland.

Iraq dossier. (2003, January 10). *The New York Times,* p. A22.

Iyengar, S., & Hahn, A. S. (2009). Red media, blue media: Evidence of ideological selectivity in media use. *Journal of Communication, 59,* 19–39.

Iyengar, S., Sood, G., & Lelkes, Y. (2012). Affect not ideology: A social identity perspective on polarization. *Public Opinion Quarterly, 76,* 405–31.

Iyengar, S., & Westwood, S. J. (2014). Fear and loathing across party lines: New evidence on group polarization. *American Journal of Political Science.* doi:10.1111/ajps.12152

Jackman, M. R. (1994). *Paternalism and conflict: Ideology and coercion in gender, class, and race relations.* Berkeley: University of California Press.

Jacoby, R. (1999). *The end of utopia: Politics and culture in an age of apathy.* New York: Basic Books.

Jacoby, W. G. (2014). Is there a culture war? Conflicting value structures in American public opinion. *American Political Science Review, 108,* 754–71.

Jameson, F. (1984). Postmodernism, or the cultural logic of late capitalism. *New Left Review, 146,* 53–92.

Jameson, F. (1991). *Postmodernism, or, the cultural logic of late capitalism.* Durham, NC: Duke University Press.

Johnson, C. (2001, September 30). The lessons of blowback. *The Los Angeles Times,* part M, p. 1.

Kahan, D. (2012). Why we are poles apart on climate change. *Nature, 488*(7411), 255.

Kahneman, D. (2011). *Thinking, fast and slow.* New York: Farrar, Straus and Giroux.

Kaplan, R. D. (2000). *The coming anarchy.* New York: Vintage.

Kapstein, E. B. (2001). *Globalization and democratization: Friends or foes?* http://www.globaldimensions.net/articles/kapstein/kapstein1.htm

Kelly, N. J., & Enns, P. K. (2010). Dynamics of public opinion: The self-reinforcing link between economic inequality and mass preferences. *American Journal of Political Science, 54,* 855–70.

Keohane, R. O., & Nye, J. S. (2000a). Introduction. In J. S. Nye & J. D. Donahue (Eds.), *Governance in a globalizing world* (pp. 1–44). Washington, DC: Brookings Institution Press.

Keohane, R., & Nye, J. (2000b, Spring). Globalization: What's new? What's not? (And so what?) *Foreign Policy,* 104–19.

Keynes, J. M. (1924). *A tract on monetary reform.* London: Macmillan and company.

Kinder, D. H., & Sanders, L. M. (1996). *Divided by color: Racial politics and democratic ideals.* Chicago: University of Chicago Press.

King, G., & Murray, C. J. L. (2002). Rethinking human security. *Political Science Quarterly, 116,* 585–610.

Klandermans, B. (1997). *The social psychology of protest.* Oxford: Blackwell.

Kolk, A., & Levy, D. (2001). Winds of change: Corporate strategy, climate change, and oil multinationals. *European Management Journal, 19,* 501–9.

Krauthammer, C. (2001, September 28). The war: A road map. *The Washington Post,* p. A39.

Krauthammer, C. (2003, January 24). No turning back now. *The Washington Post,* p. A27.

Laconte, J. (2003, January 28). The prince of peace was a warrior, too. *The New York Times*, p. A21.

Ladd, J. M. (2012). *Why Americans hate the media and why it matters*. Princeton, NJ: Princeton University Press.

Laitin, D. D. (1988). Political culture and political preferences. *The American Political Science Review, 82*(2), 589–97.

Laitin, D. D. (1995). The civic culture at 30. *American Political Science Review, 89*(1), 168–73.

Landau, M. J., Solomon, S., Greenberg, J., Cohen, F., Pyszczynski, T., Arndt, J., et al. (2004). Deliver us from evil: The effects of mortality salience and reminders of 9/11 on support for President George W. Bush. *Personality and Social Psychology Bulletin, 30*(9), 1136–50.

Lane, A. C. (1927, August 4). Rivers need room. *Christian Science Monitor*, p. 16.

Lawrence, E., Sides, J., & Farrell, H. (2010). Self-segregation or deliberation? Blog readership, participation, and polarization in American politics. *Perspectives on Politics, 8*, 141–57.

Layman, G. C., & Carsey, T. M. (2002). Party polarization and party structuring of policy attitudes: A comparison of three NES panel studies. *Political Behavior, 24*, 199–236.

Lears, J. (2003). *Something for nothing: Luck in America*. New York: Penguin.

Leege, D. C., Wold, K. D., Krueger, B. S., & Mueller, P. D. (2002). *The politics of cultural differences: Social change and voter mobilization strategies in the post-New Deal period*. Princeton, NJ: Princeton University Press.

le Grignou, B., & Patou, C. (2004). ATTAC(k)ing expertise: Does the Internet really democratize knowledge? In W. van de Donk, B. D. Loader, P. G. Nixon, & D. Rucht (Eds.), *Cyberprotest: New media, citizens, and social movements* (pp. 164–79). New York: Routledge.

Lewis, A. (2001a, September 15). Beware unintended results. *The New York Times*, p. A23.

Lewis, A. (2001b, September 22). To thine own self be true. *The New York Times*, p. A25.

Lindert, P. H., & Williamson, J. G. (2003). Does globalization make the world more unequal? In M. D. Bordo, A. M. Taylor, & J. G. Williamson (Eds.), *Globalization in historical perspective*. Chicago: University of Chicago Press.

Lipset, S. M. (1996). *American exceptionalism: A double-edged sword*. New York: W. W. Norton.

Lipset, S. M., & Rokkan, S. (1967). *Cleavage structures, party systems, and voter alignments: An introduction*. New York: Free Press.

Lukes, S. (1974). *Power: A radical view*. London: Macmillan.

Maas, P. (2001, October 21). Emroz Khan is having a bad day. *The New York Times Magazine*, p. 48.

Malley, R. (2001, October 11). Faith and terror. *The Washington Post*, p. A33.

Mann, J. (2004). *Rise of the Vulcans: The history of Bush's war cabinet*. New York: W. W. Norton.

Mann, M. (1997). Has globalization ended the rise and rise of the nation-state? *Review of International Political Economy, 4*, 472–96.

Mansbridge, J. J. (1980). *Beyond adversary democracy*. New York: Basic Books.

Mansfield, E. D., & Mutz, D. C. (2009). Support for free trade: Self-interest, sociotropic politics, and out-group anxiety. *International Organization, 63*, 425–57.

Manza, J., & Brooks, C. (1999). *Social cleavages and political change: Voter alignments and US party coalitions*. Oxford: Oxford University Press.

Marcus, D. (2011). From occupation to communization. *Occupy! An OWS-Inspired Gazette*, no. 3, pp. 30–31.

Massey, D. (2007). Understanding America's immigration "crisis." *Proceedings of the American Philosophical Society, 151,* 309–27.

Mayer, J. (2010, August 30). Covert operations. *The New Yorker,* pp. 44–55.

McAdam, D., Tarrow, S., & Tilly, C. (2001). *Dynamics of contention.* New York: Cambridge University Press.

McCloskey, D. N. (2006). *The bourgeois virtues: Ethics for an age of commerce.* Chicago: University of Chicago Press.

McCloskey, H., & Zaller, J. (1984). *The American ethos: Public attitudes toward capitalism and democracy.* Cambridge, MA: Harvard University Press.

McCright, A. M., & Dunlap, R. E. (2011). The politicization of climate change and polarization in the American public's views of global warming, 2001–2010. *The Sociological Quarterly, 52,* 155–94.

McGregor, I., Zanna, M. P., Holmes, J. G., & Spencer, S. J. (2001). Compensatory conviction in the face of personal uncertainty: Going to extremes and being oneself. *Journal of Personality and Social Psychology, 80,* 472–88.

McKinley, J. C. (2007, February 21). Tougher tactics deter migrants at U.S. border. *The New York Times,* p. 1.

McLaughlin, D. (1998). Fooling with nature: *Silent Spring* revisited. Frontline, PBS. http://www.pbs.org/wgbh/pages/frontline/shows/nature/disrupt/sspring.html

McPhee, J. (1989). *The control of nature.* New York: Farrar, Straus and Giroux.

McPhillips, J. (1998, August 17). R.I. firm used illegal aliens in Mass., audit says. *Providence Journal-Bulletin,* p. 1B.

Mearsheimer, J. (2001). *The tragedy of great power politics.* New York: W. W. Norton.

Mearsheimer, J., & Walt, S. (2003, January/February). An unnecessary war. *Foreign Policy, 134,* 51–59.

Meltzer, A. H., & Richard, S. F. (1981). A rational theory of the size of government. *Journal of Political Economy, 89*(5), 914–27.

Melucci, A. (1989). *Nomads of the present: Social movements and individual needs in contemporary society.* Philadelphia: Temple University Press.

Mendelberg, T. (2001). *The race card: Campaign strategy, implicit messages, and the norm of equality.* Princeton, NJ: Princeton University Press.

Meraz, S. (2009). Is there an elite hold? Traditional media to social media agenda setting influence in blog networks. *Journal of Computer-Mediated Communication, 4,* 682–707.

Meyer, D. (1986). The world system of cities: Relations between international financial metropolises and South American cities. *Social Forces, 64,* 553–81.

Mickelthwait, J., & Wooldridge, A. (2000). *A future perfect: The challenge and promise of globalization.* New York: Random House.

Miller, D. T. (1999). The norm of self-interest. *American Psychologist, 54*(12), 1053–60.

Miller, G., & Schofield, N. (2008). The transformation of the Republican and Democratic party coalitions in the U.S. *Perspectives on Politics, 6*(3), 433–50.

Mol, A. P. J. (2000). The environmental movement in an era of ecological modernization. *Geoforum, 31,* 41–56.

Moravcsik, A. (1997). Taking preferences seriously: A liberal theory of international politics. *International Organization, 51,* 513–53.

Morin, D. T., & Flynn, M. A. (2014). We are the Tea Party! The use of Facebook as an online political forum for the construction and maintenance of in-group identification during the "GOTV" weekend. *Communication Quarterly, 62*(1), 115–33.

Morone, J. A. (2003). *Hellfire nation: The politics of sin in American history.* New Haven, CT: Yale University Press.

Mudge, S. L. (2011). What's left of leftism? Neoliberal politics in western party systems, 1945–2008. *Social Science History, 35*(3): 337–80.

Mulhern, F. (2015). A party of latecomers. *New Left Review, 93,* 69–96.

National Security Strategy of the United States of America. (2002). *National Security Council.* Washington, DC. http://www.whitehouse.gov/nsc/nss.pdf

Nelson, B. (1984). *Making an issue of child abuse: Political agenda setting for social problems.* Chicago: University of Chicago Press.

The New York Times. (1927a, August 28). Hoover's plan to harness our waters.

The New York Times. (1927b, October 4). Coolidge projects inland waterways for flood control.

The New York Times. (1927c, December 4). Issues that confront Congress.

The New York Times. (1928a, March 29). Flood bill passed by Senate, 70 to 0, with record speed.

The New York Times. (1928b, April 29). Want government to control floods.

Nisbet, M. C., & Myers, T. (2007). Twenty years of public opinion about global warming. *Public Opinion Quarterly, 71,* 444–70.

Niven, D. (2005). An economic theory of political journalism. *Journalism & Mass Communication Quarterly, 82*(2), 247–63.

Noll, M. A. (2008). *God and race in American politics: A short history.* Princeton, NJ: Princeton University Press.

Norenzayan, A., & Hansen, I. (2006). Beliefs in supernatural agents in the face of death. *Personality and Social Psychology, 32,* 174–87.

Nyhan, B., & Reifler, J. (2010). When corrections fail: The persistence of political misperceptions. *Political Behavior, 32,* 303–30.

Olzak, S. (2011). Does globalization breed ethnic discontent? *Journal of Conflict Resolution, 55*(1), 3–32.

O'Neill, K. (2004). Transnational protest: States, circuses, and conflict at the frontline of global politics. *International Studies Review, 6,* 233–51.

Oreskes, N. (2004). Beyond the ivory tower: The scientific consensus on climate change. *Science, 306,* 1686.

Pan, Z., & Kosicki, G. M. (2001). Framing as strategic action in public deliberation. In S. D. Reese, O. H. Gandy, & A. E. Grant (Eds.), *Framing public life: Perspectives on media and our understanding of the social world* (pp. 35–66). Mahwah, NJ: Lawrence Erlbaum Associates.

Paris, R. (2001). Human security: Paradigm shift or hot air? *International Security, 26*(2), 87–102.

Parker, C. S., & Barreto, M. A. (2013). *Change they can't believe in: The Tea Party and reactionary politics in America.* Princeton, NJ: Princeton University Press.

Passel, J. S. (2005). *Estimates of the size and characteristics of the undocumented population.* Washington, DC: Pew Hispanic Center.

Penn, M. (2011, June 30). The pessimism index. *Time*. http://www.time.com/time/nation /article/0,8599,2080607,00.html

Perla, H. (2011). Explaining public support for the use of military force: The impact of reference point framing and prospective decision making. *International Organization, 65*, 139–67.

Perry, J. (2003). *Under God? Religious faith and liberal democracy*. New York: Cambridge University Press.

Pew Research Center. (2006). *Little consensus on global warming: Partisanship drives opinion*. Washington, DC.

Pew Research Center. (2013). *Majority views NSA phone tracking as acceptable anti-terror tactic*. Washington, DC.

Pew Research Center. (2014). *Views of job market tick up, no rise in economic optimism*. Washington, DC.

Pew Research Center. (2015). *State of the news media, 2015*. Washington, DC.

Pew Research Center for the People and the Press. (2003). *Views of a changing world*. Washington, DC: Pew Research Center.

Pew Research Center for the People and Press. (2004). *Online news audience larger, more diverse: News audience increasingly polarized*. Washington, DC: Pew Research Center.

Pew Research Center for the People and Press. (2010). *GOP likely to recapture control of House*. Washington, DC: Pew Research Center.

Pew Research Center for the People and Press. (2012). *In changing news landscape, even television is vulnerable*. Washington, DC: Pew Research Center.

Pew Research Center Forum on Religion and Public Life. (2011). The Tea Party and religion. Available at http://www.pewforum.org/2011/02/23/tea-party-and-religion/

Pfetsch, B. (2004). From political communication culture to political communications culture: A theoretical approach to comparative analysis. In F. Esser & B. Pfetsch (Eds.), *Comparing political communication: Theories, cases, and challenges* (pp. 344–66). New York: Cambridge University Press.

Piketty, T. (2014). *Capital in the twenty-first century*. Cambridge, MA: Belknap Press of Harvard University Press.

Pinkerton, J. P. (2001a, October 2). Not ready for prime-time: Peaceniks. *The Los Angeles Times*, part 2, p. 13.

Pinkerton, J. P. (2001b, October 23). A lot will be crushed in terrorism war. *Newsday*, p. A39.

Preston, J. (2006, July 17). Texas hospitals' separate paths reflect the debate on immigration. *The New York Times*, p. 1.

Preston, J., & Connelley, M. (2007, May 25). Immigration bill provisions gain wide support in poll. *The New York Times*, p. 1.

Prior, M. (2007). *Post-broadcast democracy: How media choice increases inequality in political involvement and polarizes elections*. New York: Cambridge University Press.

Program on International Policy Attitudes. (2012, September). *PIPA/Gfk Knowledge Networks Poll*. University of Maryland.

Public Religion Research Institute. (2014, November). *Religion and politics tracking survey*. Retrieved from the iPOLL Databank, The Roper Center for Public Opinion Research, University of Connecticut. http://www.ropercenter.uconn.edu.proxy.cc.uic .edu/data_access/ipoll/ipoll.html

Putnam, R. (2000). *Bowling alone: The collapse and revival of American community*. New York: Simon & Schuster.

Quinnipiac University. (2014). *American voters split on Obama's immigration move*. Available at http://www.quinnipiac.edu/news-and-events/quinnipiac-university-poll/national /release-detail?ReleaseID=2115

Radcliffe, J., & Fikac, P. (2011, March 4). Illegal hiring bill spurs jests, jeers. *Houston Chronicle*, p. B1.

Rapley, J. (2004). *Globalization and inequality: Neoliberalism's downward spiral*. Boulder, CO: Lynne Rienner.

Reese, S. D. (2001). Prologue—Framing public life: A bridging model for media research. In S. D. Reese, O. H. Gandy, & A. E. Grant (Eds.), *Framing public life: Perspectives on media and our understanding of the social world* (pp. 7–31). Mahwah, NJ: Lawrence Erlbaum Associates.

Rice, C. (2000, January-February). Promoting the national interest. *Foreign Affairs, 79*, 45–62.

Rodriguez, L. (2006, September 18). Immigrants see English as vital, but work, family limit time to learn. *Houston Chronicle*, p. 1.

Rodrik, D. (2005). *Has globalization gone too far?* Washington, DC: Institute for International Economics.

Rodrik, D. (2012). *Ideas over interests*. Project Syndicate. Available at http://www.project -syndicate.org/commentary/ideas-over-interests

Rojecki, A. (2002). Modernism, state sovereignty and dissent: Media and the new post-cold war movements. *Critical Studies in Media Communication, 19*, 152–71.

Rojecki, A. (2003). *Think tanks and the Washington consensus*. Unpublished manuscript.

Rojecki, A. (2011). Leaderless crowds, self-organizing publics, and virtual masses: The new media politics of dissent. In S. Cottle & L. Lester (Eds.), *Transnational protests and the media* (pp. 87–97). New York: Peter Lang.

Rojecki, A., & Meraz, S. (2016). Rumors and FIBs: The role of the web in speculative politics. *New Media and Society, 18*, 25–43.

Rorty, R. (1998). *Achieving our country*. Cambridge, MA: Harvard University Press.

Rosenblatt, A., Greenberg, J., Solomon, S., Pyszczynski, T., & Lyon, D. (1989). Evidence for terror management theory: The effects of mortality salience on reactions to those who violate or uphold cultural values. *Journal of Personality and Social Psychology, 57*, 681–90.

Rothschild, E. (1995). What is security? *Daedalus, 124*(3): 53–98.

Ruiz, C., Domingo, D., Micó, J. L., Díaz-Noci, J., Meso, K., & Masip, P. (2011). Public sphere 2.0? The democratic qualities of citizen debates in online newspapers. *The International Journal of Press/Politics, 16*(4), 463–487.

Saez, E. (2013). *Striking it richer: The evolution of top incomes in the United States*. Available at http://elsa.berkeley.edu/~saez/saez-UStopincomes-2011.pdf

Safire, W. (2001, October 8). Our relentless liberation. *The New York Times*, p. A17.

Samuelson, R. J. (2003, February 26). Earning Americans' resentment. *The Washington Post*, p. A23.

Sandman, P. (1989). Hazard versus outrage in the public perception of risk. In V. T. Covello, D. B. McCallum, & M. T. Pavlova (Eds.), *Effective risk communication: The role and responsibility of government and nongovernment organizations* (pp. 45–49). New York: Plenum Press.

Sassen, S. (1991). *The global city.* Princeton, NJ: Princeton University Press.

Sassen, S. (2006). *Cities in a world economy.* Thousand Oaks, CA: Pine Forge Press.

Sassoon, D. (1996). *One hundred years of socialism: The West European left in the twentieth century.* London: I.B. Tauris.

Schattschneider, E. E. (1960). *The semi-sovereign people: A realist's view of democracy in America.* New York: Holt, Rinehart, & Winston.

Scheve, K. F., & Slaughter, M. J. (2004). Economic insecurity and the globalization of production. *American Journal of Political Science, 48,* 662–74.

Schlesinger, P. (1997). From cultural defence to political culture: Media politics and collective identity in the European Union. *Media, Culture and Society, 19*(3), 369–91.

Schudson, M. (1989). How culture works: Perspectives from media studies on the efficacy of symbols. *Theory and Society, 18,* 153–80.

Sciolino, E., & Meyers, S. L. (2001, October 7). Bush says "time is running out"; US plans to act largely alone. *The New York Times,* section A1, p. 1.

Scott, A. O. (2005, September 11). Among the believers. *New York Times Magazine,* p. 38.

Sears, D. O., Lau, R. R., Tyler, T. R., & Allen, H. M., Jr. (1980). Self-interest vs. symbolic politics in policy attitudes and presidential voting. *The American Political Science Review, 74*(3), 670–84.

Semetko, H. A. (1996). Political balance on television: Campaigns in the United States, Britain, and Germany. *Harvard International Journal of Press/Politics, 1*(1), 51–71.

Servín-González, M., & Torres-Reyna, O. (1999). Trends: Religion and politics. *Public Opinion Quarterly, 63*(4), 592–621.

Sewell, W. H., Jr. (1999). The concept(s) of culture. In V. E. Bonnell, L. Hunt, & R. Biernacki (Eds.), *Beyond the cultural turn: New directions in the study of society and culture* (pp. 35–61). Berkeley: University of California Press.

Short, J. R., & Kim, Y. -H. (1999). *Globalization and the city.* Harlow, UK: Longman.

Sides, J. (2013, March 31). No, the 2012 election didn't prove the Republican Party needs a reboot. Available at http://www.washingtonpost.com/blogs/wonkblog/wp/2013/03/31/no-the-2012-election-didnt-prove-the-republican-party-needs-a-reboot/

Sides, L. E., & Farrell, H. (2010). Self-segregation or deliberation? Blog readership, participation, and polarization in American politics. *Perspectives on Politics, 8,* 141–57.

Simon, H. A. (1985). Human nature in politics: The dialogue of psychology with political science. *American Political Science Review, 79*(2), 293–304.

Sites, W. (2003). Global city, American city: Theories of globalization and approaches to urban history. *Journal of Urban History, 29,* 333–46.

Sitrin, M. (2012). Occupy Wall Street and the meanings of success. *Occupy! An OWS-Inspired Gazette,* no. 5, pp. 2–3.

Skocpol, T., & Williamson, V. (2012). *The Tea Party and the remaking of Republican conservatism.* New York: Oxford University Press.

Skowronek, S. (2008). *Presidential leadership in political time.* Lawrence: University Press of Kansas.

Slovic, P. (1987). Perceptions of risk. *Science, 236,* 280–85.

Slovic, P., Finucane, M. L., Peters, E., & Macgregor, D. G. (2004). Risk as analysis and risk as feelings: Some thoughts about affect, reason, risk, and rationality. *Risk Analysis, 24*(2), 311–22.

Smith, G. B. (1997). Leo Strauss and the Straussians: An anti-democratic cult? *PS: Political Science and Politics, 30*(2), 180–89.

Smith, T. W., Rasinski, K. A., & Toce, M. (2001). *America rebounds: A national study of public response to the September 11th terrorist attacks, preliminary findings.* Chicago: National Opinion Research Center.

Snow, D. A., & Benford, R. D. (1992). Master frames and cycles of protest. In A. Morris & C. M. Mueller (Eds.), *Frontiers in social movement theory* (pp. 133–55). New Haven, CT: Yale University Press.

Sobel, R. (2001). *The impact of public opinion on U.S. foreign policy since Vietnam: Constraining the colossus.* New York: Oxford University Press.

Sommers, S. R., Apfelbaum, E. P., Dukes, K. N., Toosi, N., & Wang, E. J. (2006). Race and media coverage of Hurricane Katrina: Analysis, implications, and future research questions. *Analyses of Social Issues and Public Policy, 6*(1), 39–55.

Spence, M., & Hlatshwayo, S. (2011). *The evolving structure of the American economy and the employment challenge.* Working paper, Maurice R. Greenberg Center for Geoeconomic Studies, Council on Foreign Relations.

Steele, C. M. (1988). The psychology of self-affirmation: Sustaining the integrity of the self. In L. Berkowitz (Ed.), *Advances in experimental social psychology* (pp. 261–302). San Diego: Academic Press.

Stiglitz, J. E. (2007). *Making globalization work.* New York: W. W. Norton.

Stimson, J. A. (1991). *Public opinion in America: Moods, cycles, and swings.* Boulder, CO: Westview Press.

Strange, S. (1996). *The retreat of the state: The diffusion of power in the world economy.* Cambridge: Cambridge University Press.

Strauss, B. S. (2001, November 18). The Bush-Putin summit. *Newsday,* p. B4.

Strauss, L. (1991). *On tyranny.* Revised edition. New York: Free Press.

Stroud, N. J. (2011). *Niche news: The politics of news choice.* New York: Oxford University Press.

Sullivan, A. (2001, October 7). This is a religious war. *The New York Times Magazine,* p. 44.

Swartz, D. (2011). Politics and the fragmenting of the 1970s evangelical left. *Religion and American Culture, 21,* 81–120.

Swidler, A. (1986). Culture in action: Symbols and strategies. *American Sociological Review, 51,* 273–86.

Tadjbakhsh, S., & Chenoy, A. M. (2007). *Human security: Concepts and implications.* London: Routledge.

Taleb, N. N. (2004). *Fooled by randomness: The hidden role of chance in life and markets.* New York: Random House.

Tanzi, V. T., & Schuknecht, L. (2000). *Public spending in the 20th century.* Cambridge: Cambridge University Press.

Tarrow, S. (2005). *The new transnational activism.* Cambridge: Cambridge University Press.

Taylor, P. J., & Lang, R. E. (2005). *US cities in the "world city network."* Washington, DC: Brookings Institution.

Thompson, J. M. (1928, February 5). Quick action urged on flood control. *The New York Times*, p. 53.

Time/CNN/Yankelovich Partners Poll. (1996, February). [survey question]. USY-ANKP.022396.R25B. Yankelovich Partners [producer]. Storrs, CT: Roper Center for Public Opinion Research, iPOLL [distributor].

The Times and Iraq. (2004, May 26). *The New York Times*, p. A10.

Timiraos, N. (2015). Economic mobility trumps the income gap as bigger worry—WSJ/NBC poll. *Wall Street Journal*. http://blogs.wsj.com/economics/2015/05/04/wsjnbc-poll-economic-mobility-trumps-the-income-gap-as-bigger-worry/

Todorov, A., & Mandisodza, A. N. (2004). Public opinion on foreign policy: The multilateral public that perceives itself as unilateral. *Public Opinion Quarterly, 68*, 323–48.

Tomlinson, J. (1999). *Globalization and culture*. Chicago: University of Chicago Press.

Tough, P. (2002, December 15). The year in ideas: Pop-aganda. *The New York Times Magazine*, p. 112.

Triennial Central Bank Survey. (2010). *Report on global foreign exchange market activity in 2010*. Basel, Switzerland: Bank for International Settlements.

Tuchman, G. (1972). Objectivity as strategic ritual: An examination of a newsman's notions of objectivity. *American Journal of Sociology, 77*, 660–79.

Tuesday, and after. (2001, September 24). *The New Yorker*. Available at http://www.newyorker.com/magazine/2001/09/24/tuesday-and-after-talk-of-the-town

Turner, P. A. (1993). *I heard it through the grapevine: Rumor in African-American culture*. Berkeley: University of California Press.

Turow, J. L. (1997). *Breaking up America: Advertisers and the new media*. Chicago: University of Chicago Press.

UN-Habitat. (2008). *State of the world's cities, 2008–2009*. London: Earthscan.

United Nations. (1994). *Human development report*. New York: Oxford University Press.

Usher, N. (2014). *Making news at the New York Times*. Ann Arbor: University of Michigan Press.

Van Aelst, P., & Walgrave, S. (2004). New media, new movements? The role of the Internet in shaping the "anti-globalization" movement. In W. van de Donk, B. D. Loader, P. G. Nixon, & D. Rucht (Eds.), *Cyberprotest: New media, citizens and social movements* (pp. 97–122). London: Routledge.

Vavreck, L. (2009). *The message matters: The economy and presidential campaigns*. Princeton, NJ: Princeton University Press.

Vitello, P. (2002, February 3). One economy can't fit all. *Newsday*, p. A04.

Von Drehle, D., Newton-Small, J., Jewler, S., O'Leary, K., Yan, S., & Malloy, W. (2010, March 1). Tea Party America. *Time, 175*(8), p. 26.

Walter, S. (2010). Globalization and the welfare state: Testing the microfoundations of the compensation hypothesis. *International Studies Quarterly 54*, 403–26.

The Washington Post. (1927a, October 2). Nation's first task, p. S1.

The Washington Post. (1927b, October 9). Program in Congress, p. S1.

The Washington Post. (1927c, October 30). Politics and flood control, p. 57.

The Washington Post. (1928, January 29). Task for the nation, p. S1.

Wessel, D. (2011, April 19). Big U.S. firms shift hiring abroad—Data show work forces shrinking at home, sharpening debate on the impact of globalization. *Wall Street Journal*, p. B1.

What is Occupy morphing into? (2012, September 19). *Adbusters.* Available at https://www.adbusters.org/blogs/adbusters-blog/tactical-briefing-38.html

White, J. W. (1998). Old wine, cracked bottle? Tokyo, Paris, and the global city hypothesis. *Urban Affairs Review, 33,* 451–77.

Wildavsky, A. (1987). Choosing preferences by constructing institutions: A cultural theory of preference formation. *The American Political Science Review, 81*(1), 3–22.

Williams, B. A., & Delli Carpini, M. X. (2011). *After broadcast news: Media regimes, democracy, and the new information environment.* New York: Cambridge University Press.

Williams, R. (1983). *Keywords.* 2nd edition. Oxford: Oxford University Press.

Wilson, G. K. (1998). *Only in America? The politics of the United States in comparative perspective.* Chatham, NJ: Chatham House.

Winter, N. J. G. (2006). Framing and the racialization of white opinion on social security. *American Journal of Politics, 50,* 400–20.

Winter, N. J. G. (2008). *Dangerous frames: How ideas about race and gender shape public opinion.* Chicago: University of Chicago Press.

Wittkopf, E. R. (1994). Faces of internationalism in a transitional environment. *Journal of Conflict Resolution, 38*(3), 376–401.

Wolf, M. (2004). *Why globalization works.* New Haven, CT: Yale University Press.

Wolf, M. (2010). We can only cut debt by borrowing. Available at http://blogs.ft.com/martin-wolf-exchange/2010/09/26/we-can-only-cut-debt-by-borrowing/?

Woollacott, A. (2000, October 20). It's time America woke up to the rest of the planet: US foreign policy is mainly an exercise in adhering to the past. *The Guardian,* p. 24.

World press roundup. (2001, September 21). *The St. Louis Post Dispatch,* p. B7.

Wuthnow, R. (1988). *The restructuring of American religion: Society and faith since World War II.* Princeton, NJ: Princeton University Press.

Yeager, D. S., Larson, S. B., Krosnick, J. A., & Tompson, T. (2011). Measuring Americans' issue priorities: A new version of the most important problem question reveals concern about global warming and the environment. *Public Opinion Quarterly, 75,* 125–38.

Zaller, J. R. (1992). *Information, predispositions, and opinion: The nature and origins of mass opinion.* New York: Cambridge University Press.

Zernike, K., & Thee-Brenan, M. (2010, April 15). Discontent's demography: Who backs the Tea Party. *The New York Times,* p. A1.

Zoellick, R. (2001, September 20). Countering terror with trade. *The Washington Post,* p. A35.

Note: Page numbers in *italics* indicate figures and tables.